Memoirs of a Working Man

1941 (Age 3)

1954 (Age 16

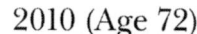

2010 (Age 72)

Almost retired

Bob Oliver

AuthorHouse™ UK Ltd.
500 Avebury Boulevard
Central Milton Keynes, MK9 2BE
www.authorhouse.co.uk
Phone: 08001974150

© 2010 Bob Oliver. All rights reserved.

No part of this book may be reproduced, stored in a retrieval system, or transmitted by any means without the written permission of the author.

First published by AuthorHouse 4/1/2010

ISBN: 978-1-4490-9349-5 (sc)
ISBN: 978-1-4520-0023-7 (hc)

This book is printed on acid-free paper.

Foreword

What's to be said about a man like Bob Oliver? We have been together for over fifty years and I still haven't fathomed him out. He is a total contradiction and the love of my life. We have faced together almost everything life can throw at us and survived; in fact, thrived.

Bob decided to write about our life, as we have little or no information on our grandparents or, for that matter, our parent's life and we wanted to pass on to our children and grandchildren our experiences and like Topsy it just grew and grew.

When I first met him he was in the army and he was often away, his letter writing was, to say the least, sparse and empty of any emotion and I, as a 16-year-old girl, was not impressed. It was only in later years that I discovered that he was dyslexic, a condition not at that time recognised in working-class schools. He was therefore treated at school as a lazy scholar and was subjected to severe beatings by his disinterested teachers, because he couldn't recognise the words on the page.

All of this is covered in his book and I am finding it difficult not to ramble on and spoil his surprise. To me, he epitomises the "stoic working man" and that's where the title of his book came from. He is honest and honourable and no one is better qualified to write about the world we grew up in.

This is our life as we see it and he writes easily about the fun things in our life, but like lots of men of his generation and background, he finds the more serious side hard to grapple with, which is why our children urged us to put pen to paper before we both go senile.

He is a good man and if you read through you will see that he is also funny. Our three beautiful daughters were lucky enough to have a great dad and our ten grandchildren are benefiting from a wonderful granddad. Life with him is like a roller-coaster ride, we go down but we fly up again and I can't wait for the next chapter.

Eileen Oliver

I would like to thank Eileen, who has critically examined all of my writing and given sound advice regarding its contents. She has been my guiding light and inspiration. The greatest wife, mother and grandmother one could ever hope for.

My sincere hope is that whoever takes time to read these memoirs will not only find it enlightening, but will also get a good laugh at my attempt at humour. Laughter is great. So keep smiling.

Bob Oliver

Early Years

Young Bob through the Second-World-War Years

Christmas presents always give one an idea of what your family think of you and, as usual, I got the normal presents: CDs of the 1950s, Old Spice, gallons of deodorant, three gallons of whisky and various other bottles of booze – indicating that I'm an old man, who is very smelly and a drunk to boot! That's now, but thinking about Christmases of yesteryear really sets the mind reeling and how things have changed.

I was born in February 1938 and my first memories go back to the early 1940s, "the war years". As you might well remember, they were not times of plenty. The first Christmas that I have clear thoughts about was in an air-raid shelter, which had to be seen to be believed. It was like a huge cellar in the middle of the garden that my dad had built. Most of the time we slept shoulder to shoulder, it seemed like there were hundreds of us, but this particular Christmas we younger kids had it to ourselves.

Thinking back, I suppose the older members of the family were out celebrating and as it was Christmas, they must have felt safe enough to sleep in the house, even though half the windows had been blown out. That suited us fine, for we had the whole place to ourselves. Oh boy did we have the "rip". But, even though the bomb shelter looked as though a bomb had found its way in and kids were strewn everywhere, Santa still managed to find us and distribute our own individual goodies and gifts. Because we had never had much and everything was scarce, we were goggle-eyed at the mere basic of things we received and to get an orange along with a bruised apple was luxury, indeed.

As I grew up in the 1940s the war ended. There was still rationing and everything was in short supply, but the grown-ups made the Christmases memorable and special. My two eldest sisters May and Josie, and especially their husbands, the "two Uncle Lens", organised games and entertained us younger kids with board games and charades. I can remember being scared "shitless" with my favourite game, Murder in the Dark, and, of course, there was always the radio.

What a wealth of entertainment the radio had to offer: *Take It From Here*, *ITMA*, *Paul Temple*, *Valentine Dial* (the man in black, with his stories that gave you nightmares but made for compulsive listening) and, of course, the incomparable *Dick Barton Special Agent*. Every weekday evening at quarter to seven came the signal that cleared the streets of kids. One moment the traffic-free roads were teaming with noisy children and then someone would shout those immortal words *Dick Barton Special Agent* and within seconds, as if a magic wand had been at work, the streets were deserted.

Without electricity and only gas for cooking and lighting, our radio was powered by a rather large battery called an accumulator. These batteries had to be periodically charged, which meant that the kids would get the task of taking it to the bicycle shop; it seems strange now, but that is where they had the charging facilities.

Our only means of transporting these huge batteries was an old pushchair. It was quite a mission, with sulphuric acid slopping about ("safety" was a word that hadn't been invented), but to live without the radio was unthinkable.

Then there were the Saturday morning pictures showing westerns starring of Tom Mix, Roy Rogers and the singing cowboy Gene Autry. For sixpence, we had a whole morning's entertainment. On the way home we would ride our imaginary horses, shooting our pretend guns, stopping only to scrounge chocolate or chewing gum from the passing American servicemen. These men in their brand new uniforms were like gods to us scruffy kids in our hand-me-down clothes that had more stitches and patches than a patchwork quilt.

Winter times always seemed to mean snow and even as a kid I hated snow. Maybe it was because the big boys compacted their snowballs so tightly that they became ice-balls and when they hit your head, you had a headache for a fortnight. I soon learned this "art" and gave the younger kids the benefit of my experience – evil little swine.

School Days

My early years didn't set me up to be a good scholar. For many years both during and after the war we were plagued with shortages, rationing and poverty but, what you have never had, you never miss. That was life and growing up in those circumstances was accepted by everyone as the norm.

School was a nightmare and a place to be suffered. Mine was an old Victorian building with concrete staircases stuck on the outside. The iron railings that once assisted the climber and prevented you from falling had been removed, melted down and turned into guns for the war effort; bars that once had decorated the windows of the former prison or sanatorium had also gone. In the winter, those concrete steps were even more treacherous. Covered in ice and snow they were a death trap, where cuts and bruises were common, but no one seemed to care and litigation and health and safety were unheard of.

Toilets were a crude affair and were stuck in the corner of the playground. A brick wall surrounded a channel to "pee" into, but most boys attempted to bridge the wall with a fountain of urine and woe betide anyone passing by on the other side. I had an aptitude for this feat and other boys watched in awe at my greatness. It's a pity my schoolwork didn't have the same elevation.

Inside the school the rooms were dismal, dreary and foreboding. They were poorly decorated and were ill lit with gas mantles; the high wooden ceilings were littered with pen nibs that had been flighted with straws.

The senior school was a little better. (The building I'm talking about, not the teachers.) I hated the teachers, who were a cross between the incompetent and the sadistic. All the young and talented adults had been gobbled up by the war, so we were left with those who were too old to be soldiers or of no use for any physical employment.

The weak masters were given a nightmare of a life by the reluctant students, often facing abuse, missiles and humiliation.

The stronger ones, of whom there were more, dominated with wicked ferocity. Being caned was a daily occurrence; I don't think I was a bad boy and the canings were handed out to me for simply not understanding the lesson. I'm sure my problems stemmed from my dyslexia and, of course, back in the 1940s, such conditions were unheard of.

Montague Road School was a place where no one was ever expelled; the reason being that this was where disruptive and badly behaved pupils were sent. It was the end of the road and so it was full of rogues and villains. Looking back, I now have a little sympathy for the teachers; only a little, mind.

I can remember hypnotically watching the fleas, head lice and nits having a merry old time on the head of the boy in the seat in front of mine. I have to stop and scratch even now. Other memories of that dreadful place were of two lads fighting with one of the teachers; the master almost had the better of them, until he tripped over a chair and then they were on him, punching, kicking and biting. He was a big man and was able to gain his feet despite the rain of blows. He tossed one lad, crunching him against the wall, and punched the other senseless and that was the end of that little episode. From then on he was held with a little more respect, although the lads involved said that if we had helped them they could have "done for him good". I wonder what happened to "Chalky White" and Lennie (the lad) Watson.

The "bullies" were nearly as big a threat as the teachers. I dreaded break time almost as much as the so-called lessons. The big lads would single out some poor kid, drag him into what was known as the "Dark House" and beat the shit out of him. Just for the pleasure and the sheer hell of it, you understand. I was one of these unlucky lads. Actually, it was really my mate Dutchy they were after, because he had swapped a tatty old toy lead soldier for a pair of roller skates with one of the big boy's little brothers. But, as always, he was conspicuous by his absence and I had to take the hammering for being his best friend.

Smoking

Even as a kid, Dutchy had strength of character. When we started smoking, he was the only one I knew that had the balls to say, 'No thanks, I don't like it.' But all of us other mugs just had to be clever and look big. How small we really were.

Most people of our generation smoked. We were brainwashed into thinking that if you didn't smoke you weren't a real man. Advertising showed footballers, cricketers and famous sports personalities all smoking and when you went to the pictures, all the film stars could be seen sucking on that awful weed, supposedly looking sexy, macho and magnificent.

I started smoking at the tender age of eight. Another brat and I half-inched a packet of fag papers from his old man and then we proceeded to walk the streets in search of fag-ends; how we didn't catch some incurable disease I don't know. After we had collected sufficient, we made our way to the nearest bombsite and began the task of converting the cigarette butts into roll-ups.

We were, of course, very ill and cannot remember a time that I have ever felt worse: my head ached, throbbed and spun, my stomach churned and I vomited profusely. My mother, God bless her, not knowing the cause of my illness made a rare fuss of me and I was waited on hand and foot. The nausea was almost worthwhile, especially the part when I was kept off school.

A couple of days later, I was recovering but still felt a bit queasy. It was a hot summer's day and as I lay on my bed I could hear the "old lady" talking to someone in the street at the front door. My interest in the conversation increased as I realised that it was the mother of my "comrade-in-smoke"!

'Bobby's been really ill, with vomiting and a high temperature.'

'So was my Terry, the little gits. You know what they've been up to, don't you?'

Mum must have broken all records for stair climbing, but even at the tender age of eight I still had a built-in desire for preservation and a yearning to see nine. I had the presence of mind to vanish before she hit the first stair. Of course, it was only a matter of time before I had the shit kicked out of me, but I still feel that had she got her hands on me at the time, it would have been a lot worse. Mind you, Terry the Squealer got more; he had me to contend with as well as his mum. It didn't stop me smoking, though. That happened when I was twenty-five and sense finally prevailed.

Truancy

Truancy from school became the easy option, especially when I discovered that young Ernie Bates (nicknamed Master Bates) was a very good forger. He used to copy sick notes written by our mums, which were accepted without question – I wonder what happened to little Ernie – and we became the two most sickly kids north of the Thames. With a combination of truancy and poor teaching, my education was somewhat lacking and the net result was illiteracy.

The River Lee was a short walk away and was one of our favourite haunts when skipping school. During the summer we would swim naked in the filthy, effluent-ridden water. The banks were lined with factories pumping out all sorts of waste; the risk of disease more than equalled picking up fag-ends from the gutter.

Then there were the "sandpits". Another extremely treacherous place for our fun and games. But when we really wanted danger we went to "The Blue Lake" – an area of land that had small lakes surrounded by peat bogs – a super place for us kids, but again rife with hazards.

Hard Times

Mum struggled to make ends meet, but somehow she always managed to produce a special Sunday lunch, while Father's Sunday ritual was typical of the day: lunch, preceded by a heavy drinking session down at the pub.

My elder sisters would set the big, solid wooden table – it had to be strong to survive the hordes of hungry Oliver's. It was always scrubbed white, but the cigarette burns from the evening card games couldn't be scoured out. The nearest thing we came to a tablecloth was an old curtain, but for the most part it was newspapers; the curtain only came out for special visitors. Come to think of it, we used newspapers for everything in those days – from wiping bums to floor covering. In the centre of the table sat this huge mountain of buttered bread. All the kids were impatiently waiting for the guv'nor to show so we could eat, but no one, not even my big brother, dare touch the bread before he arrived.

My kids find it hard to believe when I tell them we lived on bread and potatoes in those days. One particular Sunday's speciality was a rabbit that the old man had acquired and the old lady had worked the usual miracle by transforming the scrawny little beastie into a stew that would floor a navvy, with dumplings the size of cricket balls.

The dog, which had started barking when the old man came in, got a kick for his troubles. 'I live 'ere you stupid animal.' Dad's voice was slurred; two sniffs of his breath and you were giddy. He made his way unsteadily to the kitchen table, followed by a stampede of kids.

The grub was dished up and I filled my face with as much food as I could. It was always a question of he who eats fastest gets the most. The "gaffer" sat at the head of the table, his whole body slowly rotating as his eyes fought for clarity. First, he applied the salt to his meal in abundance and then the pepper. I watched the old man as he focused on the sauce bottle. Sauce in those days had a quality of its own; when left unused the vinegary substance separated and needed a good shake. He took hold of the bottle with a grip of steel and shook it vigorously.

Now, whoever had used it last had inadvertently left the top loose, so the sauce splattered all over the wall and everyone held their breath awaiting the explosion. The silence was deafening; you could have heard a feather falling onto the roof.

He seemed to sober slightly and being aware that everyone was watching, he applied what was left of the sauce to his dinner. Without the slightest flicker of emotion on his face, he turned to my big brother and simply said, 'Clean that up!' And of course, he did so without question. Dad wasn't the kind of guy you argued with.

Mum and Dad

I wish I knew more about my parents and grandparents. Unfortunately, I was born at the tail end of a large family. Mum was thirty-eight when I was born and Dad was thirty-six. This day and age that doesn't sound old, but anyone born around 1900 had two world wars to look forward to. Life was extremely hard for the working classes and life expectancy wasn't very long.

Apart from shortages, living conditions and hardships, most people smoked and this did nothing to extend their life. On the contrary, my grandparents died when I was very young, so I didn't get to know them and I was too young to realise the importance of gleaning a life history from Mum and Dad about them and their own parents.

I have picked up a few bits from my older brothers and sisters, but like me they were busy building their lives and providing for their own wives and children. Dad was born in 1902 in Shoreditch, East London, within the sound of Bow Bells and as such was deemed to be a true cockney. Mum was born in 1900 in Walthamstow, East London and she shared her birthday with Queen Elizabeth's mother. But apart from the common denominator of having lived through two world wars, they led very different lifestyles. Mum gave birth to ten children and sadly I know little about her younger life.

Apparently, Dad started his working life as a bricklayer's labourer. His mentor was my mum's dad, Jack Baldwin, who was a bricklayer, responsible for repairing the crumbling sewers of London. One of Dad's claims to fame was that he saved a man's life. According to London papers, one of the guys working in the sewers was overcome by the fumes, passed out and fell in. Dad went in after him and dragged him out. It didn't hit the headlines, but there was a nice column about it.

I was told by my eldest brother-in-law that Dad boxed in the booths around London to earn a little extra cash. He also played for Leyton Orient at football. But that was before they became a professional outfit, so there wasn't any money in that.

He had a serious motorcycle accident – I'm not sure how old he was – and the doctors said he was lucky to have survived; they believed that it was only the enormous amount of alcohol in his system that had saved his life. Then again, the accident might not have happened had he been sober. His skull was split from his forehead across the crown of his head and one of his shoulders was badly smashed. Drinking and driving, like smoking, was the norm in those days and crash helmets weren't compulsory.

In the mid to late 1950s I was sent home on compassionate leave from the army, as Dad was in hospital again with a duodenal ulcer and internal bleeding. The family were asked to donate blood – I think the body holds between 7 and 8 pints of blood – and they kept him alive by pumping 13 pints into him. Since then I have always considered the number thirteen to be lucky. Once again he cheated death, but it was cigarettes that finally killed him in 1967 at the age of 65, after drawing just one month's pension.

I am very proud of my dad. He was a very strong character, self-educated and worked his way up from a bricklayer's mate to become clerk of the works. A couple of major jobs of which he took charge, including the fortifications of Dover during World War II and the restoration of "Number 1 London", also known as "Apsley House", home of The Duke of Wellington, although no doubt there were others.

The building of the Dover defences involved a huge building project that can still be seen today, of which Dad was in charge, to protect us from the Germans, who had huge guns that fired equally large shells across the English Channel, a distance of some 18 miles. I was born on 11 February 1938, just over a year before England declared war on Germany. The Second World War was all I knew as a child and my early memories are of sleeping in the air-raid shelter that my dad had built. As you might imagine, having built the fortifications, the construction of the shelter in our back garden was well within his capabilities. He dug a huge pit in the back yard, built an underground room and reinforced it with concrete and steel. The entrance was above ground, with steps leading down, like a cellar.

The road we lived in was only a couple of hundred yards long; it was a small offshoot from a larger road and at the bottom of our road ran a railway line: a prime target for Jerry to bomb. We had a lot of near misses and it was commonplace for us to lose half the roof and all of the windows in the house. The nearest we came to copping it was a bomb that took out half of our road, which was completely obliterated, resulting in many deaths. I'm sure if they'd have been able to build a shelter like ours they would have survived even the direct hit that wiped away their homes and their lives.

I can remember one morning emerging from the shelter to see all the windows of the house smashed and the grown-ups talking. They were saying that the Blue Anchor Pub had been hit and that the police had shot someone for looting. Other nightmare memories were of sirens giving out that bone-chilling whine to warn of impending enemy aircraft attacks or the dreaded "Doodlebugs", the unmanned flying bombs. We listened with bated breath to the drone of their engines and knew if the engine stopped, it would only be a matter of seconds before the horrendous explosions that shook your very bones.

In the early 1950s the council compelled us to move for "slum clearance". I was told by an eyewitness that huge bulldozers moved in and were pushing the houses over as if they were made of paper. Apparently, they were fitted with large forks that dug into the walls of the houses and the weight did the rest. All was going well till it came up against the 6 foot entrance to Dad's air-raid shelter. The driver was oblivious to what he had hit as the bulldozer crunched to a shuddering halt and almost dislodged him from his ivory tower. Backing up, he braced himself with great determination and took another charge at the immovable object. Both forks snapped on impact, with a thunderous crack. The driver, who must have been a month short of a calendar, set to the task of fitting a new set of forks to his machine. He was about to launch a fresh attack on the enemy, when the site foreman who had been informed of the disaster, arrived on the scene.

The Foreman wasn't best pleased and he severely abused the driver, saying, 'Now look 'ere, son, those forks are rather expensive and we don't want to bust another pair, do we?' The best building-site colourful language ensued, with each word punctuated with a four-letter word and emphasis being placed on his dubious parenthood; indeed, there was just a hint of the suggestion that his IQ wasn't what it might be.

The entrance to the old man's dugout stood for months after everything else had been flattened. Experts had been consulted and following their inspection, it was decided that the only way was to blow it up. It therefore had a long reprieve and stood proud for several months while the local council saved up enough cash to buy the dynamite.

End of the War was near

Towards the end of the war as the bombing became less frequent, the old man acquired an indoor air-raid shelter in which the four youngest slept and the old shelter was reduced to a playroom. The indoor one was in the shape of a huge four-poster bed, except the posts were steel girders and the canopy was a quarter of an inch steel plate. This steel monster almost filled the room and was set up in the downstairs parlour. I think Dad constructed it downstairs because it would offer a greater amount of protection from the bombs than any of the upstairs bedrooms, besides the obvious practical reasons.

The indoor shelter-cum-bed also doubled as a play area, as most things did to a houseful of kids. I can remember having a rough and tumble with my brothers and I was sent flying from the shelter and landed bum first in the fireplace. As it was winter the fire was alight ... and so was I! Fortunately for me Billy, my eldest brother, was alert to the situation and he pulled me from the hot coals before any major damage was done and I escaped with just singed clothing. A salient lesson was learned that day, but it didn't put us off resuming the frolics next day and Mum never knew about her "almost barbecued" son.

I was 7 years old when the war ended. To me it meant being scrubbed, cleaned and wearing our Sunday best for the street party. Tables, benches, stools and chairs were lined up in the middle of the road and all the women buzzed around with tablecloths, cutlery and table decorations. A feast, the like of which we had never seen, poured from out of the houses: jellies, blancmanges, home-made cakes, Spam sandwiches and lemonade, made from some sort of crystals that were dissolved in water. We were in heaven, especially when the huge bonfire was lit. How we didn't succeed where Hitler's Luftwaffe had failed in burning what was left of London, I just don't know.

After the grub came the fun and games, organised by the grown-ups, until the kids were exhausted and falling asleep. The grown-ups were left carry on with the celebration till Gawd only knows what time. There was always someone in the street who owned a piano, which was dragged from house to house depending on who was hosting a party, be it a wedding, Christening or just a "home-on-leave" do. Anyone who owned such an instrument was guaranteed a place at the party.

We younger celebrants slid asleep to the sound of all the nostalgic wartime songs, such as *Roll Out the Barrel*, nearly always finishing with *The White Cliffs of Dover*.

I can remember the streets being decorated with flags, bunting and Union Jacks. There were barrels of beer and dancing in the street, with Mrs Flint showing off her knickers while performing *Knees up Mother Brown* ... or was it Knees up Mother Flint? To my young eyes it was the greatest thing I had ever experienced, but in today's world of plenty it needs imagination to conjure up the magic created that night by our parents. They had suffered six years of heroically stretching out wartime rations and enduring mass bombing raids, with make do and mend and all the while keeping morale high in front of the children.

It was mainly the mums who did all the work, because the dads were few and far between: killed, too old, too ill, still away in the forces or in some prison camp awaiting release. Added to this, our corner of the world had been hit by a doodlebug, destroying nearly half of our little London backstreet called Derby Road. Now, as an adult, I realise just how lucky we were, as the bombs and doodlebugs had hit all around us indiscriminately, killing some and sparing others. Although I think the Oliver's could have survived a direct hit nicely tucked up in Dad's air-raid shelter.

Even with the end of the war, rationing continued well into the 1950s. Electricity was slowly being introduced into homes, but gas and coal was still widely used: gaslights, gas cooking and coal fires. Gas cookers were common, although quite a lot of folk did their cooking in coal-burning ovens. Televisions, videos, central heating and double-glazing were still to come. I can remember going to bed with so many old blankets and army overcoats on me that we could barely move. But we were warm, especially as there were four of us in the bed.

There were a great deal of door-to-door deliveries. The milkman, the baker and the rag-and-bone man all trundled round the streets with their horse-drawn carts. The most impressive was the coal wagon, which was pulled by a real horse. It was massive. To us skinny little undernourished kids most things seemed big, but the coal horse really was a giant. It had to be, as the load it pulled was also massive and very heavy.

The deliveryman loved his horse and treated it like royalty and none dare go near it without his prior permission. We were allowed to feed it with a slice of stale bread, but he had to inspect the bread and oversee us. We had to lay the bread on the palm of our hands and let the horse take it. It was quite frightening to see those huge teeth so close to your fingertips, but the elation of having done the deed was worth it.

The coalman ran a scam, where after the bags of coal had been weighed and lined up on the flat bed of the open-backed wagon, he would make some extra bags by skimming coal from the other bags, which he would sell at a reduced cost. The customers thought they were getting an extra bag cheaply, when in actual fact they were buying their own coal back.

The housewives would stand by the front door as the coalman went through the house to the back garden where the coal shed was and they would watch the delivery being made like hawks, so as to ensure they got the correct amount of bags they were paying for. As the coalman returned after tipping, he would fold and place the empty bag at the housewife's feet, when they would count the bags together and agree a price for the extra one he had slipped in. She was happy in the knowledge she hadn't been done and she had, because she was his favourite, got an extra one on the cheap and he was happy in the knowledge that she had been done and he had obtained an extra few bob.

There was one cart that didn't have a horse to pull it and that was the seafood cart. The old boy used to push it around the streets and as he was invariably under the influence of drink, he would zigzag along the middle of the road shouting, 'Shrimps, winkles, cockles, muscles alive alive O.'

Housewives and kids alike would run into the streets with jugs and basins and the seafood man would dole out his produce from a measuring cup he kept in the back of the cart. Dad couldn't get through his weekend without his winkle sandwich on a Sunday afternoon, having slept off the Sunday lunch and his weekly booze session down the pub.

Cars were virtually non-existent; all the pollution in those days came from chimneystacks. The baker was the first to go mechanical, but he still treated his old van like a horse and cart. It was quite incredible; he would pop it into first gear and as it trundled down the street under its own volition with the back doors wide open, he would make the deliveries, running back and forth to his trusted steed, taking customers' orders from the back of the van.

He was poetry in motion and the timing had to be seen to be believed. The smell of that freshly baked bread used to drive us mad; you couldn't get anywhere near him or his bread for a free sample. He was as sharp as a needle and was up to all the tricks, and was in all probability a bit of a villain himself when he was younger. Nowadays it's hard to imagine a London street without hundreds of cars parked everywhere.

Into the 1950s and Work

My brothers and sisters left school at 14 years old. Boy was I sick when the powers that be decided to put the school leaving age up to 15; a decision that was made just before I was about to leave. This meant that I had to suffer another year of purgatory before I was able to leave and start my first job in a furniture-making factory. I was fifteen and it was 1953 when I stood on the end of a machine stacking veneer. It was repetitive and extremely boring, but it was still better than school and I was on a massive five pounds a week. This newfound wealth enabled me to buy my very own clothes and for five shillings down (twenty-five pence) and two shillings and sixpence a week (twelve and a half pence) – in other words, for about 200 years' work – I could afford to buy a tailor-made suit.

My best friend Les Dutch and I used to go to Lew Rose, a bespoke Jewish tailor in Walthamstow High Street, East London, to get fitted up by this wonderful man. I thought I looked the absolute bee's knees in my suit of black barathea. The jacket was of knee-length drape, with the obligatory velvet cuffs and collar. The 15-inch bottoms on the drainpipe trousers had a button fly and cheeky cutaway pockets; it was a cross between "Vicki" and "Teddy". The shoes were commonly known as brothel creepers, with 2 inch crêpe soles, blue leather encasing and even bluer suede: the epitome of *Blue Suede Shoes*, my pride and joy. To complete the ensemble was the hairdo: a blow-wave job stuck in place with sweet-smelling lacquer. The style was Tony Curtis, with the front cockerel shape gently dipping onto the forehead and the sides sweeping to the rear into a stunning DA (duck's arse). It was all worth every penny and, more importantly, the girls liked it; well, at least I thought they did.

I can well remember my very first kiss. Ah yes! What magic memories. I'm talking real grown-up stuff now. None of your baby nonsense. The absolute height of savage excitement, 100 per cent toe-curling, senses reeling, mind-blowing sensations. These treasured moments are to be locked into one's memory bank forever.

It was a hot summer's evening way back in 1952. I was fourteen, she was thirteen. We had met at a dance and I'm still not sure how I had managed to pluck up the nerve to ask if I could take this gorgeous creature home. I was on cloud nine as we strolled the back streets of London; you could do that sort of thing in those days without fear. We came all too quickly to her house in Sweet Briar Grove and my heart was racing with anticipation of my first kiss. It was obvious to me that she was a woman of the world, because her nails were painted bright red and because of the sophisticated way she held her cigarette, just like Betty Grable.

The streetlights dazzled me as I gazed up into her eyes. I hesitated and chatted nervously, desperately searching for the courage to take her in my arms in a gentle but passionate embrace. Bravery was overcome by anxiety as I floundered and fluttered. She gazed adoringly into my eyes and murmured in my ear, 'Err, wots yer name? Can you kiss me goodnight, 'cos I gotta go in; I'm busting for a pee!' It fair turned me off.

My black barathea Teddy-boy outfit was nearly ruined on a "Beano", which was organised by the factory social club. A Beano is an outing where two or three coach loads of yobs were let loose on some unsuspecting seaside resort. This particular year we headed for Margate and with crates of beer on board; we would be three parts to the wind before arrival in Dreamland. No, that wasn't my state of mind – it's what they called the entertainment area. A type of theme park or glorified fairground.

It was the "Doodlebug" ride that finished me off, taking its name from a German unmanned flying bomb. This mock-up version bloody near killed me. It rotated as it dive-bombed in a clockwise direction and then just when you thought it was all over, they put it in reverse!

Beer, hotdogs, fried onions and greasy chips wouldn't have been a problem, had I been brave enough to rebuff my so-called mates' jibes that I didn't have the balls to fly the Doodlebug. I was ill; I was very ill and very, very sick. Fortunately, the suit cleaned up and I was able to pull a few more birds with it; we had to rely on our "clobber", because we didn't have cars in those days.

My wage earning came to an abrupt end when I broke my arm. A bunch of us lads were up to no good when I fell from a wall, about 15 feet high. It was a bad break: both the bones in my forearm were shattered and some of the bone pieced the skin. The doctors at North Middlesex Hospital did a good job in piecing the bones together through 6-inch cuts. I was in plaster for six months, which meant I was out of work for six months with no money; in those days it was no work, no pay. There was no help from anywhere, except Mum, who fed, kept and slipped me the odd sixpence (two and a half pence).

Bush Hill Park

Mum and Dad were forced to move from Derby Road when the powers that be decided that it had to be cleared as part of the "slum clearance project". Dad found a house in the very posh area of; now wait for it, Bush Hill Park. It even had a bathroom with a bath that never had coal stored in it. Are you impressed or what? Still more amazing was that the house even boasted a TV aerial socket. We sat looking at it wondering just how they got the picture through that tiny hole. Technology, eh! Amazing.

The bath had a huge gas heater over it, but the damn thing never seemed to work, until one day my big brother cracked it. It was so simple. The old man, not wanting to waste money by burning gas, had turned the gas off to stop us using it. Arthur found the gas tap under the bath and it was hot water for us all from that time on and the laborious treks to the Town Hall for a bath were suspended. We had even been clever enough to shut the gas off after use and made sure the bathroom was steam free before he came home from work.

Our suspended treks to the town hall for a bath were short-lived. Dad got the gas bill one day and it had risen dramatically – he nearly had a baby when he discovered what had been going on behind his back. In a fit of pique, he tore out the gas heater and took it down the rubbish dump; so once again the town hall beckoned.

New Zealand

My lifelong friend and I had decided to emigrate to New Zealand. It was 1955, we were 17 years old and we were both working in humdrum factory jobs. At that time in London the traffic problem was rearing its ugly head; it had grown from a little above zero during the war years of the early 1940s, to traffic congestion on roads that were designed for horse and carts.

In those days, people thought nothing of using paraffin, or anything else, to propel their cars, vans, lorries, motorbikes or scooters. This resulted in an unwelcome addition to the already polluted atmosphere caused by factories and homes burning coke and coal, which spewed out fumes that were toxic enough to choke a horse. The London smog's were inevitable and soon followed.

Not sure if that had any bearing on our decision, but as we went through our daily routine of walking to work breathing in the fumes of London – and the boredom of standing at a machine for nine hours doing the same thing forever and a day, day in, day out – we often said, 'There just has to be more to life than this!'

So we decided that New Zealand would be our ticket to a new and more exciting life. Our first step was a trip to New Zealand House in the City of London. Dressing up in our best Saturday-night finery, we looked a perfect vision, with Les with his spanking new jacket turning the heads of passers-by. He was years ahead of his time; most people were wearing sombre, humdrum colours, so Les' jacket was a breath of fresh air. It was three-quarter length and was predominantly white with a black fleck and it had dark velvet elbows and shoulders. But the final kudos was the back of the jacket, embroidered with the emblem of the day: a guitar, of course. My outfit paled into insignificance. But boy did we cut a dash as we mounted the 149 bus from Edmonton, to embark on our venture.

Our young brains were full of excitement and expectations. As we made our historic journey we watched the population going about their mundane routines and with more than a little contempt, we chuckled in the knowledge that our lives were going to be different.

With the interview complete and given all the necessary documents to complete, we strolled about taking photos and talking of how, in years to come, we would look back at the pictures of Nelson's Column, St Paul's and the other London sights and say with affection, 'That's where we were born.'

There was no doubt in our minds that we were soon to be making that sea voyage halfway around the world, but what we hadn't reckoned on was one small but very powerful stumbling block: my mum, who foiled our plans by refusing to sign the papers, saying we were too young. Dad wouldn't get involved, muttering that he would stand by Mum's decision.

Disappointed at having "our great adventure" curtailed, we went to the pub and as I sipped my Black and Tan and Les relished his R. Whites, we discussed the army and our attention turned to serving England and the Queen – just to escape the shackles of a life of tedious monotony.

National Service was only nine months away, but to us that might as well have been a lifetime. So we decided to sign on as regulars, which meant we could go in at seventeen. The navy never entered the equation and the RAF only fleetingly crossed our minds. It was the army for us, but which mob to sign up with? That was the question. Les fancied The Pay Corps, while I was attracted to The Royal Electrical Mechanical Engineers.

After a great deal of discussion we decided to flip a coin and it was the REME that won it. OK, OK, I admit it – it wasn't quite kosher and I did cheat, but where was the glamour of being a pen pusher in The Pay Corps?

The early summer of 1955 found us in Kentish Town Recruiting Centre carrying out the ceremony that pledged our allegiance to Queen and Country. We had to have a medical so, stripped naked, someone who purported to be a doctor told us to cough. Confirming what we already knew; that we were lean, mean fighting machines. We both passed A1, which, I believe, is the top pass grade. Our reflexes, when grabbed by the short and curlies with ice-cold hands, proved we were, indeed, alive. A lesser reaction would have meant a lesser grade and possibly the Pioneer Corps.

"You're in the Army, Boy; I'm Yer Muvvah Now, Son"

Basic Training

The train journey from London to Dorset was quite special, as it was the first time I had been outside of London apart from Southend and Margate, when I was too drunk to know what was going on, and you can't really count that as countryside. To see endless rolling fields, animals grazing and trees full of leaves instead of straggly stalks scattered along the streets of London seemed like a different world. Indeed, the villages, with small groups of houses scattered few and far between and individual houses nestled in isolation among the beauty of the English countryside, were, for us, quite breathtaking.

But our mood changed from pleasure to pain when we began our basic training, which signified the start of eight weeks of hell. Blandford Barracks was a very large, basic training area and was a shock to our systems, with everyone running around shouting and barking orders. The army swapped my black barathea Teddy-boy outfit for a uniform fabric that was a little on the rough side. The sergeant wasn't very impressed with my hairdo, either; especially my DA, which had to go.

The seeming obsession for the raised voice was the first thing that hit me; the second was being lined up and marched to the barbers shop. I say "barbers shop", suggesting that one might find a barber there. Oh dear me no; this was where we found a Neanderthal, built like a brick shithouse; a former ground worker in Civvy Street, masquerading as a barber. And no one in their right senses dare tell him that his own hair hadn't had the correct treatment. He was hand picked for the job – curls, locks and DAs vanished from our crowns and many a tear was shed.

Then we were issued our kit. None of the clothes fitted and the battle dress stank of mothballs and was made from a material as thick as a board and oh, so rough on my tender skin. The boots were covered in pimples and our first task was to iron them flat and "bull" them till your drill sergeant could see his face in them.

To achieve this miracle, we were instructed to heat a large spoon with a flame from a candle, cover the boot with black polish and iron out the pimples, while impregnating the leather with boot polish. Once the pimples had been removed, all that was left was to create a mirror-like surface with polish and a couple of gallons of spit. Oh, and, of course, time and patience! Hours and hours of time and endless bleeding patience.

There was a two-week wait before our real training started, as our squad had to have it's numbers brought up to strength with National Service men. Because we were regular soldiers, special treatment was lined up for us, consisting of two weeks "fatigues". Fatigues, normally carried out by the naughty boys in the army, were delights like scrubbing baking tins in the cookhouse. Apart from the mounds of filthy, greasy baking tins there were several other pleasures to savour in the back rooms of the kitchen: potatoes to be peeled, which were heaped to the ceiling, floors to scrub and cookers and ovens to clean. The squaddies' dinners also had to be dished up.

I hated serving the baked spuds, as they were the most popular and the troops would always want more. I would call to the cook, 'They want more potatoes, sarge,' and from a position behind the scenes that only the servers could see he would put two fingers up, silently mouthing to us to give only two potatoes each. Then he would call out aloud, 'Give them plenty of potatoes!' leaving us to decide whether or not we would give them more. As the sergeant cook had more control over the quality of my life, I took abuse from the squaddies and avoided the wrath of the cook. There would often be cries of, 'Who called the cook a git?' and 'Who called the git a cook?' (Only "git" wasn't the descriptive word used – oh no, it was something to do with "Ceeing U Next Tuesday".) The best fatigue I was ever fortunate enough to get was cleaning out the cinema, which was always spotless; mainly because hardly anyone had time to use it.

Our fourteen-hour day started with a rude awakening at 5.00 a.m. The demented drill sergeant would come crashing through the billets, shouting and screaming at the top of his voice that we would be well advised to remove our hands from our private parts and place them on our socks. Not content with this, he always carried his pacing stick and caressed our ears by clattering it on the metal frames of our super-soft, comfortable beds and tin lockers. We had fifteen minutes to get dressed, run to the cookhouse with our tin cups for a bromide-laden cup of tea and then report for roll-call parade. After roll-call we had half an hour to prepare for billet and kit inspection and woe betide anyone who wasn't 100 per cent "bull-shitted up".

A half-hour for breakfast was next. Not quite what Mother made, but when one is a tad hungry one tends to eat any crap served with or without sugar. I must admit that even I, who was bought up to clean my plate, had a problem with cold fried eggs coated with congealed fat; the base of which were burnt black and the top resembling uncooked slime. Only the baked beans were semi edible, with the globules of yellow grease floating in its juices. To get this culinary delight we had to queue for fifteen minutes.

Then we had to rush to our next parade and drill, drill and more drill. Our evenings were spent bulling-up for the next day. Then, of course, in-between time there were fatigues that were the highlight of our day. Little wonder no one had time for the cinema.

The two weeks of fatigues seemed like an eternity and the arrival of the National Service men was a relief, but we didn't admit this to the Rookies, for we were the old soldiers, the old sweats, the experienced ones. We constantly bragged that we had served and what it was like to be a regular. Somehow, I don't think many were that impressed; in fact, I got the distinct impression that the verdict from the National Service men was that anyone who would volunteer for this purgatory had to be some sort of a lunatic.

The six weeks' basic training that followed was a nightmare round of bullshit, parades, inspections and drill. I began to think that maybe the National Service men had a point.

Left, left, left right left. We marched up and down, over and over again, with the drill sergeant screaming abuse at us. We were apparently "unworthy of the air we breathed" and "disgusting creatures that had just crawled out from under a stone". One of his favourite sentences, done in full volume, with the veins in his neck fit to bust and his nose 2 inches from yours, whilst spraying spit in your face was, 'By Christ! I'll move you just now!' and move us he did.

There was one guy who just couldn't march to save his life. He had zero coordination and he had this uncanny knack of moving his right arm forwards, working in wonderful harmony and in conjunction with his right leg and the same with his left; it was impossible for him to walk and use his brain simultaneously. Indeed, it was a feat that a normal soldier would find impossible to perform. I had a funny feeling he was trying to work his ticket, but it didn't work. He came in for some awful stick and was often reduced to tears. He was eventually shunted into the cookhouse to serve his time out; he was excused parades, schemes, boots, in fact, every bloody thing, being unable to carry out anything military. Even our, the most dedicated, sergeant gave up on him.

His name was Williams, but everyone called him 606 (this being his last three numbers). Everyone in the army has a number and it's truly amazing how one remembers it; mine was 23249332. I know not of any ex-serviceman who can't reel off their number without thinking about it – and this was after fifty odd years. Anyway, 606 was a bit dim; no, 606 was a lot dim, but I bet he has never forgotten his number.

Williams was a cross between Charles Hawtrey and Wilfred Brambell. For the uninitiated, Charles Hawtrey acted the fool in a film called *The Army Game* and Wilfred Brambell was the dirty old man in *Steptoe & Son*. Anyway, it wasn't long after 606 had joined the elite and began assisting in feeding us hungry squaddies that he was involved in a crisis in the officers' mess. They were hosting a mega special event, at which all the top generals; the lady mayor, the local MP, lords and ladies were to be there for some sort of inspection of an army training barracks. But first of all was lunch.

The sergeant in charge of the officers' mess was drafting in as much help as he could and the cookhouse sergeant sent over as many squaddies as he could spare; 606 among them. The army, notorious for ramming square pegs into round holes, typically and true to form decided that 606 should be a waiter. He was issued the appropriate outfit and told to go and smarten himself up; anyone who knew him would know that was a ridiculous request.

All dressed up, he thought he looked great and had at last found his niche. But, to everyone else – except the officers' mess sergeant, who had other things on his mind – he looked like a sack of cack kicked to death. The kitchen was buzzing, the tables were laid and the entire dignitary was seated, when along came 606: an apparition in blue, wandering about with a wine-stained napkin slung across his shoulder, doing what he does best – sod all and getting in the way.

A corporal grabbed him and said, 'Right, go out there and find out how many for soup.'

Enter 606. Picture the scene: shuffling to the end of the table, nearly tripping over his undone lace, he slaps his hand on General Fitzgibbon's shoulder and calls out, 'Right, 'ands up all those who want soup?'

After that, 606 was given a job guarding a deserted army camp awaiting demolition; all on his little lonesome. Wonder if he's still there.

Guard Duty

Just to fill your life completely the army laid on guard duties, during which you did two hours on and four off. The two hours on was spent alternating between patrolling the perimeter and standing guard at the main gate, while the four hours off were spent either playing cards or grabbing some kip in the bunks at the rear of the guardhouse. Boy, how we must have put the fear of Christ up any would-be terrorist. Our ill-fitting uniforms had more fluff than the Dulux dog and those berets were like pancakes over our head and ears. The webbing was hand-me-downs from the First World War and, of course, the pièce de résistance was our super-modern firepower, in the shape of a pickaxe handle.

On the road outside the main gate we watched a man march smartly by and Dutchy commented on his uniform and how snappy he looked. I had to agree and he made us look like *Steptoe & Son* (rag-and-bone men). This guy was immaculate in a light blue uniform, with a broad red strip running down either side of his trousers, a three-quarter length jacket sparkling with brass buttons and other decoration and a 3 inch black belt. His dark blue cap with its black peak, red band and gold braid seemed to hold his head rigid, while he marched in his impeccably clean shoes with a clickety-clack.

'Cor!' I commented, 'I wonder what mob he belongs to.'

'Don't be an idiot,' Dutchy mocked. 'That's a Salvation Army uniform.'

The Sally Army man got about 10 yards past us, when he stopped, turned smartly and marched passed us again.

We looked at each other and shrugged our shoulders, both thinking: what the hell is he up to?

'Maybe he's selling watch towers,' I said.

Stopping once again, he looked at us over his well-adorned shoulder. Then, turning, he briskly marched straight up to me. Sticking his chin out and with his nose in my face, he spat these words, 'What's the matter with you, soldier; don't you salute an officer when you see one?'

'Sorry, sir,' I said, trying to sound subservient, 'I thought you were Salvation Army.'

I can't remember his exact words, but there was a hint of aggravation in his voice and, of course, we were put on a charge. Our punishment was to clean fifty million guns in the armoury; well, it seemed like that. What puzzled me was how come all we were given to guard the place with was a pickaxe handle, when the armoury was chocker block with guns. Now I'm older I understand why.

The corporal in charge of the armoury was 5 foot nothing and weighed in at 7 stone wringing wet. He was an obnoxious little chap who obviously thought that because we were now so-called criminals, he had to appear tough. So when we reported to him, he stood with his hands on his hips, peering through huge, thick, horn-rimmed glasses, and began shouting instructions at us in a Mickey-Mouse squeaky voice. He apparently wanted us to move our idle bodies and jump to it.

Dutchy whispered to me, 'Don't forget to salute this time.'

Like the idiot I am, I saluted. The little man went mad and while he was preoccupied telling me, in the nicest possible way, of course, that one just doesn't salute an NCO, Dutchy moved to his rear and began to pull faces.

This all proved too much for me and I was unable to stop myself from laughing. This, in turn, made the corporal angrier. We stood there giggling like a couple of schoolgirls, while he jumped up and down screaming, 'I'll jump on you from a great height!' The thought of him jumping on us from a great height held no fear and just made us laugh even more.

The next day, the sergeant major, who was 6 foot 3 and weighed 18 stone, said something similar to us and do you know what? Neither one of us could raise a smile. Corporal Hitler had put us on a charge for insubordination. Well, at least the jankers didn't involve going back to the armoury.

AWOL

Most of the driving duties were a doddle, with hours to make any union rep in Civvy Street envious. Our guv'nor, Staff Sergeant Miles, was great and he looked after his small band of rogues like a mother hen. We were excused most chores

– early morning parades, physical training, guard duties and the like – and were given passes that said we could go to the cookhouse at any time of the day or night for a meal, a cup of bromide-free tea or whatever our little hearts desired.

There were ten of us and because we had to do odd hours and, of course, our top two drivers had the enviable job of driving the general and the colonel's cars, we were the untouchables.

Though, we did have our enemies. A certain Regimental Sergeant Eggleton looked on us as the enemy, a non-military rabble, an out-of-control mob, the great unwashed, a scab on his little domain, but he was outranked by our guv'nor, so his powers were limited. What made things worse for him was that the top man in the camp, Sergeant Major Bloy, was the most easy-going sergeant major I would ever come across in the British Army.

Although he was a fearsome-looking brute – an ex-boxer, broken nose, cauliflower ears, battered and scarred – he and his familiar Irish voice had become part of our lives. More than a little punch-drunk, he used to charge round the camp shouting and hollering at anyone and everyone, including officers. He would make second lieutenants quake as he would scream, 'Sir, sir, smarten yourself up'; 'Sir, you look like a sack of shit!' But for all our misdemeanours, he rarely charged anyone and kept matters of discipline under his control and well away from the officers.

I had my own theory about this: charges meant paperwork and it was easier for him to dish out jankers or CB (Confined to Barracks), leaving only the very serious crimes for the charge sheet. In any case, with all the trouble Dutchy got me into, I needed all the help I could get. One time he got me in a bit of bother and I feared the worst; even our very own Staff Sergeant Miles was powerless to help. Sergeant Major Bloy would surely throw away the key. But it was Sergeant Eggleton, of course, who cast his net over us.

To leave the camp for a night out on the town, one had to be suitably turned out and pass the Military Police inspection at the guardhouse. They took great pleasure in refusing us squaddies permission to leave. Dirty boots meant you couldn't shave in your reflection. Cap badge a disgrace meant he was able to look at it without sunglasses. Creases in your uniform that failed to cut your finger, a wonky tie or webbing that failed to please were all reasons we had been turned back for. One could get bow-legged running back and forth to the billet in an attempt to sign that magic book and leave the camp.

Dutchy came up with this brilliant brainwave: we would scale the perimeter fence, cut through the generals' garden, across the married quarters and to freedom. Our dress code would have never passed inspection; especially the 2 inch thick, crêpe-soled blue suede shoes. I know they didn't go too well with the uniform, but they were so comfortable and they were the only piece of civilian clothing we had at camp. After all, it was the age of the Teddy boy and a fashion statement had to be made. A great night out was had by all, but what we didn't know was that our favourite sergeant had watched us and noted our unorthodox departure.

He and two military policemen patiently waited for our return and we were unceremoniously marched to the guardhouse jail, where we spent an uncomfortable night. Sergeant Eggleton read us the riot act and he relished reading out every item on the charge sheet: breaking out of camp; failing to comply with company regulations regarding signing out and signing in; absent without leave; improperly dressed; wearing unauthorised footwear, i.e. brothel creepers, and breaking into camp. Even Staff Miles couldn't get us out of this. We were doomed. The next day, Sergeant Eggleton marched us to see Sergeant Major Bloy.

His 6 foot 2 frame dwarfed us as he stood with his clenched fist drilled into his hips and with bloodshot eyes looking dolefully at us, he said, 'So, 'twas yourself dat went out widout booking out, was it?'

It was more a statement than a question, so it went unanswered.

He turned on his heels and strode off across the parade ground, stopping halfway, where he turned and shouted, 'Double in, double in.'

This was by way of a command, to tell us that he required our company some more. Moving faster than we thought possible, we comfortably beat Eggleton, which seemed to please him.

'What punishment will I be giving you, den?'

Again, we declined to answer. We were dumbfounded. He was obviously going to deal with it himself and that meant "no charge". Eggleton's face was a picture, as he was also realising that all his work was going down the drain.

'Confined to barracks for a week and report for fatigues after work tonight. Now, double away, double away!'

A second telling wasn't needed, but we'd only got about 100 yards, when we were stopped dead by his thunderous roar. Eggleton had obviously been at work, for as we ran back, he had that slimy sneer on his face.

Bloy stuck his face into ours and snarled, 'You were wearing dem brothel creepers, weren't you?'

This time, the question demanded an answer.

'Yes, sir,' we replied timidly.

He started nodding his head and then turned around, stepping forwards, stepping back and shaping up, just as though he were shadow boxing. His huge fist hovered over my head and I felt like saying, 'It was 'im, sir, it was 'im.' His mind was obviously tortured at the thought of this heinous crime and what punishment these 'orrible little men deserved. Eggleton's eyes bulged with delight and anticipation. There was a hint of pleasure creeping across his face at our pending doom; he must have been imagining giving evidence at our court marshal, with a six-month prison sentence in Shepton Mallet being the absolute minimum.

Bloy suddenly stopped, pushed his face close to Eggleton and declared, 'Deez men, in addition to punishment already given ...' Bloy paused, deep in thought.

The excitement on Eggleton's face was positively electrifying. Dutchy and I exchanged glances, not knowing just what to expect.

Bloy continued in a coarse, harsh voice, 'Deez men, will do a weekend's fatigues as well!' He turned and strode off and as he went, he muttered repeatedly, 'As well, as well, as well ...'

Without moving our heads or a single muscle in our bodies, our eyes moved from Bloy to Eggleton. We were expecting a blast from himself; but, instead, his normal ramrod-straight back was somehow slumped, his face crestfallen and his mouth stood open in unbelievable astonishment. Without a word, he turned and marched of in semi-military fashion for, as low as he must have felt, he was still able to carry himself like a peacock on the pull. The breath from our bodies slowly exhaled and we swiftly and quietly moved in the opposite direction.

That evening, we watched from a distance but in earshot of the fatigue party as the duty corporal gave out the jobs. Our names were not on the list, so we went back to the billet and listened to Elvis Presley singing *Heart Break Hotel* on Radio Luxembourg.

We were due for guard duty that weekend. We only did one weekend in six and as it looked infinitely better than fatigues, we reported for duty and were able to witness, at close hand, the fatigue-duty roster and guess what? Our names were missing. Eggleton had really given up the ghost.

Bull (Army style)

In basic training we were taught how to march, shoot and, most of all, how to bull. I wasn't keen on the marching or the bull, but I have to admit I loved the guns. The 303 rifle was the first gun we experienced, first to drill with and then the good bit, actually getting real bullets to fire on the rifle range.

Firing the 303 is done belly down, lying on the ground. To reload after firing, one has to draw the bolt back, to allow the next bullet from the spring-loaded clip to be raised for the bolt to push it up the spout. Once this is achieved and the target has been lined up with the sights, the trigger can be squeezed, to send the bullet 800 to 1,000 yards into the bull's-eye of the target.

My aim was spot on and I could hit the bull's-eye every time, though my problem lay in that I'm left-handed and in those days, they only had right-handed rifles. Reloading was therefore a mission in itself, as I had to drop the rifle from the firing position, reach across with my left hand and complete the bolt action. So when we were instructed to fire five shots rapid, the best I could do was three shots in the time allowed.

This was the first time that our drill sergeant showed any compassion or understanding, taking the time to show me the quickest method to achieve the best results. No way could a left-hander be as fast as a right-hander, but it did speed me up. I kidded myself that this extra tuition was because he could see I was a good shot, but I found out later it was because he, too, was a left-hander. We also fired a pistol, a Sten gun and a Bren gun, and were taught to strip these weapons and reassemble then in a darkened room.

On the Road

After completing basic training at Blandford we moved to Barton Stacey, Hampshire, to complete our training. This part of the training was the ultimate fine-tuning of eager young men facing the rigours of life as a soldier; for Barton Stacey was home to the greatest trainers in the world: great men, with nerves of steel.

They took 17 and 18-year-old boys and turned them into men by teaching them to drive; army lorries, that is. Being a very young, fresh-faced boy, my driving instructor appeared to me to be older than the hills and I wondered how someone so old could still be working – after all, he was all of forty-five and a civilian to boot, as were all the driving instructors. Maybe he looked older than he was because of the job he was doing; but at the time that didn't occur to me. What I saw was a heavily lined face twitching with unnerving uneasiness. His face, although shaven, had patches of whiskers and nick marks, where the razor had failed to run smooth in his unstable hands. Never once smiling, he grunted his orders through nicotine-stained lips that were rarely without the ever-present cigarette.

We spent the first two hours driving round and round a large piece of wasteland, changing up and down the gearbox. Back in 1955, the gearboxes on these big old army lorries had what was called "crash gearboxes", so named because to change gear, one had to master the art of double-declutching, getting the gears to work in harmony with the engine. If the engine was running too fast, making a smooth connection was impossible and it would create the most horrendous crunching sounds, explaining why they were given their names. As soon as I had mastered the knack and had gained sufficient expertise we ventured onto the open road.

The amount of traffic on the road in those days was considerably less than today, but the roads weren't nearly as good, with towns not bypassed and dual carriageways few and far between. My heart was pounding as we pulled onto the road, but my tense body slowly unwound as I negotiated my way through the gears. As we trundled down the narrow country lanes I was beginning to think that this driving lark was a real doddle. Then, a few hundred yards in front of me, a lorry appeared, heading my way, with similar proportions to the huge beast I was driving. The road was not, in my inexperienced eye only; big enough to take *one* such vehicle, let alone two. I glanced agonisingly at my mentor, who seemed unperturbed, or had he fainted? I coughed nervously as the lumbering heap of metal drew ever closer. At the last moment I have to admit to closing my eyes as the left side of my vehicle brushed the hedgerow and the wing mirror on the right side came within a fag paper of the other lorry. That was my first real lesson, during which I learnt that those narrow country lanes *can* take two large motor vehicles alongside each other; but only just. Now I know what had made my instructor look so aged.

Our driving lessons began on the Monday and we took our driving test on the following Saturday, just five days after sitting behind the wheel of a 3 ton army lorry for the first time, at the grand old age of 17.

Those of us who were fortunate enough to pass were posted to camps all over the world. Dutchy and I had befriended the corporal who was in charge of issuing out the postings and he told us he had two postings for Hong Kong if we were interested. We were young, incredibly silly and had been away from Mum for nearly three months, so we begged him for something nearer home and he fixed us up with a posting to Ashford, Middlesex.

It was the cushiest posting that any squaddie could have dreamed of – especially for us – with most weekends off and just a bus ride into Hounslow, a Tube to Manor House and we were home. But we often wondered what it would have been like in Hong Kong.

At the age of 17 our driving career had begun and the mighty British Army had seen fit to give us a driving licence, which enabled us to drive anything from a jeep to a 10-ton truck. Brimming with overconfidence, it took me three whole months to destroy my first army vehicle. They should have left me driving the big stuff only capable of speeds of 40 miles an hour; a little faster going down hill with the wind behind you. But no, they gave me this lovely little Humber van – which hadn't had its speed restricted, like most army vehicles were subject to – and that was all I needed: speed, speed, lovely speed. We all know that speed in the hands of experienced drivers is dangerous, but in the hands of youth and inexperience it is a recipe for disaster.

I was only doing 65 miles an hour down this narrow country lane, when I found that I couldn't hold the road on a sharp left-hand bend and this stupid lamp post got in the way: the Humber was a write-off and the lamp post faired little better. Of course, the army wasn't best pleased and I was put on a charge and fined one twentieth of the value of the vehicle, which was assessed to be worth sixty pounds. It doesn't sound much, but I can assure you that it was a great deal of money, especially when you consider that my weekly wage was one pound and five shillings.

I was roaring round the Hampshire countryside in a nice new Land Rover three months later – will they never learn? It was very foggy with dubious visibility, but I saw no reason to slow down. After all, I could see a whole 10 yards ahead of me and the lads were waiting for me in the NAAFI. Just as I was overtaking a parked car, this brand spanking new Vauxhall Cresta appeared before me, clobbering my lovely Land Rover, resulting in the Cresta being a write-off. The driver of the VC was a highly respected local doctor and when I returned to camp, my staff sergeant looked at me with doleful eyes and said, 'Bleeding hell, Oliver, you sure know how to pick 'em and no mistake.'

But learning from previous experience and worried that another fine would bankrupt me, I managed to place the blame at the door of the good doctor. Perry Mason couldn't have done it better and somehow I managed to talk my way out of trouble and was ready for my next adventure.

Time passed and my driving skills improved; well, I thought so. When the army decided to give me a big old lorry that was capable of doing speeds in excess of 30 miles an hour, but not much in excess. I overheard the staff sergeant saying to the corporal, 'This should keep him out of trouble!' He was, of course, optimistic and it was three months, almost to the day, since my previous accident, while driving this ancient (naught to twenty in fifteen minutes) vehicle, that fate struck again.

Approaching a junction in the road where I was to make a right hand turn, I did everything right. Scanning the wing mirror, I checked the road behind. Yes, nice and clear, but still I made my hand signal – no indicators on this old girl. In the middle of a near-perfect right-hand turn, a noise caused me to glance over my shoulder. I was completely flabbergasted to see a car, brakes screeching and tyres burning the road, bearing down on me at the speed of light. I was completely powerless as a beautiful, gleaming, sparkling new Armstrong Sidley Sapphire was transformed into a crumpled wreck as it ploughed into my side, with the sound of breaking glass and tearing metal in its wake.

I jumped out of the lorry and the liveried chauffeur – yes, you read it right – clambered from the wreckage and as he struggled to separate the mangled metal, I heard a tiny super-cultured voice coming from the back seat. Unable to distinguish the words, I said, 'What, love?' Leaning forwards to hear better, I caught sight of an apparition. A little old lady, who must have been at least 200 years old, dressed in black with a fox fur round her neck, stretched out one of her claw-like hands, flicked it up and down and repeated. 'Young man, don't you have any flippers?'; she meant indicators.

'No, darling,' I replied. 'The British Army reckons a 10 ton wagon would be a bit obvious, especially with a big army arm stuck out of the window.' Being now an expert on accident procedure, I always carried my accident kit. A pen, a piece of paper and a tape measure. 'Right, mate,' I said to the chauffeur. 'Driver's name?'

'Smithers.'

'Owner's name?'

'Admiral Jellico.'

Oh my Gawd!

'Err, Smithers, who's the old dear in the back seat, then?' I inquired hesitantly.

'The Dowager Countess Jellico,' he stonily informed me.

My poor old staff sergeant aged ten years when I submitted my report, but after the police had investigated the accident I was cleared of blame, because there was a 150 yard skid on the road, a continuous white line in the middle of the road and a 30 mile an hour speed limit.

A further three months on, I drove with extreme caution and was able to break my three month jinx, but not before all the lads, including my lifelong, so-called friend Dutchy, had put me through sheer hell.

New Broom

It was a sad day: news filtered through that our sergeant major was to be posted to another camp. Our loss would be their gain. We were desolate. The new sergeant major didn't look as fearsome as Bloy, but he was an absolute bastard and right up Eggleton's street. Anyone would have thought they were in the army! Within a week of taking over he, in cohorts with Eggleton, had decided we were too soft and sloppy and in need of shaping up.

They decided that in addition to our normal day's work, we would embark on a physical training course. Our normal day began at six thirty, with morning parade at seven – if we were unable to skive out of it – breakfast at seven fifteen and report for work at eight. The diabolical duo announced that everyone – bar none except the dead – would rise at five and commence bodily enhancement.

It was a nightmare; Eggleton was in his element. Every morning at five, while all the squaddies were at perfect peace with the world, the relative calm was quashed by that dreaded man. He would burst into the billet, cracking his pacing stick on the metal frames of the beds, screaming at the top of his voice that old chestnut about our socks being a better place for our hands than our genitals.

The first morning we did some exercises and a nice little 5-mile run. This was too much for Dutchy and he soon came up with one of his "super skive" schemes.

'The empty billet!' he explained. 'They don't have a roll-call; we could grab a mug of tea from the cookhouse, dive into the empty billet and hide up. It'll be a piece of cake.'

Hell, where have I heard that before? Dawn broke and Eggleton entered with his cheery greeting. 'OK, chaps; time to rise and shine.' Or words to that effect – I don't think! Dragging ourselves from our stinking pits and pulling on our clothes, we had fifteen minutes to get it together. The cookhouse was close by, so grabbing the bromide-charged tea we took refuge in the empty billet. Inside were rows of large metal lockers that comfortably housed one body.

I couldn't believe our luck: it had worked – we weren't missed. As days passed we became more organised, stashing pillows and blankets in the lockers in the unused billet and thus our mornings grew more comfortable. One or two of the other lads caught on and very soon every locker was taken and sometimes, for the very close friends, it was two to a locker. Then the inevitable happened. Even the big – and oh so thick – Eggleton had to realise that there had been a considerable reduction in the amount of squaddies taking part in his fun-filled morning's entertainment.

So, after a head count, he must have decided that someone, somewhere, was skiving. Mind you, he still couldn't figure it out. He had checked the billets, the cookhouse and every other possible hiding place; he had even checked the empty billet and I can remember sitting in the locker holding my breath for what seemed like an eternity, listening to him stomping up and down talking to himself. 'Their feet won't touch; their feet won't touch!' Thank heavens it never occurred to him to look inside the lockers.

Then it happened: the boom was lowered. He spotted a straggler and like a Private Dick, he followed him to our hiding place. We were caught red-handed and there was hell to pay, with fatigues, extra guard duties and severe earache dealt out.

Now, I'm not going to divulge the culprit's name who was our undoing, because even after all these years the contract for his very existence is still waiting to be claimed. All I will say is that he made getting me into trouble an art form. The extra guard duties plus our own duty weekends, bit deeply into our free time and it was the weekends that were the highlights in our lives.

Sickness

The weekends were great and it was always hard returning to camp on Sunday night, so Dutchy and I caught the last possible Tube back to camp. We were always bemoaning the fact that although life was marginally better than the humdrum life in a Civvy Street factory, we still hadn't achieved the exciting new life we'd expected. What at first was a super-cushy posting was, indeed, becoming boring and irritating, especially with the arrival of the new sergeant major.

One Sunday, Dutchy announced that he wasn't going back!

'Don't be daft. They'll hunt you down; don't you remember Terry Chisholm's dad during the war; the military police were always chasing him. Not that they ever caught him, but they were always after him.'

'No, no, Bob, I'm going sick.'

'What? How can you go sick in the army?'

His devious brain had been at work again. It was something that would never have crossed my mind.

He explained his plan. 'You go back to camp and then tell them I'm ill and going to see the quack.'

'Me? Me? What about me?' I said.

He suggested that we should each take turns, so we could extend our weekends, as long as the doctor would give us a sick note. 'It's foolproof, nothing can go wrong!'

After thinking about it, I calculated that it was safer for me to go second, but my fears were unfounded and it worked like a dream. We discovered that as long as you got a medical certificate you were covered.

It was now my turn and I was thinking about my family doctor, who I would have to see to get the necessary certificate. This put my mind in top gear and off down memory lane I sped. When I was just a kid, our local GP had a larger-than-life character, both physically and psychologically. He was also a comedian to boot, with a weird sense of humour, and was always cracking jokes. I had the feeling that if someone went to him on his last legs he would have had hysterics – a trait you seldom find in the medical profession. Having said that, he was no mug and when I was a child, the old lady took me to see him with pains in the stomach – he had me in hospital for an Appendix operation quicker than a wink. To this day, I doubt his diagnosis of my condition, but it sure as hell stopped me whining about belly ache.

Over the years, he and the hospital saw a great deal of me; what with broken bones, boils, abscesses and several serious cuts. My old dear was bow-legged running me to and fro, but it was a way of life and she was used to it, all my brothers and sisters having trodden the same path. Although, to quote her, she did once say, 'You top the bleeding lot, you do!' referring to me. Somehow, I managed to survive adolescence and "Big Doc".

Anyway, it was my turn to visit the surgery and try my luck; I was on a week's leave and had a lot of time to think about the "going sick skive". At first I had my doubts and I didn't think I would go through with it, but as the week progressed the thought of going back to camp lay heavy on my mind, planting the decision firmly in my mind that I would go to the doctors first thing Monday morning.

Then I had this vision of "Big Doc", laughing like a drain as I pretended to be sick. I told myself, Bob, you have two choices: go back to camp and that malevolent Sergeant Eggleton, who needed his daily quota of blood, or try your luck with "Big Doc", with his twisted sense of humour and a slim chance of a couple of extra days' sick leave. Weighing up all the pros and cons, I finally decided that Saturday would be better. That way, if unsuccessful, I could always go back on Sunday and no one would be any the wiser.

It was long before the appointment system was introduced, so a long wait in the surgery was to be expected. Come to think of it, the appointment system makes little or no difference even these days – you still have a long wait. I sat in that waiting room for two solid hours, rehearsing my script. The waiting room was full of the dead and the dying sat perched on hard wooden benches reading old newspapers and I felt like the fraud that I was; but the thought of Eggleton enabled me to see it through. The place was dark, uninviting and miserable.

The receptionist's presence was dominant, daring anyone to break the fearful silence. She sat in her huge, comfortable chair at her desk in the corner; in those days, the doctor's assistant wasn't just a receptionist, she was also a nurse, a secretary, a cleaner, a personal aide and a tyrant to boot. This one was older than my driving instructor; she must have been 50 if she was a day. Tall, skinny, hard-faced and hook-nosed, wearing thick horn-rimmed glasses: a formidable figure.

Finally, it was my turn and the superior voice called me. 'Mr Oliver.' The "Mister" seemed to stick in her throat, the "Oliver" spewn from her mouth in disgust. She peered over her glasses and snapped, 'Come this way.'

The hairs on my neck bristled and my heart lodged in my throat. Nervously entering his den, I was dwarfed by his enormity; even sitting down he seemed to tower over me. He hadn't changed a bit, his bulky features booming with amusement.

It was as if he had just been watching the *Tony Hancock Show*. A fleeting thought flashed through my mind: someone must have died.

'Well, Robert.' He always called me Robert. 'How's the army treating you?'

I was puzzled; do I answer his question or do I go into my headache routine? Bloody hell! I thought, the last time I complained of a stomach ache he had half my innards removed. What will he do for a headache?

'Come and sit yourself down, laddie.' Oh yes, and he was a Scot. A jovial Jock. I always reckoned he was so happy because he was in a good position to inflict misery on the Sassenachs! 'Well well, Robert,' he repeated himself. Then, still smiling, he leaned forwards; his eyes had narrowed and were completely divorced from the rest of his jubilant fizzog.

It was as if he was searching for something. Then, as if by telepathy, a look of total recognition crossed his features. 'How long do you want off and what can we find wrong with you?'

His words stunned me but, quick to recover, I stammered, 'A wweeek … err, a cold!' The thought that there was a catch never entered my head. What a fool; how naive.

My greedy eyes watched as he wrote out the sick note, my hands caressing each other in anticipation. His gold false teeth sparkled as he offered me the certificate saying, 'Unfortunately, Robert, because you're in the army and not strictly on my books, I'll have to make a small charge. It'll be two shillings and sixpence per day; so that'll be twelve shillings and sixpence, please!'

I was left with eight and a half pence or, in those days, one shilling and nine pence; or, as my dad would say, a chip (a shilling), a sprat (sixpence) and a joey (a thrup'ny bit). This had to last me ten days, till the next pay day: needless to say, I couldn't afford too many trips to the jovial Jock, but one must count one's blessings and, after all, there was always the old lady to sponge off.

Dutchy, of course, overdid it, going off for six whole weeks, and the military police arrived on his doorstep with an ambulance, whipping him off to a military hospital. After undergoing some serious examinations he was pronounced fit and returned to camp. He said they had told him they would send an ambulance to him on the first day of any future sickness, to ensure that he received the best of medical attention. Good, ain't they?

Schemes

Every now and then the monotony was broken and an announcement was made that we were going on a scheme. Yes, even in REME workshop barracks we had to play soldier every now and then, when the well-oiled machinery of the British Army moved into action. It was winter and bitterly cold and we spent our nights in sleeping bags in tiny little tents called bivouacs. The thing that sticks in my mind most of all is not being able to get my feet warm and lying in my sleeping bag curled up and rubbing my feet with my hands. There were icy winds and freezing rain; the old wags said that if it snowed it would be warmer. Oh, how I prayed for snow; well, when you're seventeen you believe anything.

As on all schemes, we played war games in which there was a hill we had to defend. Anyway, the captain told Dutchy and I to dig a slit trench. It was getting late, it was dark and we were cold, miserable, hungry and knackered. The ground was like solid rock, even after we had broken the frozen crust, but we managed to get down a couple of feet. Then Dutchy had this masterly idea – here we go again! 'Look,' he said, 'we'll only have to fill it in tomorrow, why don't we kneel in the trench for the inspection, so it looks like it's up to our necks? In the pitch-dark the captain will never know the difference!'

Something at the back of my mind kept telling me this latest plan wasn't as masterly as Dutchy made out, but there you go – I'm easily led and gullible to the bitter end. Anyway, I went along with him and come the inspection we knelt down, scrunching ourselves into the hole, and saluted smartly when the captain came by. To my amazement, it worked and we passed inspection!

After doing our bit on guard we crept into our bivouacs and I fell into the deepest sleep I'd had since coming on the scheme. Unfortunately, it was short-lived, for I was rudely awakened by shouting and hollering: the enemy had decided to attack. One can only assume that someone, somewhere, had got bored and decided to use us to elevate their monotony.

My tent was on a slight incline and in my deep sleep I had rolled and was well and truly entangled in the sleeping bag and the bivouac. Like a demented man in a straitjacket, I struggled to get free. Sticking my head out of the tent flap, I witnessed a truly magnificent vision: the clouds had disappeared and the moon shone bright, the frost was as thick as the pile on a new carpet, the stars sparkled and the naked branches on the skeleton trees glistened in the moonlight. When, crashing through the night, came the captain, screaming, 'Turn out the guard, stand to the guard.'

Now this bit was the most beautiful vision of all. Only half dressed, his pistol and belt in one hand, while the other hand clutched at his trousers containing only one of his legs, the other leg revealed a pair of saucy pyjamas. He took a huge leap into the air, anticipating a deep drop into the safety of Dutchy's slit trench, only to discover the protection wasn't even thigh deep! He looked to the heavens as if in prayer and seeking divine guidance, he threw his hands in the air and screeched, 'Oliverrrrrrrr!' Me? Why me? Tell me, why me? Why not! 'Dutcheeeeeeeee!'

Goodbye Trouble

Dutchy and I managed to stay together for nearly two years and this was very rare, as the army have a habit of moving people about. So when he was called to the office and told that his unused talents were needed in another place, it didn't come as a real surprise. With the National Service men being demobbed and others being posted away, I was now one of the most senior soldiers in the motor transport section, without my right arm, Dutchy, and his mad ideas to get me into trouble and with my driving skills improving all the time. So Staff Sergeant Miles decided to promote me to Colonel's Driver: the cream of the MT section, where there was most definitely no guard duties and no parades.

When the general's driver was on leave, it was my duty to take over and drive the general's old Humber and that was something special. What a cushy life I was having – too bloody cushy. The novelty soon wore off and I was missing the excitement of getting Dutchy into trouble. Whoops! I mean him getting me into trouble; nearly let the cat out of the bag there.

Time for some real Soldiering:

The Paras

Watching the sergeant major and, of course, the colonel, who were both ex-Paratroopers, I decided that I needed something more and that the Paras was the real army, for which I would volunteer. But there was a problem: they told me that I couldn't transfer to the Paras, as I had less than two years to serve and would have to sign on for another three if I moved rank.

While driving the colonel one day, I plucked up enough courage and had a word with him. I told him the truth about being keen on joining the Paras, but gave him a little bullshit about signing on for an extra three years, saying that if I passed the Para course and it was as good as I thought it would be, I would sign on. Not sure if he fell for the bullshit or if he wasn't keen on my driving, but within three days I was on my way and once again I was leaving behind a great bunch of lads.

The training course for the Paras was all you would expect it to be. Assault courses, running, unarmed combat, running, arms training, running, gym training, running, log racing, running, milling and more running. But the thing that surprised me was that there wasn't any "bull". Sure, we always had to be clean and tidy on parade, but the thing missing from previous camps was the "bull". Furthermore, the atmosphere was different. Because we were all volunteers and keen to qualify, there wasn't any thought of skiving; not that we could hope to get away with anything and, of course, this time I didn't have my old mate to lead me astray.

Milling was quite an ordeal. The squad was lined up – tallest on the right and shortest on the left. 'Move, move, move your idle bodies.' Yes, some things never change! 'Number from right to left in twos.' This was the signal for the squaddies to shout as loud as we could. 'One, two; one, two; one, two,' right along the line. 'Odds one step, forward, march.' The final word of any command in the forces was always ten pitches higher than the others that were screamed and spat out as if in an uncontrollable rage. It always had the desired effect: one moved one's idle body as quickly as one could. We now had two lines. 'Front rank, about face.' The guy now facing you had now become your enemy.

The next command was for both lines to number from the tallest to the shortest. A square was formed and the sergeant would shout out a number and the two squaddies with that number would enter the square. Without finesse or skill of any kind, they would, for one minute, "mill". This meant that you attempted to punch the shit out of your opponent and anyone who dared to box their way through the minute was subjected to three minutes of physical abuse with the physical training instructor. These instructors were the best of the best; in peek physical condition, they were awesome beasts to be feared. I wouldn't have relished three minutes with any of them, so my head went down and my arms went every which way. Milling for one minute seemed like an eternity and I thought it would never end.

The log race was an experience that is only good to look back on. We were divided into teams of nine. A line of telegraph poles lay on the floor and we were told attach toggle ropes to one of these poles. The team leader ran in front, pulling his toggle, which was tied to the front of the log. The other eight were paired to carry the log; four each side. The race was a mile long over tank tracks – an arduous terrain to put it mildly. The pain was immense, with blood, sweat and tears, and with bodies aching and lungs fit to bust; even the milling seemed attractive during this particular activity.

In most races our team acquitted ourselves reasonably well and once, we came a respectable fourth out of ten teams. There again, once we came last, but that was owing to our leader collapsing halfway round and his caring team running right over him, leaving him well and truly sunk into the mud. I was third back from the front and didn't see him go down and only realised we were leaderless when my left boot found his back, followed swiftly by my right boot finding his left ear. The poor bastard must have wished he had dived into the nearby stagnant pool of slime and filth. A lesson had been taught: one does not go down when one is the lead runner.

The "holiday-camp billet" was Maider Barracks, Aldershot, which nestles in the beautiful Hampshire countryside. The accommodation still retained its World War I charm but made maintenance a slight problem. The cookhouse had its own unique, beguiling allure, with specialities like half-cooked corned beef fritters lying on a bed of congealed fat. My other non-favourite was fried eggs; they had an unusual way of preparing this dish and try as I may, I find it impossible to emulate.

The finished article has a slightly overdone underside, with flakes of black clinging longingly to the dark brown surface. The top is completely uncooked, with the yolk a very pale yellow, suggesting it had an extremely undernourished mother, and the so-called white of the egg in reality displaying a mouth-watering grey appearance that resembled a jelly-like substance found in the intestines of a frog. For all these delights and more, one had to queue in a line of 100 yards plus; with a whole thirty minutes to complete one's lunch break in. I existed mainly on glucose and chocolate from the NAAFI. Even if we had time to queue, the cookhouse food was only consumed by the strong of stomach or the starving National Service men, who couldn't afford the NAAFI.

Abingdon: The DZ

By the end of the course, our trainers had eliminated half our numbers and they had quietly disappeared; we, the rest, moved on to Abingdon to learn how to parachute. All that had gone before was an endurance test, to decide who was to become a Para and who was to be rejected.

Abingdon was an RAF camp and we thought we had arrived in heaven. The food and accommodation was something we had never encountered before in the army; breakfast was always superbly prepared and was preceded by a choice of cereal – it was unbelievable luxury. The billets were clean, the beds were comfortable and there were even curtains at the windows.

Memoirs of a Working Man

Can you believe that? Curtains! I was shocked to hear the "Brylcreem Boys" complaining and when I told them they should try Aldershot; they declined, commenting, 'We joined the RAF to avoid the squalor the army had to offer, thank you very much.' I think they had a point.

Our first lesson was how to hit the ground at 20 feet a second and survive. Army parachutes were designed to get the troops down as quickly as possible, for obvious reasons. Nowadays, they have chutes that you can drive with precision, land on a sixpence, stand up and casually walk away. When we hit the ground, we had to have legs, knees and feet together, with elbows tucked well in.

The line of drift, the way the wind was taking you, determined how you presented yourself to the ground. It was practice, practice and more practice. Leaping from a mock-up aeroplane – the back of a lorry – a controlled jump from 30 feet was made in a harness, in a hanger. Then there was the outside 70 foot training jump, where we hit the ground at an authentic speed.

Finally, we were ready for the real thing. Parachuting is the second-best experience in the world, though balloon jumps were the scariest. As the balloon hoists the cage up there is plenty of chat, but the higher you go the talk diminishes, the temperature drops dramatically, the cage sways in the breeze and the people on the ground shrink to Lilliputian size. Was it the cold making me shiver or was it fear?

The cage is an open basket with an open door and a bleeding great gaping hole in the floor. It's all very cold-blooded and you felt very vulnerable; unlike the aeroplanes, where you are all closed in. Stumbling from the cage, you face a sheer drop; parachuting from an aeroplane you have to leap into the 200 mile an hour slipstream of the plane, whipping you away, with your chute opening, hopefully, before you know what's happening. Once the chute is open you feel like you have all the time in the world as you float down, absorbing the scenery and sucking in the atmosphere.

But before you can take time to admire the view, you must check the parachute, kick out twists in your rigging and release the 90 pound (41 kilo) weapons' container that's strapped to your legs, checking first to see that no one is beneath you. After all, you don't want to a drop 90 lb weight on one of your buddies' chutes. Once released, it drops and hangs on by a 30 foot nylon cord from your harness. Only then do you have time to enjoy the whole scene. And what a scene – truly breathtaking.

There isn't any feeling of falling; just floating timelessly on air, with the impression that it would go on forever. But, suddenly, the dream is shattered when, at about 70 feet from the ground, the sensation of falling appears at an alarming rate and the earth leaps up, hitting you like a train rushing a tunnel.

To get our Wings, we had to make eight jumps: two balloon and six from an aeroplane. The best jumps by far were from the "boon of the Beverley Aircraft". This was a huge plane designed to transport trucks, Land Rovers and heavy goods. The boon is a section on top of the plane sticking out beyond the rear and it has a large hole in the floor, used to drop goods or bodies.

This was far better, because it meant that you just stepped into the hole in the floor and didn't have to propel yourself into a slipstream. In addition, we were spared the fearful roar as the instructors removed the side doors, the noise sending chills of fear through our bodies; but, of course, you must never show that there are butterflies in your stomach or the terror that is coursing through your veins.

Well-ard or What! I think "or What"!

Para training at Abingdon was without a doubt the best time in my years spent in the army. It was a culmination of several things: living conditions were excellent and the instructors weren't out to test our very existence. They were RAF instructors and we all had great respect for them; they were no-nonsense gentlemen, there to teach us, not break us. The physical pressure was off. Everything was new. The practice and training interesting, the jumping exciting and, of course, our group of lads were great, the army having moulded us into a team.

We ended our training with a night jump, which was quite spectacular. The night was as black as Newgates knocker, with a thick blanket of cloud shutting out the moon and the stars. Our only means of navigation were the lights on the DZ, lights from buildings and, in the distance, from towns and villages. As trained, I tried to focus on a point to assess my drift, but try as I might I couldn't work it out. Then I peered straight down in an attempt to see the ground, but again it was all in vain; I couldn't see a damn thing.

It soon became apparent why I was unable to work out my approach to the ground, when my knees struck my chin with some ferocity. My descent had been completely vertical. That was the nearest I ever came to a stand-up landing.

My luck was better than one of my mates who, we were told, had been taken to hospital with broken legs having made a bad landing. But that wasn't the case, as we found out later: he had landed on the flat concrete roof of a bunker; the building was a bombproof hanger. However, it wasn't this that broke his legs. He told us later, 'I thought I'd hit a road; it was pitch-black and I couldn't see a hand in front of me. I looked around for the homing light, rolled up my chute and was just congratulating myself on a brilliant landing on hard ground, when I stepped off the bunker.'

We were presented with our Wings and the holiday was over. All good things must come to an end and it was back to "Murder Maider Barracks", Aldershot.

Manoeuvres

The Para training had honed me: I was as fit as a fiddle, 10 stone wringing wet, without an ounce of fat on me and, of course, full of self-importance. We were told that at 07:00 hrs the next day we would be setting off in convoy to a place called Otterburn, to take part in manoeuvres, and that the scheme would last for a month.

The thought of getting away from "Murder Maida Barracks, Aldershot" was greeted with joy and excitement, because it wasn't nicknamed "murder" for nothing. It was the absolute pits and was by far and away the worst barracks I'd had the misfortune to serve in. Even the knowledge that it meant a month living rough and under canvas wasn't a deterrent and the fact that I hadn't a clue where Otterburn was didn't even enter the equation; as far as I was concerned, it could have been in the Soviet Union.

As it happened, it's situated on the English side of the Scottish Border, 300 miles from Aldershot. The journey took two days to complete, stopping overnight at a place called Tamworth. The same journey today could be accomplished in five or six hours – cones permitting, that is – but in those days, before motorways and bypasses, every town and city en route had to be crossed using the old roadway network. The November weather was unkind and the further north we went, the worse it became: mist, fog and drizzle; typical autumn weather.

Our approach to Otterburn seemed a signal to the Gods that a welcome was due and the heavens opened up; this was my first experience of northern weather. London born, I had never ventured further north than Watford and I was quickly discovering that the northern weather was harsher than I was used to. The rain is definitely wetter up there, it's certainly colder and it's generally bloody awful. No wonder they call us "soft southerners".

Otterburn was an established camp, designed especially for manoeuvres, and the accommodation was all set up. As you can imagine, in the 1950s it was sheer luxury – I don't think. The tents afforded shelter for four squaddies with four lovely camp beds, but the ultimate comfort was the floor covering. Well, that is to say that the floor wasn't exactly covered – they were of timber construction and were aptly named duckboards, for they floated and bobbled on a stream of water that passed through the tents; only retained by pieces of nylon cord attached to the camp beds.

Sleeping was a nightmare; not only did the rain hammer unrelentingly down onto the canopy, but we had to have all our kit on the bunk with us, for fear that it might at best get wet or worse, get washed away, never to be seen again.

I was allocated to drive the recovery vehicle and my co-driver and I had been instructed to pick up a signalman, proceed to our appointed map reference and await instructions. So it was that the well-trained, super-efficient Para machine moved into action.

The signalman was a right big head with a mouth to match. He made me look positively refined. You know the type: open your mouth and he has done it, been there and got a bigger one. Now I don't dislike Brummies, but this guy went a long way to create an everlasting prejudice in me. I know we shouldn't be swayed by a person's looks and the way they talk, but his every word grated on me and he had the look of a cockerel on heat. Long, thin neck with the biggest Adam's apple I have ever seen, his chin vanishing from below an extremely large, hooked nose and eyes bulging beneath bushy eyebrows. It was years later when I heard Jasper Carrott described as looking like a ferret in a suit that I decided it summed up Signalman Jones perfectly.

Our four-wheel drive recovery vehicle took us across some horrendous terrain in our search for our assigned map reference. We slipped and slid through the rain-soaked countryside and still it rained; northern rain, that is – none of your soft southern stuff. We made it, managed to find a bit of shelter from the driving rain, camouflaged our vehicle, put a brew on and settled down to await further orders.

A couple of hours passed with my mate, who could sleep on a clothes line, snoring contentedly, while "big head" the signalman was playing with his radio in the back of the lorry. "Bravo golf, bravo golf" and all that nonsense. Anyway, the signalman nudged me, pointed to his radio set and said, "Ere, you should hear this lot! They're going potty. Been trying for hours to locate the recovery vehicle! And they're not answering! Boy are they going to get it in the neck!'

I grabbed him by the throat and snapped, 'You dozy, bleeding great pillock! We're the recovery vehicle! What do you think all this sodding equipment is for? Mountain-bloody-neering?'

When we finally arrived at the location, to which we had been summoned, we found a scene resembling something from World War One, with about fifty squaddies up to their necks in mud, soaked by the uncompromising rain and thoroughly miserable. We were not flavour of the month. A couple of 10 ten ton lorries were bogged down to their axles in the quagmire, with the captain barking orders at the cheerless "other ranks" as they attempted the impossible. What they really needed was a recovery vehicle.

The game plan had been simple. The recovery vehicle would be conveniently situated close by. A ton lorry would get bogged down, the recovery vehicle would be alerted and, like the cavalry, would charge across the horizon to the rescue. When we didn't respond to their call, the captain sent a messenger to our appointed map reference, returning later to report, 'No sign of the recovery vehicle, sir.'

Don't look at me. It wasn't my fault; the stupid co-driver had misread our instructions and we ended up 10 miles north. If we'd been in the Gulf, we would have ended up in an Iraqi prison.

They had been calling us continuously, while my co-driver snored and my signalman received signals. Meanwhile, the captain, in his infinite wisdom, had decided, against the advice of the sergeant, to attempt his own recovery, by using another 10 ton lorry. The end result was, of course, two stranded vehicles.

He spluttered and choked on his words, but all that came out was, 'Get them out, Oliver, get them out!'

With the sergeant's expertise and our equipment, we hauled them out in no time at all. But don't let the time factor fool you – it was by no means an easy feat and my co-driver and I sweated blood while the sergeant directed proceedings and all the while that swine Signalman Jones was sat sniggering in the dry.

It wasn't all bad and we did have some laughs, but the main thing I remember about Otterburn is the rain. For twenty-eight days solid we didn't see the sky. Soaked and soggy, I often longed for the squalor of "Murder Maider Barracks".

Foreign Parts

My time spent in the Paras was interesting; activities meant that we were never allowed to get bored, with something always going on. The training never seemed to stop: assault courses, parachuting, shooting, yomping, schemes and war games. A far cry from the time I had spent in the army before joining the Paras. It was a very exciting time in my life, especially when the call came to serve in foreign parts. Apparently, in those days, Britain had a treaty with King Hussein of Jordan and he had requested troops to protect his borders from unfriendly neighbours.

The problem was that the call came in 1958 when I was due for demob. The notice on the board said that anyone with less than six months to serve would have to stay in Aldershot. My saving grace was the army's need for experience and volunteers were required from all who were due for demob to sign on for an extra six months. I was first in the queue, but there was another problem: Eileen. We had been courting for over a year and I dare not tell her that I had signed on or I would have got a "Dear John" before leaving. So I just left that bit out and told her we were being posted overseas.

We didn't know where we were going, it was all very hush-hush, but the issue of khaki shorts gave us sort of a clue and suggested it wouldn't be to chillier climes; though with the army one could never quite be certain. On the aeroplane we were told that we were destined for Jordan, but that we were going to regroup in Cyprus. More firsts for me: it was the first time I had been abroad and the first time I had ever been in a plane when it landed; I was used to exiting before touchdown.

We found ourselves assembling just outside Nicosia. As with any military movement, it was all hustle, bustle and organised chaos. We pitched our tents and, oh joy, dug latrines. Then up went a huge marquee used by the Greek Cypriots to sell us anything and everything. First thing to be heard was a jukebox, which blared out rock 'n' roll music "all around the clock". The strange thing was I never actually observed any money being put into the machine. Then one day I saw why. We were sitting chatting and sucking back a few pints of Keo, the local brew, when one of the lads strolled over to the jukebox, expertly open it, ran his fingers across the keys inside, closed it up and strolled off, leaving us with a free, non-stop music fest. The Cypriot owner wasn't at all chuffed with his takings and took the matter to the captain, who in turn gave us a lecture on honesty.

That same evening, the owner brought a friend and together they spent an hour making the jukebox break-in proof. Grinning triumphantly, they departed. At that same moment, a squaddie appeared, produced a screwdriver and with a flick of the wrist, there was a loud cracking sound and the jukebox was as open as the Grand Canyon – the music continued.

We were plagued by flies – I had never seen so many flies in my life – especially around the latrines. Our super-deluxe lavatory was a huge pit with a plank of wood across it and it was surrounded by a hessian screen, with no roof, thank God. Anyway, one day the inevitable happened: we all suffered from the dreaded "berri berri", "the Bombay squirts", "Delhi belly" or whatever you want to call it. This had to be the closest to hell as I ever want to get, sitting on that plank of wood covered in flies, the pit emitting a stomach-churning, unbearable stench. The funny side is the mental picture I still have of a row of squaddies, shorts down, bums out, grunting and groaning with heads clasped in hands.

One day we were lying in our tent during the midday siesta, when "Loopy Lennie" leaped from his camp bed and started running for the lavvy. We all knew what he was going through and our worst dream became Lenny's nightmare as I watched him speeding across the wasteland. He was within 20 yards, but didn't make it; he came to a sudden halt, standing there with his head bowed, looking the picture of dejection, as he slowly dragged his way, step by wavering step, to the fly-ridden bog.

I turned to Harry the Rick and said, 'Chuck me over Lenny's shorts and just in case, some boots.' Lenny was nicknamed Loopy because of his nerves. Everywhere he went he would run his hand along anything that was handy. At every opening or entrance he came to, he would stop and adopt the position as if he were jumping from a plane. After making several attempts to get through, rocking back and forwards he would make a final effort and zoom off. No one ever took the mickey out of him and we all looked after him like a mother hen. The reason for his affliction was that one day he was in a plane about to make a jump, when the guy behind him stumbled into him and they both went out of the door together. As they hit the slipstream they began spinning. The guy who was behind Lenny was somehow thrown clear, leaving Lenny entangled in all the parachute straps of the lads that had gone before. He was hanging out of the plane door being buffeted by the slipstream and crashing into the side of the aircraft for several minutes before the instructors could haul him back in.

He was very shaken and was never the same again. The army psychiatrist, in his infinite wisdom, decided that the best treatment for him was to be with mates. Apart from his trouble with getting through doors and the obsession with running his hand along everything, he was saner than the rest of us put together. He must have known he was doing it, because I had him in stitches when I said, 'Right oh, Len, put your boots on, rub the tent pole three times and I'll treat you to a beer.' To this day, I suspect he was working his ticket.

Roughest, Toughest Motor Journey on Earth

The day came when we had to leave Cyprus. We had to take the heavy equipment by boat from Famagusta down to Egypt through the Suez Canal, into the Red Sea and up the Gulf of Aqaba. It was on the Red Sea that I experienced seasickness. Our boat was the first one through the canal and we had to wait for the others to catch up. The Port of Aqaba was shallow and so the boats were flat-bottomed.

As I sat on the deck in the burning sun watching the arid coastline of Saudi Arabia, with the sea like a mill pond and only gentle ripples across its beautiful blue surface, I was unaware of the flat-bottomed boat gently rolling, the coastline appearing and then disappearing. The realisation that I was soon to be calling for "Hugheee" over the side came too late. I can't remember a time when I have felt so ill.

On the approach to the port we could see four countries: Egypt, Saudi Arabia, Israel and Jordan. Unloading seemed to take an eternity; we were all getting edgy and were eager to get going, but what we didn't realise was that we were about to embark on the roughest, toughest motor journey in the world from Aqaba to Amman. The lorry I was driving was, like all the others, loaded to the brim; even the cab was full, with barely room to change gear. Every vehicle towed a trailer; mine was a 200 gallon water tank – a good thing to have nearby when you're in the desert.

There were no roads, just a narrow dirt track, and the order of the day was "drive on the right". Right of what? I thought. As we skirted awe-inspiring canyons and gorges, the vehicle in front of me just seemed to sink from view. Then my heart lodged in my throat as I began to descend the steepest incline I have ever encountered. The 200 gallon trailer began to push me hard and the once fearless 19-year-old boy shook like a leaf and wished that someone else had the water trailer.

I can vaguely remember looking up to see a vast canyon with a winding track that was barely wide enough to take a car, let alone a convoy of large lorries towing trailers. It snaked down one side and up the other, with sheer drops in places that gave one an uneasy feeling between the legs and palpitations that shook the whole body. Fighting all the way down, I managed to keep control of the vehicle. Going up was also very hairy, but after the descent it was a picnic. I found myself shaking long after we had left it behind. Later, there were other wadis to negotiate, but none of them seemed as bad as that first one.

Out of the desert and into the mountains we trundled, when I suddenly became aware that I'd lost sight of the vehicle in front. Putting my foot down on the accelerator, my speed shot up to more than 20 miles per hour. And believe me; this was exceptionally fast for the conditions. The truck and trailer bounced from rock to hole, swaying violently along the dirt track. Suddenly, I crashed to a halt and sank axle deep into soft sand. Shaken, I climbed out of the cab.

The silence was deafening. I was alone, terrified, in a foreign land thousands of miles from home. Scouring the mountainside my eyes fell upon an Arab waving and shouting what seemed to me like abuse. This is it, I thought, I've strayed across the border and there are thousands of marauding Arabs about to descend and slaughter poor me.

Reaching inside the cab, I grabbed my Sterling sub-machine gun and loaded it. Keeping the gun out of sight and peering across the bonnet, I watched the lone Arab close in. Shaking, I was about to blast him from the face of the earth, when it became obvious he was only trying to tell me I should have turned right at the cliff face. I should then have proceeded across the rickety-rackety bridge that I'd seen a long way back, but never dreamed passable. Waving my appreciation I climbed back into the cab. Crossing my fingers, I slipped the gearbox into four-wheel drive and found first gear.

Thankfully, that beautiful low-geared Rolls-Royce engine eased me out of the soft sand. About 200 yards back along the track, roaring up to me came the captain, ranting and raving like a maniac. He was stating the obvious, by telling me that I had taken a wrong turning; with the bleeding water supply, they weren't about to lose me.

Out of the mountains and back into the desert, we were now in the land of mirages. Around us lay vast lakes and swamps and cool, sparkling pools of water that could be seen but never reached, because it was never there in the first place. The first day we travelled for thirteen hours, covering about 90 miles, before bedding down for the night under the bright desert stars. Huge bats winged over us, unidentified rodents scurried around our field kitchen and a breeze sighing through the dust dunes sounded like waves breaking on a distant shore.

At the crack of dawn, at about 4.00 a.m., we were told to move our idle bodies, as we had to be in Amman before dusk and with less than half the journey covered we had our work cut out. Our journey seemed to last a lifetime as we floundered through the dunes as best we could, edging around hillocks of black rock shimmering in the blazing sun.

We stopped at midday to eat and refuel. We had halted in the centre of a bowl, fringed at the horizon with grotesquely misshapen, jagged black hills. All round us dust devils and whirlwinds snaked and twisted high into the sky, where the sun appeared a deep red behind a haze of dust. It was a sight I will never forget.

As we closed in on Amman we passed through small villages. I had never seen people living like this – the poverty was appalling. Young children hobbled along with the convoy, crying out, begging for food. Their homes, if you can call them such, were makeshift shacks without sanitation. All these things are etched in my memory forever.

The first sign to tell me we had made it was the speed we were travelling. Suddenly, we were on a tarmac road.

Return to Cyprus

Things quietened down and tensions eased. A small group of us who had passed our demob time were told that as soon as we could get back to Cyprus, we could return to England and Civvy Street. Unfortunately, to return to Cyprus via the Gulf of

Aqaba wasn't an option. Our only hope was by aeroplane, but there was also a problem there, for there was an embargo on air traffic across Israel and the Brits being British will always stick to the rules. But thanks to the Yanks, who care not for rules, we only had to wait a few days. Late one night, our sergeant rounded up those of us due for demob and told us that a Yankee Globmaster was about to take off for Cyprus and if we wanted to get on it, we should grab our gear and skedaddle to the air strip; at the double, of course. This we did without hesitation.

Now the Yankee Globmaster isn't a passenger aeroplane – it's England's equivalent to the Beverly – so the American pilot gave us a pep talk. Because we were about to fly over restricted air space, we would be flying at a very high altitude out of reach of radar. It would be very cold and we would experience deafness, ear popping and maybe even some light-headedness. But we were young, we were fearless, we couldn't care less and we were on the move.

When we arrived in Cyprus there were more problems. The Greek Cypriot terrorists had become very active and the wives and children were being evacuated back to Blighty, so we squaddies had to take a back seat. After a few weeks we were given a choice: wait for space on an aeroplane or take a boat that was leaving from Famagusta the next day – six of us decided that the ten-day boat trip was the best option, as we would at least be on the move. We stopped off at Gibraltar, but we weren't allowed off the ship, as we didn't have the appropriate dress. This was very frustrating and I vowed I would return some day and explore The Rock.

After Gibraltar, we moved on towards The Bay of Biscay. The sea became hostile and the mountainous waves dwarfed our ship and crashed all around us. Strangely, I didn't succumb to the dreaded seasickness, finding the awesome sight of those wild and fearsome waves exciting. The boost of adrenaline must have overcome any thoughts of seasickness; unlike the awful experience I had been subjected to on millpond calm seas of the Red Sea.

Demob

After three years in the army, I was sorely tempted to sign up for another three-year stint. I had enjoyed the life and in the three years I was with them, the good times well outweighed the bad, with the army giving me a wealth of experiences. Apart from an education in life, they gave me an opportunity to discover that learning could be a pleasurable and fulfilling experience and unbeknown to me, it planted the seeds for my love of words.

Then there was the physical side that turned a little weed into a very fit young man and the discipline that taught me to respect myself and others. The army also gave me the opportunity to travel; not a thing to be understated, because travel in itself is a great education. But the thing that made me decide to leave the army was the married quarters. They were grim and I observed with horror the hovels that the wives and children of the squaddies had to live in. Eileen and I were courting at that time and there was no way I would let her live like that.

It was "Lust" at First Sight

Eileen

Eileen was born in West Hartlepool in 1940. The youngest of six children, she had a very difficult childhood. Starting life in the North East of England, she was born in an air-raid shelter with bombs dropping all around; the German bomber pilots were after the nearby docks. In the poverty of the thirties, two of her sisters had died in childhood; this was before Eileen was born, but she knew that her parents had suffered because of their loss. At the age of 6, her parent's marriage broke down and her mum took the two youngest children and left Hartlepool to live with relations in London in 1946.

Things in London proved more difficult than her mother envisaged and Paddy (Eileen's dad) wrote stating that he wanted the children back and that he would take legal steps if necessary. His motives were simple: he thought that if the kids came back so, too, would the mother. Alas, this was not the case and Mary brought back the children but returned to London.

Eileen was raised by her dad, who had to work or starve. In those days, the only help you got was from your own family. The 6-year-old Eileen had to be looked after by her 11-year-old brother Tom and an older married sister, who was a great influence in her life but was in the throes of rearing a wonderful family of six kids of her own and so had more than enough on her hands already.

Her eldest brother had been a prisoner of war and although he survived the Japanese slave-labour camp while working on the Burma Railway, he never fully recovered and died in 1951. Eileen was sixteen when her father, who she worshipped, died suddenly without warning – it was probably the most earth-shattering event in her short life. After he died, she was obliged to move to London with her mother, who had since remarried.

Not an ideal situation for a 16 year old naive girl or a 56-year-old woman, who didn't really know each other and didn't particularly want each other; but that was the situation and they both had to live with it. Her stepfather was a very selfish man and added to this, he was violent when drunk. She took many a beating during these years for nothing more than just being in the wrong place at the wrong time.

His alcoholism came as an even bigger shock, as she had never seen her own father drink let alone be violent, so life at that time was to be endured until she could leave, which is when I came along.

Jobs were plentiful in those days and she soon found herself working in an office nearby as an office junior: filing, typing, carrying messages, anything but answering the telephone, because she still had a Northern accent, which wasn't acceptable; telephonists in Eileen's day had to speak like the queen, using BBC English.

Eileen had no social life at that time, being a stranger to the area and having been uprooted from her friends and family. Looking back on it now she was in shock. She sat in night after night, with seemingly no interests apart from writing to her sister and friends back in Hartlepool. In desperation, her mother took her along to the local priest, Father Brown, who suggested that she join the parish youth club, Eileen was mortified at the idea, but her mother was insistent and so a terrified Eileen presented herself at the parish hall, where the gentle Father Brown took in the situation and asked a very attractive young girl to look after the newcomer. That was a great stroke of luck as Hilary was exactly the salve needed to heal Eileen's wounds.

Hilary was, and still is, vivacious, level-headed and, above all, kind and she became Eileen's best friend and a rock to lean on; she helped her a great deal to settle into life without her father.

Although her home life was less than tranquil, with her mother and stepfather's violent outbursts, thanks to Hilary, Eileen found a full and happy social life, especially when a "shining white knight" swept into view. Well, not quite "shining", not very "white" and definitely far from "knightly". It was I! Bolshie Bob; an arrogant young swine, who was full of himself. Well, who isn't at 18 years old?

I now find it inconceivable to imagine life without Eileen and I bless the day I found her. She is without doubt the best person I have ever known. On my part, it was "lust" at first sight when we met. She was a beautiful 16-year-old girl – good-natured, friendly and outgoing – while I was 18, big-headed, full of myself and still in the army. We first met at a dance and we immediately fell in love, dancing close and clinging to each other as if the world was ours and we would own the world till the end of time.

Actually, it wasn't quite like that – I was cocky, arrogant and brash and I told her it was her lucky night, as she would have the great pleasure of me taking her home. Eileen's current boyfriend of the time was also in the army and was away at the time serving Queen, country and sergeant major. Well, it happens to us all and I seized the opportunity with both hands. She was deliciously refreshing; without a trace of any make-up, in a time when all young girls had two faces: the one you could see and the one under half an inch of powder and paint. Although she had a scrubbed-clean, innocent look, she was built like Marilyn Monroe and carried herself with natural dignity. Little wonder I had aspirations.

I thought I was on to a good thing, but it turned out that she was a good Catholic girl and anything more than a kiss was for after marriage. Bugger my luck … What I didn't know was that Eileen was looking for an excuse to ditch this other guy and I was supposed to be a convenient, temporary replacement. But I managed to get my hooks into her –couldn't get anything else – and slowly the lust turned to love and although it took a little longer for Eileen, I do believe she was beginning to like me just a little.

I was home on leave once and we had planned to go to the pictures. She had been discussing me with her brother prior to me collecting her for an evening out. She had told him how she knew that I didn't have much money and she wanted to 'go Dutch' that night, but was worried that I might see it as an insult and be upset. She and Tommy rehearsed what she would say, so as to let me down gently. Commeth the hour, commeth the man.

When I arrived, she took me into the hall and said, 'Bob, I know you don't get a great deal of money being in the army and I was wondering if you wouldn't mind if we went Dutch tonight.'

'Blimey,' I said, 'I was hoping you were going to pay for me as well!'

I can still recall the day now – how can I ever forget it, when Eileen still reminds me of the story after all these years?

Even though I was born in London, I knew little of the city sights. It was Eileen with her unquenchable thirst for culture that had us visiting London's places of interest. We would catch the bus to Manor House Tube Station and then travel into the city on the Tube.

We had a stormy courtship and Eileen chucked me more times than I can remember, ordering me never to darken her doorstep again. But I was clever enough to know that I could never be the equal of Eileen and if I let her slip from my grasp, I would be the loser. So at every opportunity and whenever the army allowed, I was back knocking on her door. I still hadn't got the message that a bunch of flowers would have put me in her good books; I had to rely on my charm to get me by.

'I thought we agreed that it was over?' Eileen said on one of my returns.

'Wot yer doing tonight?'

'Well, err, nothing really.'

'Well then can't we do summat togevver?'

Ah! what a bleeding charmer and no mistake. How could any girl resist me?

My full name is Robert Anthony Oliver and whenever I went out with a girl, I always told them my name was Tony Roberts, just in case I needed an excuse to vanish. It was Boxing Day morning 1957 and Eileen and I were walking along Tottenham High Road; there weren't many people about and best of all – not one single shop open. Then a loud voice broke the peace and came dancing on my eardrums. It was Dutchy from across the road.

'Hiya, Ollie!'

'What did he call you?' Eileen enquired.

'Just a nickname,' I explained. 'It's short for Oliver.' I was biting my tongue as I said it.

'You told me your name was Tony Roberts.'

'No, no, no,' I stammered. 'Tony Roberts Oliver, but you can call me Robert Tony Oliver … err, or anything you like.' After all, what's in a name?

It was just as well she found out the truth, because Eileen was the girl who was to become my one true love. Anyway, we survived the topsy-turvy courtship and our relationship begun to settle, when I was posted overseas.

When I came home I was greatly relieved to find that she hadn't found anyone else and I was able start courting her in earnest.

I was invited to Eileen's mum's house for Christmas dinner. It was very cold in the winter and she lived in a draughty old Victorian property, a two-up two-down. The living room was about 10 foot square and doubled as a dining room. Crammed into that tiny room was a three-piece suite, a dining table, four dining chairs, a sideboard, the obligatory black-and-white television and a budgie cage, complete with stand and bird There was hardly room to pull a cracker. The 10-year-old Christmas decorations had been resurrected from the cupboard under the stairs and were very much the worse for wear for having been buried with all the other junk also jammed into such places. In the living room was a gas fire, making it the only warm room in the house, with everyone huddled around trying to avoid the draughts from windows and doors. Tommy, who was at that time serving in the Merchant Navy, was home between trips and was suffering from the cold after the hot, sunny climes of the tropics, so he spent a lot of time huddled in this room.

If the gas fire was the most praiseworthy thing to be said about the house, the toilet must have been the worst. An outside loo, it was definitely not the place to linger in the winter. The pipes were always frozen and one had to take a bucket of water to flush it. Ah, happy days! If you forgot to take your own warmed-up paper, you were forced to use the frozen bits of newspaper, cut to hand-size sheets, hanging stiff as cardboard on a piece of string.

That particular evening there were ten of us crammed into the tiny living room. A group of us played cards, shouting and screaming at each other, while Eileen's mum sat inches from the 9 inch black-and-white TV. Every now and then she would nod off and when we thought it was safe, we would switch to the other channel; we only had two channels in those days and no remote control. It was like a trigger point for Mary, for no sooner had they turned it over than she would wake up, lean forwards, hit the button and say, 'Bloody telly. Keeps turning itself over.'

Tommy, even in that warm, overcrowded room, still wore a thick woolly pullover and he struggled to deal the cards, rubbing his hands together and blowing on his fingers. The card game wasn't a Christmas activity; it was a way of life whenever we got together.

We mostly played four-handed cribbage, with arguments raging and the banter hilarious. But the stakes were high: one penny a dozen and a big shilling for the game.

Tommy's silence was unusual; he had the look of a man who had problems. It wasn't the cards – he had the need to visit the most unpopular room that wasn't in the house, where one only went when driven by desperation! Finally, he had to give way to nature and he began to prepare himself.

On went another chunky pullover and a duffel coat complete with hood. He stood at the door, hyping himself up, gritting his teeth and sucking in his breath. Then he made the ultimate effort and burst through the door, not stopping to close it behind him. Everyone screamed, 'Close that bloody door!', but he was gone into the freezing night. Less than five minutes later he was back, with his nose glowing red.

'My Gawd!' he exclaimed. 'I went out there with 7 inches and a wrinkle and come back with seven wrinkles and an inch!'

Religion

Eileen is a Catholic and I'm an atheist. When we started courting in 1956, Eileen's mother was appalled at the thought that she was going out with a non-Catholic boy and when we got married in 1960 she still found it difficult to come to terms with it, saying it would never last. My mother was as equally shocked at the thought of me marrying a Catholic and almost as bad was the fact that she came from the North East of England.

'A Catholic northerner! What on earth could be worse for a family of cockneys? Bobby, are you sure? You do realise you'll have loads of kids by marrying a Catholic!'

Now this was from a woman who had ten children and she was Salvation Army! Both of my parents soon fell in love with Eileen and said if we did break up, Eileen would be welcome instead of me. Bloody good, 'innit?

I remember once Mum telling her, 'You know, my dear, Bobby is alright until he gets in one of his moods.' Thank God she didn't listen.

Down on One Knee

Following my demob from the army I decided I would propose. As we strolled through Kew Gardens in 1958, the sun shone, the birds sang, the air hung heavy with the wonderful scent of floral abundance and romance hung dripping on the very leaves of the trees.

Impulsively, I swept her off her feet and sat her down gently. Falling to my knees, I took her small, soft hand in mine. Kissing her fingertips I gazed longingly into her eyes, saying,

'My darling, I'm deeply in love with you; will you make my life complete and consent to be my beautiful bride?'

Nah, not really, what actually happened was that we were sitting in Eileen's front room watching *Bronco Lane* on the telly and when the adverts came on I said, "Ere, girl, do you fancy going to Black Lion Yard tomorrow to get an engagement ring; my mate tells me they do some really great second-hand bargains.'

Eileen was unable to resist my debonair approach and we caught the bus to Petticoat Lane to buy the ring. The engagement ring that Eileen chose was quite special to her and even though it was an icy-cold November day, she refused to wear her gloves and flaunted it everywhere we went.

Well, romantic I wasn't. I wish I'd have had the imagination to have done it in the spring in Kew Gardens, though at least we celebrated our engagement in style. There was no party, we couldn't afford that, so I booked us front-row seats at the Finsbury Park Empire to see chart-topping Cliff "Move It" Richards and the Shadows. It was fantastic; a great night with wonderful entertainment.

To get married we needed money and both sets of parents were unable to help financially, so it was all down to us. We both worked full time and I did as much overtime as I could lay my hands on. Holidays were out of the question, but because we were legally obliged to take time off from our normal jobs, Eileen would get temping work with agencies for the fortnight and I took casual labour anywhere I could, including the company where Eileen was employed. I suppose we were lucky there was plenty of work available for us to do in London.

Bob Oliver

On one occasion I did a driving job, delivering wicker baskets and furniture to shops all over London. The vehicle they owned had to be seen to be believed; I wish I could remember more about it. All I can remember was that it was a pre-war monster, an absolute bitch to start and had to be kept running at all costs. Most of the shops I delivered to were reasonably easy to find, but I did have problems with one particular drop. I knew it was close by so, following my London A–Z, I turned up a road that led into Oxford Street. Drivers were flashing their lights and waving at me, but because I was deep in concentration I dismissed it from my mind.

As I pulled up to the junction of Oxford Street, I was deciding which way to turn, when I noticed two rather large London policemen watching me with a puzzled look on their faces. My first thoughts were that the wing of this old pre-war monster must have fallen off and that was why the other vehicles had been trying to attract my attention. However, one of the coppers turned his head and gestured at the sign above him. My eyes were drawn with his and then the penny dropped and with it came the sudden realisation of my dilemma. The sign they were alluding to was a one-way arrow, suggesting that I had driven some 500 yards the wrong way up a one-way street.

I clasped both my hands over my face in a sign of contrition, while one of the policemen strolled nonchalantly over. Looking at my vehicle with a certain amount of disgust, he said, 'Do you realise that this is a one-way street, sir?'

It was on the tip of my tongue to reply, 'But, officer, I was only going one way.' But common sense prevailed and I decided that a humble approach to the situation might be advisable.

Putting on my best country accent I replied, 'I'm so sorry, sir. I be a stranger in these parts.'

He accepted my apology and told me to move on. He went to walk away, but I called him back and asked him directions to my next drop. He looked amazed at my cheek, but pointed right, saying, 'It's the second left off that road over there, but you can't turn right here, you have to go left and around the block to it.'

It was interesting work and even though the pay was a pittance it was still a bit extra. What with Eileen typing in any office the agency sent her to and working for Vernon's pools on Saturdays, checking the pools coupons – no National Lottery in those days – we managed to save enough for the "big day". Vernon's pools was a sweat shop in East London and to this day she pales at the sight of a pools coupon.

Wedded Bliss

When Eileen and I were married on 10 September 1960, Les was my best man and a better man you couldn't get. He looked after the ring, made sure I had a half-crown, so I could give gold and silver as part of the wedding ceremony and, most importantly, he took me to Woollies, where he made me splash out on a tie costing ten pence (old money).

Tommy, who was giving Eileen away, was somewhat the worse for whisky – pillaged from Eileen's mum's cocktail cabinet. He wasn't so much a lush as susceptible to a case of the old nerves. All he had to do was walk down the aisle with Eileen and nod when asked, 'Who giveth this woman?' So what was making him nervous I'll never know.

Unfortunately, but hilariously, Eileen's mum broke the heel off one of her expensive Italian shoes as she stepped into the church. Making her grand "Bride's Mum" entrance, she was forced to hobble the rest of the way down the aisle, red-faced, like a one-wheeled handcart. Our priest had a minor heart attack, so start well it didn't. But that wasn't the end of the disasters. The band that we had booked for the evening didn't turn up and the photographer was pissed out of his head; ours was his fifth wedding that day and he had joined in the toasts at every one! All in all a most disparaging day. But we were young and in love and nothing was about to spoil it for us.

The Wedding Day

In 1960, a great year for me,
Went to church, to wed my bride to be.

Up the aisle, my dazzling belle,
With brother Tom, "drunk as hell".
She got him there, up to the altar,
She dare not stop, she dare not falter.

Dejected Mum, with shoe in hand,
The heel had snapped, on entrance grand.
Both happy clans were there to see,
My blushing bride to marry me.

> The smell of whisky caused the blush,
> Of brother Tom, the family lush.
>
> The parish priest would do the thing,
> Pronounce us wed, with crown and ring.
> Came over faint and said, 'Dear me!
> My heart is failing, can't you see?'
>
> With heavy heart we watched as he
> Was helped into the presbytery.
> Father Brown said, 'Don't panic, Bob,
> I'll step in and do the job.'
>
> Crown was given, as was the ring,
> The vows were made and we did sing.
>
> Off we set into life so bold,
> Forever us, to have and to hold.

I feel sure that Eileen agreed to my proposal of marriage in the first place because of my charm, personality and the life of luxury that I was offering her. The honeymoon was one to be envied by royalty; it set me back a tidy penny, I can tell you.

During the journey we floated almost dreamlike in sweet anticipation of things to do and exotic places to see. The caravan site had a lot of good points: the toilets were less than 100 yards from our caravan and we could get water from there as well. True, we didn't have electricity, but the gas lights and gas cooking facilities were more than adequate.

The site was situated in a beautiful spot and you could imagine what it would be like when they finished the developments. Mind you, it was a good job we bought our wellies, for there had been a lot of rain and it was very muddy.

The sea wasn't too far away and the bus ran twice a week. Once you got into Clacton there were all sorts of things to do. It was a pity we ran out of money after four days and had to come home.

But before we came home we did have a little adventure. I had a ten-shilling note (that's fifty pence in today's currency) and as we drove out of Clacton we spotted a man sitting on a chair in a field in front of a small aeroplane. A sign read: ten shillings for a ten-minute flight over Clacton. So we blew our last ten bob on the flight. It was worth it and the pilot, who was obviously an ex-RAF pilot, complete with handlebar moustache, took our photo and said, 'This will remind you of what you did on honeymoon.' How on earth did he know?

It was touch and go if we had enough petrol to get us home and the car was sucking air as we pulled up outside our new home, which we were looking forward to getting settled into. We called it "our little corner of the world". It was only one room and we had to share a toilet and washing facilities with six others, but it was our first home. It was actually my parent's home and they let us live with them until we could afford a house of our own.

After two years in our one room, the novelty had worn off and our attention was once again drawn to lands aplenty on the other side of the world; we looked at Australia, but Eileen favoured New Zealand. Eileen was getting edgy and wanted babies – silly girl – but we were in no position to bring children up in a one-bedroom place and getting a real home of our own wasn't even on the horizon. We completed all the emigration preliminaries, but I wasn't 100 per cent sure, so we let fate decide. We set a date and said that if we didn't get our own place by that time we would go.

Emigration was placed on the back-burner when we were given the opportunity to buy a two-bedroom, ground-floor maisonette in Walthamstow, East London. That decision deprived Australia of two keen and determined immigrants and prevented us from making yet another dramatic change in our lives.

The two-bedroom flat was very small, but compared with our one room with shared facilities, it was enormous. Taking on a mortgage was a big step and we only managed get the loan by telling the building society that I was earning more money than I actually was. Of course, I had to back up my little white lie with hard proof. I was able to do this because I had a friend who worked in the wages department and he waylaid the letter from the building society and with the information I had given him, the fraud was completed. I will be forever grateful.

To make the down payment we sold everything we had, but that wasn't enough and we had to borrow to make up the difference. This made our early years of marriage financially very tough: we both had full time jobs and I worked every minute of overtime that was available.

Eileen was heavy pregnant with Sally, when we were hit a very hard blow below the belt. I had borrowed some cash from a friend for legal fees when buying the house and had been using his post office book to repay the money. Every week we would pay in as much as we could. Our debt to him was down to fifteen pounds; that might not seem a lot nowadays, but then it was a week and a half's basic wage. I had done an enormous amount of overtime, so we had decided that we would settle the outstanding amount, give him back his post office book and celebrate with a bottle of cider. I placed the fifteen pounds in the book and put it on the shelf behind the clock. That night we were burgled. It was heartbreaking; we had all the stuffing knocked out of us. Eileen was very tearful being so near to giving birth. Upon reflection, we realised that she was up and down in the night running back and to the loo and could have oh so easily bumped into the burglar and I dread to think what that shock would have done to mother and child.

I had left a small vent window open that I'd thought a cat would have had difficulty getting through. I called the police and when I showed him where entry was gained he said, 'Well, sir, you might as well have left the front door open!' At this, Eileen burst into tears and the embarrassed copper couldn't apologise enough.

When the fingerprint men came on the scene, my passing remark to them was, 'Surely if he had form he would have been wearing gloves and wouldn't have been silly enough to leave his prints?'

'You'd be surprised, sir!' came the answer and sure enough they matched his prints, as he already had a record, and the police caught the culprit. We, of course, didn't get anything back and our struggle continued to pay off our debt.

At the court hearing, the burglar confessed to fifteen break-ins. His defence lawyer made a plea for leniency on the grounds that at one break-in of an 87-year-old lady, although he emptied her purse of all her cash amounting to two shillings and eight pence, he didn't steal her rosary! Thank goodness this plea fell on stony ground and his case was referred to a higher court.

I never did get to hear what sentence he got. If it was now, he would probably be given a slap on the wrist, two hours of community service on half pay and a free psychological consultation. The thing that I will never forget is his name – Ivor Albert Millward – and if I ever get my hands on him I'll make sure he won't forget mine.

Sally was born in a nursing home in Walthamstow in 1963, which curtailed Eileen's working career, even though I had suggested she could take the baby with her. After all, she *had* been lazing around the hospital for three whole days.

Not All Work

It wasn't all toil and graft; we had a lot of good times and often entertained friends and family in our little flat. We still had little or no furniture, but you would be surprised how many could eat their dinner around a coffee table. After we had eaten we would play cards and board games and I soon discovered that Eileen was a bad loser. Indeed, I dare not put hotels on Pall Mall during our games of Monopoly, otherwise the board would be propelled skywards as she considered that as cheating.

Sally's Arrival from Eileen's Perspective

I look back on my daughters' birthing experiences – the personal care, the whale music, the birthing baths – and cannot help but compare my lot with theirs. From the outset, the midwives called the medical shots and little or no consideration was given to the mother. Fortunately, I had an easy pregnancy with no morning sickness, which was doubly fortunate as at that time doctors were prescribing a drug called thalidomide to aid this awful condition. I was booked into a maternity hospital in Walthamstow and a couple of days after my due date, with no baby in evidence, a very businesslike nurse informed me that I was to be induced after the weekend; apparently, they needed the bed. I apologised for the inconvenience they seemed to think I was causing and did my level best to right my wrong – I scrubbed the house from top to bottom, had hot baths galore, ran for buses and even took castor oil (yuk), but the net result was a lovely clean house, no toilet paper and no baby. So the following Monday a very tearful me, accompanied by Bob, arrived at the hospital for my appointment.

And what a performance that was. Bob was sent away – 'You've done your bit, Mr Oliver.' And I was bathed (again), measured, weighed and given an enema (oh joy). Finally, I was wheeled into the theatre to have my waters broken, before being put into a green and beige room, where I was left alone to wait.

After an hour or two things started to happen and in my terror I rang for the nurse. She put her head round the door, had a quick look and said, 'Oh, for goodness sake, you've hours to go yet. I'm trying to have my lunch; don't bother me again until things really get going.' Nowadays, of course, I would have strangled her with her stethoscope, but in those days I was young, inexperienced and not in the least bit scared, so I gritted my teeth, sat back and waited. Oh, things happened all right – Sally was about to leap into this world with only me to catch her. Luckily, a young and kindly nurse happened by my room and within a few moments Sally Ann came into our lives.

How can one describe seeing your baby for the first time? Well, you can't – it's joy, wonder and love all rolled into one and this feeling happens with each and every child. Bob eventually arrived at visiting time with apologies for being late. Apparently, he was feeling stressed and so he'd gone to the cinema. Great! I'm huffing and puffing his firstborn into the world and he was off watching *El Cid*!

By this time I had joined other new mothers and their babies on the ward and I watched the other fathers arriving loaded down with flowers, chocolates and all sorts of goodies. Bob, however, came in empty-handed. Now I know my beloved is loving and kind, but sadly he's lacking in the "thoughtfulness" department. Having checked that Sally had the correct number of digits and after a quick look round the other cots, he announced that I had done a good job and that ours was the best baby in the hospital.

'Right,' I said, 'where's my flowers?'

He looked at me and, typically bemused, said, 'Why? Who's dead?'

'You if you don't come up with the goods,' I hissed. 'I want flowers and some fruit next visit.'

True to his/my word, the next day he arrived with flowers and fruit; the flowers had been beautiful dahlias. I say "had been", because he had bought them from a market stall and the journey to the hospital hadn't exactly been kind to them. He had cycled down and as he'd pedalled furiously with them dangling from the handlebars, he'd left a shower of petals behind him on the road, arriving with just a bunch of stems! Likewise, being September, the market was having a glut of plums, so having failed with the flowers, he handed me a huge brown paper bag of overripe plums – oh joy.

After he'd gone, in my innocence I handed the plums out to the other girls in the ward, realising they wouldn't last long. We were all breastfeeding our babies and the full impact hit the babies the next day. We used terry nappies in those days, which were supplied by the hospital. The nurses were tearing their hair out trying to keep up with the laundry and they sent the sister in to find out what the problem was. All fingers pointed to me and the plums and the look on her face said it all

In those days, we had to wait the full ten days before we were allowed home and Bob had arranged for us to go home in style, having hired a car with a chauffeur. The very superior chauffeur insisted on carrying my bag, but as he picked it up, the clasp broke and all my smalls cascaded to the floor. I quickly shoved them back in, but it still left us with the small matter of the broken clasp. 'Not to worry,' said Bob and he reached into his pocket for a piece of string to tie round the bag. I doubt very much that Bob gave the snooty chauffeur a tip.

An Exciting Career Change

The factory where I earned my crust didn't have a sick-pay scheme and was prone to lay-offs. I had worked there for four years and had survived the redundancies, but because of our financial commitments I was ever aware that I couldn't afford to be out of work; not even for a short time. So the time had come for a change in the hope that I could secure a "job for life"!

It was in 1962 that I left the factory and joined the post office in Clapton, London. My only form of transport was Eileen's very old bike, which just happened to be stuck in a low gear. Yes, I know it wasn't the hills of Matlock that I had to negotiate, but believe me, that 6 mile trek from Walthamstow at half four in the morning was tough going. The journey home was even worse after a day's work plus overtime. Good job I was young and fit in those far off days.

After my initial training as a postman, I was let loose on my own and as the junior I had the toughest round. Everything was based on seniority. Each year, the list of duties – that's what they called the rounds or walks – went up on the board. The senior man signed first and so on, until it came down to the dogsbody: me! I didn't have a choice, just what was left.

The second day that I was allowed on my own I returned with a bundle of letters. The guv'nor said, 'What's those, then?'

'Oh, they're for Ikeworth House (a block of flats on my round); the lift has broken down,' I replied in all innocence.

All eyes on the sorting office turned on me. The guv'nor's mouth was wide with astonishment and for a moment he was speechless. After he regained his composure, he snapped, 'Stairs, Oliver; use the bloody stairs!'

I did a swift about-turn and made for the block of flats. You rarely did the same round on the second delivery, so it was a terrible sin to bring back letters for your fellow postmen and, of course, the guv'nor was only interested in the mail being delivered.

It was the very same block of flats that gave me a nasty turn one day. This time, the lift was working and I always went to the top and worked my way down. Coming out onto the top landing, a sort of long balcony, I walked along delivering the letters. The balcony was very narrow; about 3 feet wide, and halfway along, I was surprised to see a deck chair in the gangway. It was facing away from me and I could see the top of a lady's head. There was a stream of sunlight coming down between the surrounding buildings and the woman was obviously making the most of the short time left before the sun disappeared from the balcony.

I had difficulty getting passed, but then I heard a voice say, 'Can you manage, luv?' I turned and looked down. The sight I saw was quite disturbing for a 24 year old. There she lay on her deck chair, naked as the day she was born. Unfortunately, a page-three model she was not. I would place her in the region of about sixty plus; her wrinkled breasts had given way to gravity and had disappeared under her arms and her large belly wobbled as she shifted position.

One of her legs was raised and her foot was placed on the door jamb – seeking to gain maximum sunlight. She didn't turn a hair as I struggled past, saying, 'Nice day for sunbathing!' It placed an entirely new slant to the phrase: the property is in a pleasant location, offering a balcony with a view. It took me a long time to recover from that experience, I can tell you.

I was doing my second delivery one Saturday morning up on Clapton Common, when a little old Jewish lady came to the door and said, 'Postman, do you think you could make a phone call for me? My daughter is in hospital having a baby and I want to find out how she's doing.'

Thinking the old dear was on her own and in need of help, I went into the house to make the call for her and was surprised to find a young guy pacing the floor. He was an Orthodox Jew in all his regalia: hat, ringlets, the lot.

The old lady saw that I was taken aback and said, 'He is the father of the baby to be, but our religion doesn't allow us to use the telephone on the Sabbath.'

The guy was obviously stressed out, so who was I to question anyone's religion? I dialled the number and asked how Mrs Cohen was. 'Well, Mr Cohen,' the nurse said, 'your wife is doing very well, she is fully dilated and we are expecting the baby to be born within the next few hours.'

I didn't tell her that I wasn't the dad, I just relayed the message. The guy nodded his gratitude, the old lady gave me a shilling and thanked me and I carried on with my round. I remember thinking, blimey, the things postmen have to do is anyone's guess.

After a year I was able to climb up the seniority ladder, with others retiring or leaving. This time, my promotion was to a Red Devil in the form of a postman driver, feared by all; even the London taxi drivers moved over when we approached. We were the elite of Her Majesty's Royal Mail postmen and even though I had an army licence, I still had a week of intensive driving training to do, followed by rigorous driving and Highway Code tests. All the training was in vain, because there is something about sitting at the wheel of a post office van that transforms the human frame into a being that is definitely not of this planet. Hence, the nickname we earned of the "Red Devils".

I remember one time I was driving round our area picking up mail, when I arrived at one post office to find cars doubled parked outside. I treble parked, blocking three quarters of road. When I came out, a policeman was directing the traffic around me. I loaded the van, he saluted me, I saluted him back and then I drove off. I glanced in my mirror to see him getting out his notebook and taking the particulars of the cars that had double parked. Yes, we even had traffic problems back in the 1960s, but the post office vans were a law unto themselves.

Talking about "a law unto themselves", in the East End of London, the Kray Brothers were the dominant force of the underground criminal fraternity back then and I later discovered that on one particular round I covered, they were alleged to have carved up Jack "The Hat" McVitie, whose body has never been found to this day.

The Big Freeze of 1963

It was the 1963 winter freeze that left the greatest impression on me. I was still a postman in London at the time, still pushing a bike 6 miles each way to work on Eileen's old boneshaker, still stuck in the low gear. Anyway, that particular winter seemed to go on forever.

My daily bike ride took me through some huge reservoirs in East London, which were frozen solid right through to late April. It was a wonderful sight, but it was a constant reminder that the winter was relentless. What I didn't realise at the time was that if it was bad in the concrete jungle of London, it must have been hell in the country, where a spoon full of snow will lie forever.

As it was, our destiny lay neither in London nor with the post office. Sally had filled our maisonette and Eileen was getting the itch for another baby – we had to move. We looked to buy locally but found it out of our price range and then we tried looking further a field, but the story was always the same: too expensive. I'm of the opinion that if we hadn't been priced out of London, I would have made a career in the post office.

From London to Suffolk

Pub Grub

Eileen and I moved from London to Suffolk in 1965 and Leslie Albert Dutch once again featured in shaping our destiny. He and his wife Carol were going through the same problems we had experienced, living in one room and looking for a home of their own. Les told us that he had seen an advert in the paper for houses within our price range of £2.300 in Suffolk, leading to Les, Carol, Eileen, Sally (who was nearly 2 years old) and myself going house-hunting in the wilds of Suffolk. As Londoners, it was like venturing across the vast Badlands of America in search of Deadwood; we felt like true pioneers in every sense of the word.

At that time pub life was suffering because of the drink-driving laws that had been introduced and a lot of pubs in and around London were turning their attention to offering meals to boost their flagging business. Little did we know that these modern newfangled ideas hadn't yet reached the sticks. We had seen food adverts on the telly: "Call in at your local for the best of British food!" and so after traversing the roads of Suffolk for a few hours we decided to stop for lunch. When we spotted a little seventeenth-century inn snuggled on top of a hill in the middle of nowhere, we agreed that this was the place for us and we left the girls in the car while we went to investigate.

As we entered the dark, dismal, smoke-filled den, the buzz of conversation ceased and the sound of silence was deafening. All eyes were on us as we approached the bar; even the cribbage team stopped to observe "the strangers". The landlady had a cigarette hanging from the side of her mouth – largely ash dangling precariously over a customer's pint of ale. She was old and grey and didn't seem too pleased to see us.

Turning her attention to the customer she was serving, she pushed his pint towards him, took his money and shuffled to the till. It was then I noticed her men's tatty slippers and wrinkly legs; or could it be she was wearing dirty skin-coloured stockings? In this light it was difficult to tell.

The customer grunted, calling the "vision" behind the bar Vera, and as he moved away, conversation once again began to buzz in the bar. The landlady stared at us silently, challenging us with her rather intimidating eyes. Les spoke, 'Could I have a menu, please, Vera?' He was always the pushy one.

'Menu?'

'Yes, we would like to order lunch; you know, the TV advert: The best place to grab some grub is at the local pub.' And then he added with a smile, 'Call in at your local for the best of British food!'

Vera looked blank and then snarled, 'This is a pub; we sell beer.'

Once again, the bar fell silent. A pub selling food – never heard the like.

'No food, then?' said Les.

'We got crisps.'

'Cheese and onion?'

'Plain only.'

'Any nuts?'

'No.'

'How about a glass of R Whites lemonade?'

We looked at each other and knew that this was a remark too far as the dart player lowered his dart, turned and stared menacingly.

As we made our fast, ungainly exit, I said to Dutchy, 'We should have known when we saw the two horses tied up in the car park.'

The new houses we were looking for in were located in the small village of Kedington on an estate called Westward Deals, built in what had once been a cornfield. Land was being bought by developers who had realised that houses in London were quickly becoming far too expensive for young families and so they had cashed-in on the situation. The new estate was only partly built, but we were able to view a finished show house and a plan of the finished site.

We were lucky with these houses in as much as they were built to a high standard and they were within our budget. The kitchen /diner really impressed us and the rooms were, to our eyes, huge. We made the decision on the spot, chose a plot number and wrote a cheque for £50 as a holding fee. The cheque wiped our account out when cashed. Les and Carol chose plot number 123 and we chose 49, because it was one of only a few on the estate that had the garage at the side of the house and it backed onto open fields. We loved the Suffolk countryside on sight, and we still do, and we then set about selling our flat.

I applied to the post office for a transfer to Suffolk, which proved to be easier than I had dreamed, as they needed a postman in Haverhill almost immediately. I explained to them that I had to wait for my house to be built and this wouldn't be for about three months minimum. But such was the need for my expertise that the post office found me digs with a wonderful elderly lady *and* paid for me to lodge with her until our house was completed.

I had been a London postman for three years before we made the final decision to move to Suffolk. Jobs were still quite plentiful and had my transfer request been unsuccessful I would have been happy to take my chances. At that time the house was the most important thing, with Eileen now pregnant with Beth, our second child.

The lodgings were good and my landlady looked after me very well, but it meant me travelling back to London after work on Saturday, only to be back for a 5.00 a.m. start on the Monday. Needless to say, the weekends were very short. My old 500 cc BSA motorbike could kick some speed out, but it was before the M11 was built and the journey took me two hours. To make the weekend longer, I travelled back in the early hours of Monday morning: I got up at 2.00 a.m., was on the road by three and in work by five.

It was just a matter of time before the engine on my old Beezer blew up. Well, it didn't actually blow up, but it did make some strange noises, before emitting large amounts of deep blue, almost black, smoke. I was on my way home, it was Saturday afternoon and I was going through Bishops Stortford. The locals weren't amused and when I had to stop at the traffic lights I was completely engulfed.

In those early days, I didn't belong to the RAC; credit cards weren't for the likes of me and with only ten shillings and five pence ha'penny in my pocket, my only priority was to get home. It was just like the scene from the film *Blues Brothers* when they arrived in Chicago after the chase and their car disintegrated. My motorbike had motored her last journey, but the old girl had got me home, even if we did leave a trail of pollution behind us. How she got me there I will never know, for she literally gave out her last gasp as I pulled up outside 113 Gloucester Road, never to spark into life again.

This setback left me with a 1920 pushbike that my dad had given me as my only form of transport. The problem was that the bike was in London and I needed it in Kedington. Fortunately, it was in the days before "Beechings Rail Cuts" had fully taken place and we had a rail link via Cambridge to Haverhill. I simply tied a label on the handlebars, put it in the goods van, picked it up at Haverhill Station and rode off into the sunset to Kedington 3 miles away.

The Arrival of Our Second Child

Beth was born in a small back bedroom on a sunny but freezing day on 14 April 1966. The midwife Nurse Kay was a lovely Irish lady, who also acted as nurse of all trades. Checking on Eileen in the throes of labour, she took a professional look at her and announced to a rapidly panicking me, 'Oh she'll be OK for a little while. I've just got time to nip round and give Old Mr Orriss his bath.' I did question her timing and she reiterated that it would be fine. 'She isn't distressed enough,' she said. Eileen's pleas to the contrary fell on deaf ears; she had vanished down the stairs.

Nurse Kay was accurate in her assumptions and Beth did, indeed, wait until her return before making an appearance. It was the first time I had witnessed such a miracle as I wasn't allowed any part in Sally's birth at the hospital and it left me in total awe. Nurse Kay wanted me out of the way, but I was having none of it. I had missed the delivery of our firstborn, so there was no way I was going to miss this one. I was there at the conception, I told her, and I also wanted to be there at the birth. But this was at a time when a man's place was downstairs pacing the floor and smoking himself green, not assisting with the birth as the modern-day man does today; Eileen always said I was years ahead of my time.

When Nurse Kay sent me off for something, in an attempt to get me out of the way, I ran downstairs shouting, 'Keep your legs crossed, Eileen; don't you dare have that baby till I get back!' Anyway, I was down and up those stairs before the next contraction and Nurse Kay finally had to concede that there was no getting rid of me. Eileen was sucking furiously on the gas and air as Beth emerged into the world: another perfect and beautiful daughter. It was a most magical moment – a bit messy, but magical nonetheless.

Eileen told Nurse Kay afterwards, 'I don't think I felt any benefit from that gas and air at all.'

To which the nurse replied, 'No, you wouldn't; the tank has been empty for years!'

After the birth, with me following Nurse Kay's instructions by the letter, she had to admit I was a good boy and Eileen didn't do too badly, either. Apparently, Nurse Kay'd had a bad experience once with a dad being at the birth. At the crucial moment, the father had fainted, falling and splitting his head open. So there she was with the baby's head presenting and the father was on the floor with a wound to his head. She later told us that she had to kick off her shoe and press her foot hard down on his head to stem the flow of blood, leaving both of her hands free to deliver the baby. That's why she wasn't too keen on the idea of me being there.

While Eileen was "confined", her mum was to act as a stand-in housekeeper and the plan was for me to drive the Panther down to London, pick her up and bring her back. However, on 14 April 1966, it was snowing. Yes, snowing! There were huge flakes falling from the sky and our next-door neighbour said, 'You can't pick your mother-in-law up in that sidecar in this weather.'

'No, no,' I replied, 'her luggage will be in the sidecar and she'll have to ride pillion.'

Joyce, our neighbour, shook her head in disbelief and said, 'No way, Bob; here, take my car,' and she handed me the keys to a brand new Ford Zephyr Six.

I didn't like the idea in case it got knocked, but she told me not to worry as it was fully insured. Eileen and I, not to mention her mum, will always be grateful for her generosity that day. After the motorbike it was unadulterated luxury and I floated along, warm and cosy, and on a high owing to Beth's birth; two perfect babies, how lucky can one bloke be.

As I drove through Epping Forest, the snow formed a white sparkly blanket over the forest, like a scene from a Christmas card. I couldn't help smiling as I thought about what it would have been like on the old motorbike. I wouldn't have been admiring the view, that's for sure, and my fingers would have been frostbitten to say the least; thermal gloves hadn't been invented back then.

Mary thought she had died and gone to heaven. To make sure all and sundry noticed the car, she went round knocking on the neighbours' doors, telling them she would be away for a few days in Suffolk, staying at her daughter's "country residence", while looking after her latest grandchild. The neighbours had never seen the like of a car before and many a curtain twitched as we set off. I wonder what our departure would have been like had I turned up on the motorbike.

Beth's Arrival from Eileen's Perspective

Beth was born on a cold and snowy day in April and again we managed to produce perfection. She was pink and perfect, but the house, pre-central heating days, was chilly, so Nurse Kay wrapped her up in her little yellow carry cot and shoved her in the airing cupboard, the warmest part of the house, where she slept peacefully. The great advantage of having babies at home in those days was that everyone in the village knew the midwife's car and as soon as she had gone, the neighbours would investigate. It was lovely to show off our latest wonder and one of the most generous gifts I've ever had was given to me that day. We had only been in our new pad a few months and the gardens weren't anywhere near established – indeed, some were little more than mud tracks – but one of my neighbours Joyce Orriss came in with three daffodils. They were the only flowers she had managed to grow and she made them a present to us; no one can give you more than everything they have and I will never forget her generosity on that day.

Wetting the Baby's Head

There were a few memorable events that happened in 1966: Beth's birth and the lesser event of England winning the World Cup, which gave me the greatest sporting memory of my life. But Eileen gave me the best moment of that year by giving me the second of three beautiful daughters.

Eileen had chosen Sally's name and so I got to choose Beth's .We had been given a book on names and even as she lay sleeping in the cot we still hadn't decided. I thumbed through it and nothing seemed to be good enough, until I came upon the name Beth.

'That's it!' I declared and pointed to the name I had chosen.

'Do you mean Elizabeth?' Eileen asked.

But I was adamant it was to be Beth and as we both loved it that was it – job done! At least it was until Eileen's mum got to find out. She wanted the baby to be named after her and although Mary is a lovely name, it wasn't what we wanted. She spent the three days prior to the Baptism wandering around the house muttering and hinting, but all her efforts fell on deaf ears.

The church was a lovely twelfth-century priory; a peaceful and inspiring place and, despite Henry VIII's best efforts, most of which still stands today. The day of the baptism at Clare Priory loomed stormy, dark and dismal, but it didn't detract from the ceremony. We were met at the door by Father Mahon – a lovely bloke who loved football, so we were on the same wavelength – and Mary collared him – no pun intended – and had a few words in his ear. He was slightly embarrassed when he approached us and he whispered, 'Mother wanted me to have a word with you about the name.'

'Good try, Mum!' said Eileen.

'Father, you know well that Mother isn't always right!' I added.

Although I have no religious leanings, it meant a lot to Eileen and it was a lovely ceremony. Afterwards, Eileen asked for a blessing – thanksgiving for a healthy and safe confinement. Sally was only 2 years old and wanted to be in on the act, so she followed the priest and, holding her mum's hand, took everything in as only a child can.

A candle was lit and passed to Eileen to hold while the blessing took place and as it was such a dark day outside, the little chapel lit up wonderfully. We stood in silence, all except for Sally who, staring at the candle, piped up with her little 2-year-old voice, 'Happy birthday to you.'

Ceremony over, we whipped home for tea, sherry for the women and beer for the blokes while the baby was passed around, my mum insisting that she was the image of me and Eileen's mum insisting she looked like her. A couple of sherries each later, they didn't care who she looked like.

Culture Shock

Local Wildlife

My transfer from London to Suffolk was a culture shock; the change from me being a soft London postman to a small town postman was a little more than traumatic. In London, the shifts were straightforward, the walks were compact and if you had a mind, you could progress and seek promotion. There was always the opportunity to do plenty of overtime to earn the much-needed extra cash. In London, I was working from six in the morning until ten in the evening six days a week, though little or no overtime was available in Haverhill. In the country, you had more chance of winning the lottery than getting promotion. With only one guv'nor' and eighteen postmen, there just wasn't the scope for doing anything else except pushing a bike. I could have lived with that, but the real tough part was the walks – as they were laughingly called. Apart from the parcel delivery, everything else was delivered on bikes.

The bike Dad had given me was great and was a lot easier on the legs than Eileen's old monster, so after the railway had shipped it to me I made the trip to the sorting office on it. This meant that I was not only doing a day's work on a bike, but was also biking the 3 miles to and from work. Boy was I saddle-sore.

The post mistress didn't like me: I was too brash, always questioning and, what's more, I was a cockney. My penalty for not conforming was to be given the toughest delivery in the area, covering one of the villages and all the surrounding farms. I biked 16 miles in the morning and 10 miles in the afternoon, in all weathers and conditions. Added to this, I still had to get to work and back on that bloody bike; I was now doing 33 miles a day. Crikey, was I fit; knackered but fit. The other big problem with being a country postman in those days was the hours.

Not only was it a six-day week, but your day was also split. You started at 5.00 a.m. and after an hour and a half of sorting, you made off into the wilds on your "Iron Horse" (the post office bike) with 40 lb of letters and packages to deliver. You returned three hours and 16 miles later, lighter in load and a few pounds lighter in body. Then came the worst part of the day: three hours to kill before starting work again. I was in lodgings and without my transport. Well, at least I had plenty of time to study my chess tactics.

The first thing I had to learn was to forget London rules; I had entered a completely different world. In London, all a postman was interested in was the name of the street or block of flats and the numbers; if the address wasn't clear or was, as we called it, an insufficient address, the letter went into what we called the dead letter box. It was then up to the postman higher grade (PHG) to track down the destination, adjust the address and put it back into the system.

In the country, they didn't know what one of these was, as I found to my surprise. The old local lad who taught me the round had set me up sorting out the delivery and had sloped off for a cup of tea. By the time he got back, I had it all sorted and bundled up and was loading up the bag.

'Hoi,' he said in that beautiful Suffolk drawl. 'What you got there, then?' He was pointing at the miscellaneous pigeon hole that was crammed full of Letters.

'Oh, them. They're for the dead letter box; insufficient address,' I told him.

He gave me a look to kill, picked up the bundle of letters and started in on me. 'Mrs Bloir is the thatched house next to the old bakery. Mr Wiseman is number two Stone Cottages ...' he stopped for a moment, looking hard at the next one.

Ah hum, I thought, that one has him stumped.

He then shouted across the sorting office, 'Did Cyril Coote's daughter Pat marry a Mizon?'

Young Neezer Smart, who was neither young nor smart, looked up and said, 'She did that and they moved into the Old Gables a couple of weeks ago.'

I was dumbfounded. All that was on the envelope was Mrs P Mizon, Withersfield, Suffolk and the postmark said it was from Cornwall. But here it was about to be delivered within twenty-four hours of being posted. It had been hard enough for me to come to terms with learning all the house names, now it seems I was expected to learn everybody's name and their family history as well.

John, the old local postman who was teaching me the round, had a striking resemblance to the singing postman of *Hav Yew Gotta loight, Boy?* fame. He had a dry sense of humour, or should I say weird sense of humour. I'm sure that his face had never experienced a full-blooded smile and for the most part, the only way you could tell he was amused or even receiving any kind of communication was a faint movement of the eyes.

We set off on our trek into the countryside. It was still pitch-black, even after two hours in the sorting office; daybreak was still slow in arriving. The wind gusted, swirling the drizzle into our faces, while John moved effortlessly along. I, meanwhile, struggled and strained every muscle in my body in an effort to keep up. I didn't want to appear to be a soft Londoner. After a couple of miles we started to ascend a steep, narrow country lane. It was sign posted "No through road", so I foolishly presupposed it wouldn't be far. Anyway, 2 miles up and beyond the back of beyond, we came across an old farmhouse; it looked like it was something out of a Peter Cushing horror movie. Surrounded by swirling mist, the thick blanket of cloud occasionally broke and the moon gave me an eerie glimpse of the spooky building.

My trainer stopped and took from his bag a stainless steel bicycle pump and held it in his hand. Without a word, we made our approach. There wasn't any sign of sign of life; no lights, no noise, nothing. The hair on the back of my neck bristled and if it weren't for my companion, I would have been more than a little nervous, even though he was strange enough himself and not an ideal escort into the unknown.

Then my silent questions were answered as the still of that early morning was broken by two of the largest dogs I have ever seen. They came bounding towards us, snarling and barking. They were either laying in wait for us or we had disturbed their slumber with our footsteps on the gravel path. Before I had time to think, I looked around and my compadre had disappeared, vanished, scarpered, leaving me to fend for myself.

This was the only time in my life I had cause to be thankful for my trusty old post office bike, for it was the only thing between me and jaws of the two ferocious beasties. I was trapped up against a tree with the bike wrapped around me. Now I understood what the stainless steel pump was about, but all I had was a bundle of letters to ward them off. Not very effective, as you might imagine, and their slavering jaws came perilously close to my flesh as I waved my hands and shouted abuse in an attempt to deter them, to no avail.

One dog has a certain amount of courage, but two are awesome. I had a vision of being stuck there forever or being eaten alive and minutes seemed like hours, until at long last a light came on in the house and a grouchy old farmer emerged, sporting a dirty old Sexton Blake raincoat over an even dirtier pair of pyjamas and with a disgusting pair of dung-laden wellingtons.

He growled at the dogs and they departed back into the barn from whence they came. He then growled at me as he snatched his post from my hands and without so much as an apology or a "kiss me arse", he stomped back into the house. I also took my leave as swiftly as my wobbly little legs would push me, before those vicious animals realised I was once again on my own.

The farmer was obviously upset that I had awoken him from his slumber. My impression of farmers had always been that they were up before God; oh, how foolish I was. I now know that it's the farm labourers, not the farmers who are the early risers.

I found my way back to the road where my hero waited patiently. Silently, he mounted his bike and travelled on with me in tow. The adrenaline coursing through my veins had subsided and I once again became aware of being wet and miserable, while I wondered what the hell I was doing in that God-forsaken place.

I kept well away from that particular farm, returning his letters to the sorting office marked up "dogs loose". After a week, the PHG rang him saying that if he wanted his mail he must ensure his dogs were locked up. By this time I had saved up and purchased a brand new, second-hand stainless steel pump.

My introduction to the post office bike was to lead to a hate of cycling; I was saddle sore for months. I was about to embark on a nice leisurely ride round the town to collect the mail from the post boxes, when I stepped outside and hesitated as dark looming clouds gathered overhead. Stopping to unpack my waterproofs, I was about to put them on, when one of the old local lads said, 'Don't you worry, boy, you won't be a' needing them. That won't rain. My old grandad always used to say when the wind is in the east and the clouds are moving north and the cows are a' standin' that's a sure sign there won't be no rain.'

So thinking that these old local boys understood the folklore of the countryside, I took his advice, jumped on my bike and pedalled into the distance. Upon reaching the point of no return, the skies darkened further and the heavens opened. By the time I had finished the collection I was like a drowned rat. The knowledgeable old local pretended he couldn't hear me come in as he sat in the dry and warm sorting the post. I squelched up to him gave him a look to wither and said, 'Sod you and sod your bleedin' grandad.'

Hellions Bumpstead was another village I was given; this was only a 12 miler – a piece of cake after the 26 miles of Withersfield and Sturmer. Anyway, one farm I was delivering to had a vicious-looking dog that, when he appeared snarling and slavering, would strike fear in Arnie Schwarzenegger. Naturally, I would beat a hasty retreat, leap on the bike and zoom down the farm track.

This happened three days on the trot and I returned the letters marked up "dog loose". The afternoon postman obviously didn't have the same problem, as the letters were never there the next day. On the fourth morning Bill, the PHG, called me over and said, 'Bob, I have a message from Jim for you.' (Jim being the afternoon Postman.) 'He wants to know why you are marking up those letters "dog loose".'

'I thought that was obvious,' I replied.

'Well!' Bill continued. 'Jim says not to worry about that dog. Not only is it 200 years old, but it's also as blind as a bat.'

That morning I put it to the test. I was very wary, as I had been spun yarns by these old locals before. Parking my bike, I gingerly approached the farm and true to form, the dog appeared, doing what he does best. I was some 20 yards from him and I slowly walked a few yards to the left. The dog's head remained unmoving, barking at the empty space where I had stood a minute earlier. Still not 100 per cent convinced, I moved quickly to the right. Still no head movement. Could this really be true or was he just waiting for his opportunity to pounce?

There was a 3 foot brick wall close by, so I scaled it and crept quietly by the drooling dog's head, which was still fixed firmly ahead. It wasn't until I trod on some broken glass that his attention changed. It was true, he was, indeed, blind and he was so old that even walking was an effort; it took a long time for me to be able to live down being scared of an ageing, blind dog, I can tell you.

It wasn't only dogs I had trouble with. I was doing a parcel delivery in one of two post office vans that Haverhill had at the time; you should see their fleet of vans now – it's like a yard at Carter Patterson's. But I digress – I roared up to the farm gates in my usual London-trained, inimitable fashion and leapt out of the van; oh, how great it was to be driving and not on that accursed bike. Anyway, through the double gates I went, when a litter of pigs got out and I spent an hour and a half with the farmer rounding them up. A lesson learnt being always to close gates behind me.

Deliveries to this particular farm were, like many others, always made at the back door. I opened the kitchen door, placed the parcel on the side and started to walk back, when their dog made an appearance; a particularly large, nasty collie with rotten teeth. I knew this dog and as long as I didn't turn my back on him I would be OK. I picked up a piece of wood and, backing away, waving my new found weapon like Errol Flynn in one of his swashbuckling films, I made the gate and bolted it behind me. I was feeling cocky and clever, but as I turned the sight before me stopped me in my tracks.

The post office van was one of those with sliding doors and I had left the door open. It was a horse that I saw, or should I say part of a horse, with its head and shoulders in the van. I couldn't get Neddy to shift, no matter what I tried. I pushed, pulled, nudged and I even climbed on its back and tried the John Wayne approach, but all was to no avail. Food must be the answer, I thought. But the only thing resembling food that I had was a packet of extra strong mints.

I took one and pushed my hand into the van and offered him the tasty morsel. To my great surprise, he took it and munched it with relish. At last I had his attention. The next time I offered it but held back a little, his head following my hand as I slowly enticed him out. His bulk was still barring me from the van door, so I backed further away to the rear of the van and he followed as I ran round the van, jumped in and slammed the door. Thank Gawd for Trebor mints. Apparently, the baker has a similar van and he always treated Neddy to a stale loaf.

A New Way of Life

Number 49 Westward Deals became our home in September 1965. There was a new way of life to learn, as there were no daily buses and most of us hadn't any transport, so we came to rely upon the delivery van men. These were your butchers, bakers and greengrocers, who would come round the estate every day to sell their wares from the van; of course, the prices were overinflated and those of us who were used to shops just round the corner really suffered.

There was a bus for the housewives every Wednesday and this went into Bury St Edmunds, where there was a market, shops and crowds. The market was a riot and an auction took place where you could buy a pig, a bag of spuds or onions (or both if you were flush), geese, ducks and even ferrets. Eileen would load up with as much stuff as she could carry or afford and then she would hotfoot it back to the bus, where the driver was invariably having a kip. Harry was a great character and would say, 'Stay there, my dear, hold that baby and I'll fold up your pram for you.' He would then carry all the groceries for you, stash them and help you to your seat; a far cry from the bus conductors we were used to in London ... or today, for that matter.

Although the house was now habitable, the garden looked like Flanders field. The builders had used our plot to store bricks and the diggers had done a magnificent job of churning up every inch of it. We had ruts that were dangerous if a child fell into it and a washing line was out of the question; even if we could have put one up we certainly wouldn't have been able to get to it.

But we had other worries: my post office wage had lessened owing to losing my London allowance and overtime was sparse. Add to that the rates – council tax – which had to be paid in advance in those days and we were completely broke. In this atmosphere we sat at the breakfast table one day and Eileen opened yet another brown envelope.

'Oh no,' she cried, 'not another bill; who do we owe twenty-five pounds to?' She passed it to me and burst into tears, 'We have nothing, absolutely nothing; how will we pay?'

I looked at it with dread, smiled and passed it back to her. 'It's the Premium Bonds, you daft bat,' I said tenderly. 'We've won twenty-five quid on the sodding Premium Bonds.'

We blew the lot on bills and three weeks later we won the village Ernie, blowing our £6 winnings on turf for the garden. We couldn't afford to do the lot, but after I'd dug the back-breaking clay soil and levelled it off a bit, it was ready for turfing; at least, enough for Sally to play on and Eileen, now pregnant with Beth, to have a washing line. The pleasure she got watching her nappies flap on that line was remarkable. Women, eh!

Central heating wasn't part of the deal and that's when we discovered the disadvantages of having a big house – it was perishing. Eileen would get 2-year-old Sally out of bed in the mornings and wrap her up in a blanket and place her on the couch with a hot water bottle until she could light the fire and defrost some of the ice that had formed on the inside of the windows. The fire heated the living room only and that was it – zilch. With no money and with a baby on the way we had to put up with it.

I think those were the roughest years we were ever to endure financially and many of the young families and couples who moved up from London at that time really felt the pinch. Alas, many marriages broke up; only a few lucky ones, like ourselves, stuck together through thick and thin.

Just as our furniture from the single-roomed dwelling had been swallowed up by the maisonette in Walthamstow, it was now the same with our three-bed semi in Kedington, Suffolk. Our new home was to us a palace, but it was a palace without double glazing or central heating and being brand new it was very damp; though, we made it as comfortable as we could with our limited resources and sparse furniture. The best thing about the house was the lovely views – to the front were similar houses to ours, but the rear garden backed onto open fields and for two townies that was really something special.

The need for some sort of transport was urgent. The cheapest to buy, run and accommodate us all was a motorbike and sidecar. We didn't deem it a luxury but an essential and so it was that I had to grow up and invest in some sensible transport.

The brand new 650 Panther had a state-of-the-art two-seater sidecar – okay, the back seat was only a child seat, but it was ideal for Sally.

The Arrival of Our Third Child

In 1967 Eileen got herself pregnant ... again! I can't be held responsible, as I thought she was leaning across to look at the alarm clock.

Sally was a perfect baby: slept through the night at six weeks and cut her teeth without a murmur; actually, if it wasn't for the rosy cheeks one would never have suspected she was teething. Sally was walking at nine months and she sailed through her infancy with hardly a hiccup. We really thought we had it cracked and there was absolutely nothing to this baby lark ... Oh boy! were we about to get a rude awakening; Beth, on the other hand, was a completely different kettle of fish.

The poor kid really suffered. She was very young when Eileen rang the doctor, suspecting measles; that was in the days when you could actually speak to one on the phone.

Memoirs of a Working Man

'No, no!' he replied. 'Beth is under a year old and is being breastfed; she can't possibly have the measles, Mrs Oliver!' He did, however, agree to make a house call. He walked in, took one look at Beth and said, 'She's got measles!' Medical history in the making.

Of course, it didn't end there; Beth caught every childhood complaint known to man and then some more. Naturally, it wasn't only Beth who did the suffering and for months on end we took turns to sleep. Having said all that, she grew to be hardy, beautiful and strong, shrugging off viruses and infections that flattened others, and now that she has grown up she has more than made up for our lack of sleep. Now, our third child was on the way and Eileen's expected date of delivery was June 1968.

At about that time there was an announcement in the local paper that on 22 June the Co-operative Society were to celebrate their centenary. We found out in May of that year that the Co-op, as part of their celebrations, would award parents of children born on their centenary date vouchers to the tune of twenty pounds – twenty quid! Now that was a lot of cash in 1968 and my brain began doing overtime. 'Right!' I said to Eileen. 'That's the date, gel; you must exercise self-control until the twenty-second.' Eileen told me later that our neighbour had overheard me saying this to her and thought that I was a right swine for saying such a thing … Yeah! And?

At 6.00 a.m. on 22 June 1968, I delivered Emma into the world with a little help from Nurse Kay in the same back-bedroom! Oh, and Eileen also did her bit. It wasn't a straightforward birth and I … or was it Eileen, had to work really hard, as Emma was born with one arm looped over her head. But we managed it and got the twenty quid in Co-op vouchers, which was like winning the pools. Well done, Emma, for arriving right on time. Oh, and Eileen as well, for her part.

Emma's Arrival from Eileen's Perspective

This was a magic time as both Sally, now four, and Beth, now two, slept right through Emma's entry into the world and when they awoke that day, all was ready. Their new sister had brought them presents and Bob brought them in to meet her. They were wearing little pink-and-blue nightdresses and, still sleepy, they tiptoed in to the bedroom. I still have emotional moments when I think of that day: the sun was streaming in, the girls were still cosy from their beds and all five of us were perched on the bed from under which Bob produced a box of chocolates – and I hadn't even nagged him this time. So there we were: the Olivers against the world and chocolates for breakfast.

Three Beautiful Daughters

I took a week's holiday from work to look after Sally and Beth. This time, we didn't bother bringing Mary up from London to help, as the last time I found that I did the work while she read the paper and my job was made even harder looking after her as well.

The next day the doctor paid a visit to check out Mum and baby. He came downstairs and told me, 'You have a beautiful baby daughter, Mr Oliver.'

I replied, 'I have three beautiful daughters, doctor.'

'Of course, of course,' he spluttered. 'But some men are disappointed they didn't have a son.'

I will never understand the mentality of people who are disappointed at not getting the baby they "ordered", when surely all that matters is that Mum and baby are fit and well. I know that in some countries boy babies are considered a benefit and girls a burden, but in our affluent world that shouldn't apply.

I asked the doctor if they were both healthy and he answered, 'Yes; apart from Mrs Oliver's blood pressure being a little high, but it's nothing to worry about.'

When I replied, 'Then that's all that matters,' I think I went up in the doctor's estimations.

Eileen told me later that one of his own children had been born with immense disabilities .The doctor then went on to explain that Eileen would be allowed downstairs in a couple of days and that he'd told her she must come down facing backwards, so that if she felt faint she wouldn't fall. I didn't like to tell him that she had already been downstairs and that when his car had pulled up outside, I'd sent her packing from the kitchen; she'd been peeling the spuds. Knowing from experience that he would expect to examine her and find her still in bed tending the newborn, she ran upstairs two at a time with the baby in her arms and jumped into bed. No wonder her blood pressure was up! After the doctor had left I called to Eileen, 'He's gone; I've put the potatoes back on for you. You can come down now, but watch that blood pressure; I've got enough on my plate without worrying about you running up and downstairs.' I can't repeat her reply, because children might read this.

Although things were financially tight, we managed. I can remember having nothing to eat in the house apart from a bag of spuds and some flour, so Eileen would organise a game of it. We would play chip shops with the kids, in which we would cut the spuds up into fish shapes, batter and fry them and pretend to the kids that we had our very own fish shop. With Eileen on the frying pan and me the server, Sally, Beth and Emma would queue up and pretend to be customers. Sally would be first and she always "lived the experience". 'Fish and chips, please,' she would say. 'Right it is, madam,' I replied and passed it over to her. She would give me pretend money and the other two would follow suit and those mock fish 'n' chips were fabulous.

But we slowly improved our situation with careful spending and hard work. Both of us knew that with a will to succeed we would get by. The children thrived in this country atmosphere, the village school was excellent and with the third one at school, Eileen could take a part-time job. It was always when Eileen could also earn a little cash that we found we could actually afford little extras, like clothes, carpets and even a short holiday.

Our first family holiday was funded by an insurance policy pay-out; this gave us the princely sum of £50. Can you believe that the fifty pounds paid for two weeks at a Pontins holiday camp near Lowestoft for all five of us, including a taxi there and back, as we had no car?

Tony the Terror

Way back in the 1960s the girls were three, five and seven-ish. Emma was three and she had a close friend who lived next door; his name was Tony and he was a little terror, but we loved him.

I was working on the post at the time and got up at 4 o'clock to start work at five. As soon as Tony heard me up and about through the dividing wall between his house and ours, he would get out of his bed and come knocking on our front door. I opened the door, to see him standing there in his Cowboy pyjamas, cowboy hat and carrying his toy rifle, saying, 'Wanna play wiz Emma.'

The first time it happened I took him home, but as their house was in darkness and all were asleep, I took him back to ours and put him to bed with the still sleeping Emma. Then I told Eileen that we had an extra kid in the house, jumped on my bike and headed off to work.

Morning after morning he persisted with his early morning visits and no amount of ticking him off could stop him. His father put locks on the front door well out of reach of the little bugger, but still it didn't stop him; he got out of the back door, instead. This, too, was bolted. His next escape route was through the window. I suggested handcuffs and shackles might be preferable at one point. His early morning rovings were finally blocked when all the doors and windows were locked and barred.

The Kedington Meadow Lark

Every year the Village of Kedington hold their annual "Meadow Lark" to raise funds for the village. In the early years, Eileen and I were roped in to run one of the sideshows. The first few years we volunteered to do the hotdog stand and then we were promoted to the shove-halfpenny stall. Every year without fail we made a fortune for the village funds.

Then we really entered the big time. We were told that we had been allotted the coconut shy and that year we made history for the Kedington Meadow Lark. We were the first ever stall ever to *lose* money! The organiser wasn't best pleased.

'How the hell did you manage lose money?' he declared in amazement. 'Was there a deadeye Dick knocking down the coconuts like ninepins?' he asked.

'Well,' I replied. 'For a start, you must realise that I assumed that the coconuts had been donated, like many of the prizes on the other stalls, and anything we took was profit. No one told us you'd paid good money for them and would get cash back on the returns.'

We'd had this brilliant scheme to attract customers. The plan was that when a small child came along to have a go we would let him or her win, thus attracting the older punters who would spend a fortune trying to beat the kids. I had attached a piece of string to one of the coconuts and when a kid threw the ball, I would pull the coconut off the cop with the string; the idea being that we would make huge bucks and all the kids would get a coconut – pah! The word spread like wildfire and all the customers we got were under five. We even had an eighteen month old baby in a pram with his mum assisting him to chuck the ball. Well, how could I not? Not only did we lose money, but we achieved yet another first for the Meadow Lark: we ran out of coconuts before time.

Despite the fact that we'd made a lot of kids very happy that day, we were never invited to run the coconut shy ever again. Instead, we were relegated to the "Bowling for a Pig" stall.

The Duck Race

Every year our village puts on the Village Duck Race, in which each of the dozens of ducks is numbered and the villagers buy a numbered ticket, which corresponds to their selected duck. This annual event raises money for the local church and is normally, depending on the weather, a happy family event, with entire families cheering-on their chosen duck.

Our village shop advertises this event in the window and was surprised to receive a visit from the local bobby, who had noticed the poster and decided to investigate the matter.

'Allo, allo, allo. Wot 'av we 'ere, then?' he said, calling the attention of the proprietor. "Av you done the necessary, sir?'

'And what might the necessary be then, constable?' came the reply.

'Well, there's the question of 'aving a police presence, the closing of the roads leading to the race area and then there will be a charge to cover our expenses, you know. And of course, then the laws of health and safety have to be adhered to. Not to mention the Animal Rights people; we can't afford to have them rioting in protest. Will all these ducks be properly looked after?'

'Well, constable,' the proprietor explained, 'the ducks are plastic and the race will take place in the river.'

'Ah, well in that case have the river authorities been advised and will there be any danger to the wildlife, fish, etc.?'

This story is true from a certain point of view, only the details have been enhanced by the writer with a little poetic licence.

Twas the Night Before Christmas 1967

Michael Vaughn was a lovable Irishman, but when someone made the mistake of calling him "Paddy", his smiling face changed: he would frown, clench his teeth and snarl, 'Me name's Michael; don't call me Paddy!'

Like a lot of Irishmen, Michael loved his drink. It was Christmas Eve, Eileen and the girls had caught the bus into town to do a bit of shopping and they were to meet me after I had done my round, so that I could bring the Christmas Goodies home in the sidecar and save Eileen's arms. My round completed, I returned to the sorting office to find that Michael was a little the worse for drink and hadn't delivered his mail. His round was a village just out side of town and his deliveries that day didn't amount to more than twenty-five letters and he couldn't see the point of pushing a post office bike 15 miles for such a small amount of mail.

The post mistress had other ideas and the PHG told me that she had said that if Mr Vaughn didn't deliver his round he would be sacked. Grabbing Michael by his collar, I dragged him out of the sorting office with him yelling, 'Bejesus, I tort

Scrooge died years ago!' He was of course referring to the post mistress.

I then had to meet Eileen, to explain that I would be delayed. I bundled him into the sidecar and roared off to complete his delivery. His condition didn't improve as at every house we visited they insisted that Michael had a little tipple, something he was unable to refuse. I, on the other hand, was driving. Michael wasn't cut out to be a postie and a few weeks later he took another job and left the GPO without a stain.

Eileen's Version of Events

I remember this particular Christmas Eve as one of my real "Christmas moments". I had taken the girls to get the last-minute shopping and the streets were packed. It was a typical December day, the weather dark and damp. The girls were so excited and like all young children on Christmas Eve, they were totally lost in the atmosphere and the magic of it all.

Shopping done, we sat waiting for Bob in the only cafe in town: The Oak Room Cafe; dishing up wonderful home-cooked food which was served by equally wonderful ladies. It was almost closing time when Bob dashed in to tell me that Michael was drunk on duty and that if he was to avoid Michael getting the sack he would have take him and deliver the mail.

Given all this, what were the children and I to do? There were no buses at that time of day, we couldn't afford a taxi, I had several bags of heavy shopping, I was pregnant with Emma, the cafe was about to close and by now the girls were getting hungry – oh joy.

The problem was solved by one of the ladies in the kitchen, who had overheard our predicament. She told Bob not to worry, they were only closing early so that they could have their staff Christmas dinner and would the girls and I like to join them. 'Besides,' she said, 'What's a Christmas party without kids.'

So as Bob dashed out into the cold damp evening with a drunken postie and the girls and I had a slap-up feed. What a magic meal that was. The windows of the cafe had all steamed over so that the outside Christmas lights became a multi-coloured blur. I looked round the table at these wonderfully kind ladies and watched as they took my girls onto their motherly laps to pull crackers with them, sort through the paper hats and pop them onto their heads. I felt so grateful to these kind semi-strangers who had taken us in, fed us and kept us warm and as if that wasn't enough, the Salvation Army had taken up position outside and they'd blasted out *Silent Night*.

That was the most Christmassy I have ever felt. These days, we get lost in the melee, rushing round in frantic efforts to spend as much as we can, but that real feeling cannot be bought and I wish I could have it again.

Poor, shattered Bob finally came back for us and the ladies had put together a doggy bag, so that he wouldn't be left out. They waved us off like family, the girls and the shopping in the sidecar and me clinging to Bob from the back of the bike. Thank you, ladies, and God bless you everyone!

Union's Branch Official

The lads had elected me as the Union's Branch Official and I constantly did battle with the post mistress, who would have served better in Victorian times. I had some Union experience from previous jobs and completed a correspondence course, acquiring a book of post office rules that was invaluable over some of my disputes with her. She must have sighed with relief when I handed in my resignation.

My time with the post office spanned a period of seven years; three years in London and four in Suffolk. I made some good friends and had some great and interesting times. It was the death of one of those friends that shifted my life in another direction. His name was Sid Purkiss. An old local boy, he was a nice, gentle old man, who deserved a long and happy retirement. But, unfortunately, he was killed by a car while delivering the mail.

The ironic thing was that he was only two weeks off retirement and his sixty-fifth birthday. I managed to negotiate a full pension for his widow.

Eileen had for some time been trying to get me to leave the post office, as the hours weren't good, the money was poor and there were no prospects of promotion. She and the kids often caught the bus into Haverhill and met me from work. While she waited she would watch the postmen go off on their bikes in all kinds of weather. She told me later that she watched one particular old postie wrapping his scarf around his neck as he braced himself against the biting wind and set off to complete a particularly arduous round; of course, quite a few of them were getting on in life. She would often say to me, 'Bob, I don't want you pushing a bike round 26 miles of countryside at their age.' It was Sid's death that got me thinking and Eileen became even more determined that I should leave the post office.

Moving On

Existence in the Sweat Box

When I told the post office lads that I was going work in a pork processing plant, they all said I wouldn't last five minutes in a factory. Well, I lasted twenty-four years. I left the post office in 1969 and my basic pay was sixteen pounds a week. Haverhill Meat Products, jointly owned by Sainsbury's and Canadian Packers, paid me thirteen pounds and thirteen shillings, plus three pounds training bonus, giving me a grand total of sixteen pounds and thirteen shilling a week.

Everything the lads had told me about the factory was true: it was a sweat box – you slogged from the moment you clocked on doing work that was both boring and repetitive. The monotony was occasionally broken when one of the office girls had to walk through our department; the catcalls and whistles made them blush and I'm not sure if they enjoyed it or not, but it did us the power of good.

Another way of relieving the boredom was to sing. The team that I was working with were without a doubt the best singers by far. On one occasion, after giving our rendition of *Bridge Over Troubled Waters*, the foreman came over and I could have sworn that he had a tear in eyes when he said, 'That was really lovely, lads.'

Because the work was hard as well as mind-numbing, there were the inevitable and long periods of silent graft. The only thing that kept me going was the wage packet and thank goodness overtime was in plentiful supply.

I had been working in the processing department for a little over a year, when I applied for a transfer to the curing cellar, which was slightly more interesting. My application was successful and the work proved to be a lot more interesting, but the conditions were worse. Because of the process of curing the meats, the area had to be refrigerated and dimly lit – it was also very damp – but I was able to earn more and went on to get a chargehand's job.

About eighteen months later, we once again began to look at emigration as a means to escape the drudgery and improve our lives. At that time Australia was still hungry for healthy young families and so we applied to Australia House and they arranged for us to be interviewed in Ipswich. I had the distinct impression that it was the kids being interviewed and we were only of secondary consideration at the time.

Our interviewer couldn't get much out of Emma, as she was only eighteen months old, so he moved on to Beth who, at three and a half, was quite shy and she clammed up and snuggled closer to her mother. Then he made the mistake of starting a conversation with Sally who, once started, couldn't be stopped and she filled him in with our whole life story. Anyway, after we had completed all the paperwork, we returned home to wait and see if we were to be accepted.

Meanwhile, back in the factory, I had decided to apply for a management position. But our lives were yet again dictated by events when we received communication from Australia House saying we had been given the stamp of approval and it was just a matter of arranging a sailing date. A couple of days later I was told that I had been accepted as a manager at the factory: emigration was placed on the back boiler, our destiny was set and we were once again reserved for England and Saint George.

Life as a foreman was very interesting. Over my years spent in management I was in charge of several departments, my last being the formulation department, where we made sausage meat. This department was made up entirely of men, whereas the sausage hall was predominantly women. There were quite a few of the women who, shall we say, weren't averse to spicing up their lives with a little extra marital activity and, of course, a great deal of the men were only too willing to oblige. I recall one particular incident when one of the guys, who was very much a "Jack the Lad", overflowing with testosterone, turned up for work in a horsebox. He parked it in the car park at the furthest point away from the factory. At lunch time, a group of workers were looking out of a window overlooking the car park, when they observed "Jack" furtively approaching the horsebox and climbing in the back. A little while later he was followed by a female, who also climbed in the rear of the horsebox. I assume they were listening to a very funny radio programme, as the box was rocking with jollity. The word soon spread and when the girl returned to work there were choruses from the other women of "Clippety-clop, clippety-clop" as she walked back to her work station. But from the Men there were cheers and, 'Get in there, my son!' Talk about double standards.

Another incident was when an irate wife, who didn't work at the factory, had been told by a well-meaning friend that her husband had been having a "carry-on". She came charging on site carrying a carving knife seeking revenge. It's not too clear as to which of the guilty parties she wanted to carve up; perhaps both.

The factory was big and fortunately, she was unable to find them. It was reported to the security office that a crazy woman was charging about the factory baying for blood. Eventually, a personnel officer calmed her down and relieved her of the knife. There were many other stories going about, but I'm unsure if they were figments of the storyteller's imagination or not.

In all my years as a manager I only had to sack one bloke over a stupid dispute about overtime. At that time we had a strict overtime rota, but this guy wouldn't accept that some other guy was ahead of him on the rota. He ranted and raved with his nose an inch away from mine and was totally out of control, but I would not budge; it was not his turn and had I given in, it would have been unfair on the others. Incensed at not getting his own way, he was foolish enough to punch me, hoping I would retaliate, resulting in both of us getting the sack. But with so many witnesses to the incident I had the presence of mind to put my hands in my pockets, showing him that I wasn't about to be provoked. When I told him he was sacked he punched me again. I was able to ride the punches and then I told him that if he didn't leave site, I would sue him for assault. At this he left; I heard later that he bitterly regretted his actions and it was a long time before he got another job.

All the other guys in the department were a great bunch. They were all as supportive of me as I was of them and a grander bunch of blokes didn't exist. Alas, I was to experience more problems with mindless militants in the Union than I did with the staff in all the departments under my control.

A Union Man

The threats and intimidation were oh so real. Join our Union or else. As the pressure on me mounted, I told Eileen to take our three young daughters to stay with her sister in the North East of England. I had already witnessed the power they wielded and just what they were capable of.

But first let me take you back to 1955, when I started my first job in a furniture factory. The shop steward at that time approached me extolling the virtues of being part of the Union. This was in the days before total "closed shop" and when one had a choice in most industries. I took the advice of my brother and brother-in-law, who was a shop steward himself, to join and paid my subs, but I never got involved in Union business.

I dropped out when I joined the army and following my demob in 1958, I started work in a factory making gas cookers, refrigerators, etc. Once again, I joined the Union and began to take interest in Union affairs. I soon began to realise that at that time, the working man was still fighting a battle for a "fair deal" for pay and conditions. OK, it wasn't as bad as the days of the Toll Puddle Martyrs, but nonetheless there was a great deal of unfairness.

In 1962 I left factory work to become a postman in Clapton, East London. This was when my involvement in the Union really accelerated.

The Conservative-dominated 1960s saw a more concerted effort to control wage levels. This precipitated a spate of negotiation and arbitration between the UPW and the government. The initial wage increases were too modest for many, leading to strikes in 1964. A national all-out official strike was avoided when a more substantial pay increase was achieved later that year.

During my seven years in the post office, I was elected to do different jobs for the Union, including Branch Secretary. We had moved from London to Suffolk, but a country postman wasn't to my liking, so in 1969 I returned to factory life in a food-processing plant.

It was there that I joined the TGWU and my involvement never waned. The management were of a closed-minded attitude and they totally mismanaged the workforce , forcing the workers to strike; not for money, but for the reinstatement of a senior shop steward, who had been sacked for holding a meeting to discuss a problem with the other shop stewards; an unpaid meeting at that. The incompetent, high-handed management were unable to understand that the workforce would actually strike over a principle with no money involved. After a few days, they caved in and reinstated the senior shop steward.

Nationally, a wind of change was blowing throughout the land and there was a slow and gradual shift of power from the incompetent managers – who were living in the past and refusing to change bygone practices, even though the signs were there for all to see – to the ever-growing Union militants.

At that time, the country seemed to be run on the "old boy" network, where prime jobs were given to people who went to the "right" schools and knew the right people, with secondary concern given to whether or not they were up to the job. Consequently, the management seemed to live in one world and the workforce another.

Meanwhile, not surprisingly, the Unions were beginning to gain momentum and the power shift continued. Communist extremists seized their opportunity and infiltrated the Unions in top positions. Slowly, the power axis shifted and the Unions became the miss-managers, abusing their power. The closed-shop scenario became widespread and even good companies were forced to dance to the Union's tune. It was during this time that I applied for the position of foreman.

I had dropped out of the TGWU Union, but always a Union man at heart, I then joined a management Union. The factory in which I was working had its fair share of extremist Union officials and because of management incompetence, they were able to manipulate the workers to establish a strong negotiating position. The Union and the company signed a closed-shop agreement for the shop-floor workers and were pushing to get the junior managers in as well. The majority of the junior managers did join, but a small group of just five foremen resisted and wanted the right of choice. The company Managing Director assured us that as part of the management group, we had the choice and didn't have to be Union members.

As time passed, the pressure from the shop stewards mounted, with suggestions that if we didn't join the TGWU their members would refuse to work with "Black-leg foremen". Then came the insinuation that they couldn't be held responsible for members taking things into their own hands and that they couldn't rule out physical violence. One rather large, intimidating shop steward told me, 'They know where you live, mate; I wouldn't like to think what might happen.' To which I told him, 'You ain't no mate of mine, mate, and if anyone goes near my family I'll come looking for you, mate!'

The threats and intimidation were oh so real. It was then that I wanted Eileen to take our three young daughters to her sister's, out of harm's way. She refused and I was constantly worried that my stubbornness would cause hurt to my family.

We, the remaining rebel foremen, met to discuss the situation and exchanged stories of being pressured into joining. At that time we were all united in our opposition, but I told them that the day would come when the company would sell us out and we would be given the option to "join or no job". I know how they worked and while they were using direct pressure on us, they would also be threatening the senior managers with industrial action. Some of our group refused to believe the company would do us down.

The senior managers were so distant from the workforce that they thought the district official would be able to get the workers out on strike to obtain a closed shop for foremen. Not realising a great number of workers had minds of their own and although they would strike for bad management and bloody-mindedness, there was no way they would support the Union practising bad management themselves.

Unfortunately, the previous Labour government had thrown open the doors and had given corrupt Unions the powers that they were now misusing and managers were then frightened of their own shadows. One by one, we were called in to see the MD and were told that they had agreed with the Union that all junior managers would have to join up. I refused, saying that I belonged to another Union, but the MD wasn't best pleased with me and he said that he couldn't do anything else for me. I replied that he and the company had let us down badly and I explained that they had done nothing at all for us, anyway. Incidentally, this stopped my promotion prospects for the rest of my time there, because I had forcibly dared to tell the guv'nor a few home truths.

After the meeting with the MD, we were told we had to have a meeting with district official of the TGWU. His arrogance was evident as he announced to us that we would now have to sign up or leave the company. He handed out forms for us to fill in, but I screwed mine up and chucked it in the bin.

'You'll be sacked!' he screamed.

'Well, then I will just have to consult my Union about that,' I replied as I played my trump card.

His face was a picture. He coughed and spluttered and red-faced with rage, he stuck his nose in my face and screeched, 'You will resign from that Union and join mine or face the consequences.'

My reply was unprintable. The rest of the group were forced to join, but because I'd been with the management Union for several years since becoming a foreman, I was able to use it to my advantage. I consulted with my district official, who checked how long I had been a member and asked me one question. 'Do you want to transfer to the TGWU?'

I replied that I would prefer to be represented by him, so he told me to leave everything to him and in a couple of days I received a copy of a letter that he had sent to the TGWU. It was a masterpiece of the written word, putting the TGWU District Official firmly in his place.

Fortunately, I had a great working relationship with my lads, so threats that they wouldn't work with me came to nothing and although the company transferred me to take over in other departments, my reputation as a firm but fair foreman followed me and I was always able to get the best from my department.

It's a sad fact of life that I was forced to use one Union to stave off the unwanted attention of another. Margaret Thatcher later changed the laws that had handed power to the Unions. My concern is that some people in power, whether management or Unions, will always misuse it and I hope the pendulum won't swing too far back.

There were, of course, happier times at the factory, like the years competing for the Wilkinson Sword Top Team Trophy.

The Wilkinson Sword Trophy.

At the age of 20 in 1958, I had just been demobbed from the army, I was 10 stone wringing wet, with not an ounce of fat, and I was as fit as a fiddle. Work, Eileen and playing football kept me in good shape over the years. But by the time I was forty, Eileen'd had enough of me getting kicked and battered on the football pitch and after seeing a squash match on the telly, she decided that would be a far better sport for me.

I didn't take a lot of persuading, as it was taking longer and longer for me to recover from the lumps, bumps and bruises from my exploits on the football pitch. Knowing little about squash, I spoke to a friend who played league squash and he gave me a couple of lessons and entered me in the sports-centre league; in the bottom group, of course. Each group had six players and the top two were promoted, while the bottom two were relegated; except for the bottom group that is, as there wasn't anywhere to go.

Eileen had envisaged me playing once a week for an hour, coming home slightly puffed out. Following a short rest I would then be expected to do any chores she had in mind for me. She should have known better; after all, we had been together since 1956. For me, it's not good enough to just dip my toe in the water; I have to be completely submerged.

It wasn't long before I was playing five, six and sometimes seven days a week. On the days I wasn't involved in a league game I was practising with a friend. It was a little late in life for me to be taking up squash at the age of 40. Most of the opposition were under 30 and had been playing for a lot of years, but I was fit and keen and I fell in love with the sport.

I also joined the factory league and I managed to reach the top group in both leagues, but was relegated to the second division where I held my own. The top group in both leagues were a class above the rest, but I thought that at my age it was a great achievement and a privilege to be in their company, even if it was short-lived.

The Wilkinson Sword Top Team tournament was, to me, an unknown quantity and I was later to discover that it was a tournament between all the factories in the area. One had to be very fit to take part, for it consisted of many different sports: five-a-side football, relay running, obstacle course race, swimming, tug of war and various gym tests.

The factory I worked for had their team of five young, *fit* lads and one girl, ready and finely tuned. They had been practising all year in readiness. Most of the events included all six members of the team taking part in a joint effort to beat the other contenders. Except for the gym test, which was performed on an individual basis, and while the guys competed in the five-a side football, the girls fought it out on the netball court.

Their captain David was super-fit guy who played semi-professional football. Shortly before the tournament was about to take place he was red-carded playing football and was sent off. This meant he was banned from playing and as The Wilkinson Sword Top Team Tournament was affiliated to the FA, it meant he was unable to take part.

The search was on for a replacement. The team manager came up with a couple of suggestions, but the others in the team couldn't agree and time was getting very close, so Alan

Seabright, the team manager, told them they would have to go along with the replacement he chose.

On the Thursday of the weekend tournament Alan, with whom I had played football, knowing I was fairly fit, approached me and said, 'Can you swim, Bob?' I told him "Fishy" was my middle name. He then asked, 'Are you doing anything on Sunday?' – going on to ask me if I would take part, explaining what was involved. I agreed to be there and to do my best.

Unknown to me – Alan told me later – all the others were aghast when he told them their replacement for David the super-fit footballer was a bald-headed 41-year-old geezer.

'That's it!' they said. 'We ain't got a chance in hell!' They knew the competition from the other entrants was of a very high standard.

As the tournament took place they began to realise that I wasn't the old duffer they'd expected, especially as I shouted and screamed them into action, urging these kids on, and not only that, but taking the lead. Age sometimes has some advantages, with shyness not a problem. Eileen has always said I only know one way – balls out and up front! As we began to win event after event, it started to dawn on us that we could actually win this trophy.

The tug of war was particularly exhausting. I've never known an event to sap strength as that one did. My saving grace was that the others looked in a worse state than me and I wasn't about to let the youngsters know how knackered I was. We came second in that event and the competition became fiercer, but we had victory in our sights.

Memoirs of a Working Man

The relay race was the last event. This turned out to be the clincher and we had to beat our closest rivals for the trophy. The whole team was taking part. It was decided to put our girl first and they put me last, as I was considered the oldest and it was so thought that I would be the slowest. It was my turn and our team was placed third, our closest rivals in second place.

There was only 2 yards in it when I set off. I had to make it and make it I did, overtaking both leaders. There was absolutely no way I wasn't going to win. Linford Christy couldn't have done it better; my adrenalin was at boiling point and I was still high. Spurred on by my team, I crossed the winning line first.

We won the tournament and they made me Captain and sent me up to receive the trophy, but what made it special for me was that Eileen and my three daughters were there to witness their old dad showing the youngsters a thing or two. My team carried me on their shoulders round the sports centre while they did a lap of honour and the packed hall whistled and cheered. I looked up at Eileen and the girls, who were in the spectators' gallery, and their grins said everything.

On the following Monday I went to see Alan and I overheard him telling two of the team, 'See, I told you about Bob; he ran faster, swam faster and completed more gym tests than any of you.'

They stood there nodding and agreeing. That was a great feeling and every time I look at the trophy I feel a warm glow of satisfaction.

The following year I said I wouldn't take part but would coach the team and there wasn't an inch of that tournament that I didn't run with them, screaming and urging them on, until I had the great pleasure of watching them win again. The following year was just as successful and that trophy became ours again. By that time, we had built a reputation of being unbeatable and we carried that honour for a few years. All good fun, but nothing can beat the feeling of winning that trophy for the first time.

One last endearing memory I have is of the father of our girl member, who came to me a few days later and said, 'Bob, I want to thank you. My daughter is so proud to be part of the team and she puts the winning entirely down to you, for driving her and the others on; she said she was more scared of you than losing.'

Retirement? What Retirement!

For many years my main ambition was to retire early – I had a burning desire to finish work at 55 years of age. My determination to take early retirement was spurred on by the premature death of my father, who died aged 65 after drawing only one month's pension.

In 1992, at the tender age of 54 and after twenty-four years working there, I had the opportunity to take early retirement/ redundancy. The package was good and although it was a year before my plans, I grabbed at it like a starving man would a slice of bread.

I hadn't completed the necessary twenty-five years to qualify for a gold watch, but oh boy was I in for a surprise. On my last day one of my lads, Peter Rook, called me into the spice room, where he was in charge of blending the spices for the pies and sausages. Thinking he had a problem I accompanied him. To my great shock, all the lads were in there waiting for me and they presented me with an inscribed gold watch. What an absolutely fabulous send-off.

My retirement was spoilt because I was so young. I wasn't allowed the luxury of disappearing into my office at home to study Italian, play chess or write my letters and stories. I had to go to the Job Centre and register as unemployed. After a short while I was called in for a "help you back to work" interview, during which I was told about the different courses that were on offer.

One particular course that caught my eye was computer literacy, as I was half interested in learning about computers and, more importantly, it would get the Job Centre off my back. I attended a further interview at the local training services centre. The guy running the training company was obviously suspicious that my interest in computers wasn't really to enable me to make a career change, but to return to the "great unwashed" employed. I had, after all, worked for forty years, with the only break being three years in the army.

He told me that my age was a factor that might restrict my chances of employment in the computer world and with my experience in management I might be better off sticking to that line of work. I couldn't very well tell him that I'd had enough and just wanted to do the things I enjoy, without being committed to regular hours and, above all, management responsibilities. Having a flash of inspiration, I told him that the way forwards was computers and to have an understanding would be a bonus. He reluctantly put me on the list, saying that is was very long and I might have to wait. A long wait would suit me well, because it meant the Job Centre would leave me alone.

Shock! Horror! Only five days after my interview, a letter arrived telling me to report on the following Monday to commence my computer literacy course.

The teacher seemed to be more concerned with the rest of the students and just shunted me into a corner with a keyboard and a set of instructions and told me to practise. The rest of the class were given far more exciting things to do – they were all females and their age ranged from 18 to mid 30s. Was I becoming a victim of sexual discrimination?

I gave teach the benefit of the doubt, thinking, maybe they already had keyboard skills. After thirty-five minutes of play, the teacher told me that George, the managing director, would like to see me in his office.

'Sit down, Bob.' George swivelled gently on his huge leather chair and looked long and hard at me. All sorts of things buzzed around my brain as I wondered what the hell was going on and I tried desperately to pre-empt his questions. 'Bob – this computer course … I have the feeling that it's just a time-filler for you.'

'No, no, no,' I said. 'I'm really interested.'

He sat so far back in his chair he was almost lying down. His hands were clasped around the back of his head, his eyes fixed on the ceiling, and it sounded like he was singing a song, 'Yes, yes, yes, yes!' Suddenly, he sat bolt upright and stared me straight in the eye. 'Look, Bob; I'll come straight to the point. We have some new guidelines from the government and I have very little time to implement them.' Can you imagine what was going through my mind?

'I need a good man to set up and supervise the new scheme and I have it on good authority that you're just the man for the job.'

I later found out that a friend of ours, Rosie, who not only works for the training company but is indeed second in command, had met Eileen on one of her shopping excursions and Eileen happened to mention that I was on her waiting list. Knowing they were about to start a new scheme, she told George that I was the main man. Thank you, Rosie. Do me a favour – don't do me any favours.

So there I was, on and off the dole too soon for any real enjoyment and then on and off my training course in thirty-five minutes flat, once again back in work.

I did enjoy the work and I lasted for two years, but I told George and Rosie that as much as I delighted in their company and found the work more than satisfying, it wasn't what I had in mind for my old age and by this time I had passed my intended deadline for retirement. They then offered me part-time work, but I wanted freedom from the commitment of having to be at work every day.

The Job Centre took me off their leash after I showed them my pension forecast, proving I'd paid enough to cover my pension and they didn't have to pay my stamp, and because I was in receipt of a pension, their interest in me vanished.

I had a couple of months of complete bliss. Then son-in-law David, who was venturing into business for himself, discovered that I was available every time he was in need of help. So I found myself in the building trade as a skivvy to my son-in-law. We would drive for miles to the different building sites where he was contracted to work and his plea for me to help him out on occasion turned into three and sometimes four days a week.

The problem was that the work was very physical and not really suitable for a man of my advancing years. Eileen kept telling me that I was fit and could handle it, but she didn't have to do it. Besides, I had other fish to fry. So I made sure that I became unavailable with a stack of excuses that could have filled "Billy Liars Joke Book".

My plan was simple: I figured that with my pension and Eileen's wages, we could live in reasonable comfort. Nothing special – food on the table, a bed to sleep in and the odd holiday. A simple but happy life. After a couple of months, my dream – yes, I, too, had a dream – was suddenly and unceremoniously put into an irretrievable situation when Eileen came home from work and told me she had put in her notice to quit work. I glanced up from my sunbed and said, half interested, 'Got another job, then?'

'No, I haven't got another bloody job. If you can loaf about and not go to work, I'm going to join you. And besides, I want to spend more time with our grandchildren.'

'But, but, but …' She had my full attention.

'No buts – I'm not going to work any more and that's final!'

How unfair is that? I ask you. How fair is that? I tried logic and posed the question, 'What about all those years I was working and you were sitting at home doing nothing?' But she wouldn't have it; all she did was make some stupid excuse about having three daughters to look after, a part-time job and housework; as if that's work.

She could have worked evenings when the kids were in bed, but no, she elected to sit at home and do zilch. But you can't use logic with women and all my arguments fell on deaf ears. All this meant I had to look for a part-time job to make up the shortfall.

On a parallel dimension Richard was also in the throes of starting his own business. He's an engineer and he asked me if I could work with him on a Saturday. His idea was that I could keep a machine running in the morning and in the afternoon we could clean the factory. It worked well and as David had taken on a couple of blokes, my excuse book was needed less. One day a week – I could manage that, no problem.

But Richard on the other hand realised that although I hadn't any engineering background, he could point me in the right direction and like a clockwork toy I would perform with robot-like efficiency. His business was growing and he persuaded me to work a couple of days during the week as well as my cleaning duties on Saturday. 'Just till I get established, you understand,' he told me. I could feel myself getting sucked in. But it wasn't too physical, so I went along with it.

Anyway, the two days developed into four days and I was putting in more hours than when I was working full time. After a couple of years he had increased his staff in the factory, but the administration side of the business was suffering. I saw this as my opportunity to get a cushier job and volunteered to sort the front office out.

This worked well for a couple of years and suddenly I was closing in on sixty-five. I suggested to Richard that it might be a good idea if I trained my replacement, as there was no way I was working past sixty-five. But once I'd trained my more than able replacement, he was still reluctant to let me go, so I returned to the workshop. The company thrived and the orders increased. The need to run the machines at the weekend was paramount, so I reduced my days to just Saturday and Sunday. When I reached sixty-five I said that was it, but my silver-tongued son-in-law convinced me to work just one day a week and because I'm so gullible and just an innocent at large, I agreed to work just Sundays. I thought I might retire when I reached seventy. Bloody seventy – now that sounds really old!

Well, as I write, seventy has been and gone and I'm still doing one day a week. Retirement? Well, maybe one day. Watch this space!

Relocation Relocation.

Time flies by.

In the wink of an eye the sixties had vanished, leaving only memories. England had won the World Cup, I had married Eileen, we'd lived in three homes, I'd left the post office and we had three beautiful daughters; a memorable decade, indeed.

Eileen explained to me that just because I'd held her hand while she was giving birth that didn't mean I could take all the credit. Women, eh! It was in 1974 that we made our momentous move from Kedington to the Gatelodge, Little Wratting. We had started our married life in one room and lived there for two years. We then bought a two-bedroomed, ground-floor flat in Walthamstow in 1962. Then, four years later, we moved out of London into a semi-detached house in Suffolk. From one room to a flat and then a semi was never going to be enough, although in the early years a detached property was unthinkable for us and was far above our station. But as time moved on, my yearning to own a detached house grew and grew.

Again, we found that the step from a semi to a detached was financially out of our reach. We changed direction and decided that the only way we could achieve our ambition was to look for something that wasn't in pristine condition. It was Eileen who spotted a sign saying "detached bungalow for sale", but we couldn't see the property as it was hidden behind years of overgrown elder and brambles.

We found the Gatelodge and it was love at first sight, for me but not so for Eileen. By this time our little home in Kedington had central heating was nicely decorated and so very comfortable. Not so the Gatelodge, which was derelict, with an overgrown garden and windows boarded up. Once we'd prised open the boards and climbed in, the first thing to hit you was the smell of damp, with smelly green fungus growing up the wall. The floorboards were rotten, wet and collapsed, the plaster had fallen in chunks from the walls and the whole place was a picture of neglect. But I could see beyond all that and I knew in my heart we could put all that right.

It had been empty some time and was therefore used as a toilet by the passing tramps and derelicts. In Eileen's eyes, this wasn't the house of our dreams, but once outside in the garden it was an oasis: apple trees in blossom, the grass was about 3 feet high and the kids were running through it laughing and calling to each other. Birds were singing, the sun was shining and the location was perfect. And if you ignored the birds and the kids you could hear silence. Yes, this was the place for me; I only had to convince Eileen … and then the bank manager.

Eileen told me later that even as though she was dead against it and had totally dismissed the very idea, she saw the look in my eyes and knew there would be no stopping me. I just kept saying, 'We can do this, gel; we can do it.' And do it we did. Even though the Gatelodge was detached, it was tiny, with only four cramped rooms, but the garden was huge, with plenty of room for an extension.

We made an offer which was accepted, so we put our present house up for sale and I got permission from the owners of the Gatelodge to do some work before contracts were exchanged. A bit of a risk, I know, but I was about to move Eileen, Sally, Beth and Emma from a comfortable home into a shack, so I had to at least get it habitable.

I was working from two 'til ten in the factory, so during the week I worked on the house from 6.30 a.m. until it was time to go to work and all day Saturday and Sunday, turning down all offers of overtime. I ripped the old floors up, stripped the plaster from the walls and tore away the out-of-date wiring and plumbing. I laid solid concrete floors and from the mains water supply outside I ran a pipe into the bungalow and stuck a tap on the end.

John Yendell, a friend of ours who was in the RAF, was an electrician and he made a deal with me. As he was stationed nearby he could get home every weekend, but obviously that was when his wife liked to go out for shopping etc., so if I could get Eileen to take his wife out, he and I would rewire the bungalow: the skilled and the dogsbody. I robbed his wife of his company for quite a few of his weekends off. Not only did he wire up the bungalow, but he would come over at every opportunity to give me a hand at whatever I was up to. He just loved the project; I suppose it was because it was so far removed from wiring up Phantom jets.

Another friend of mine was a plasterer before he went into the factory and he agreed to do the plastering on the cheap if I did the labouring. So the place was wired, plastered and we had a tap on a hose giving us water. The toilet was a little crude

– in a brick lean-to outside the four walls of the bungalow, connected to the main drains, but with no water for flushing, so that had to be bucketed. Time had overtaken me and we had to move in. I had knocked down a couple of walls, so the four rooms were reduced to three, and I put up a temporary partition to make them our sleeping quarters; the three girls one side and Eileen and I the other.

I had earmarked one of the other rooms for the bathroom and that had to be my top priority. Another room had to be our kitchen/dining and living room. We had an architect draw up plans for an extension and we proposed to double the Gatelodge in size.

Our first night in the Gatelodge was memorable as the girls, in unfamiliar and frankly crude surroundings, slowly filtered into our bed one by one, having been frightened by a scratching sound coming from the old wooden front door. I can tell you that five in a bed isn't very comfortable, but Eileen wouldn't hear of them going back to their own beds until I'd sorted out the noises in the night. I told them it wasn't anything to worry about, just a rat, and Eileen did her nut, having scared the living daylights out of them. My punishment was to sleep in their bed, while Eileen and the girls slept in the other one. It was nearly two weeks before we returned to status quo.

There were, of course, rats and the place was heavily infested with mice, having been in a rural position and empty for so long. So a cat was the order of the day and what a cat it was. A friend who had several gave one to us and the girls named it Polly; Polly Oliver.

Memoirs of a Working Man

It was young but not a kitten and within just a few weeks it had cleared the place out and was going further afield for breakfast, dinner and tea. The rabbit population also began to suffer, even squirrels weren't safe, and one day she bought home a full-grown pheasant. She stashed it in a shed and it kept her fed for a week.

A dog was the next acquisition: a Rottweiler pup. We got her cheap because she had a rough coat and for some reason, breeders only like smooth coats on Rotties. Our three daughters were eight, ten and twelve, the dog was seven weeks and the cat was six months; oh, and I almost forgot, the hamsters. They were as old as the hills; indeed, they were so old that even the cat didn't give 'em a second glance. The animals slept in one room and we slept in the other. I wanted to put the animals in with the kids, but Eileen held out.

Just outside the front door was a pile of sand, a heap of hardcore, 6,000 bricks – that I had bought Eileen for her birthday – and a borrowed cement mixer. The windows of the house were still broken and boarded up and anyone would be forgiven for thinking that the place was empty with no one living there.

One hot summer's night at about 2.00 a.m. we were all fast asleep, when a noise woke Eileen up. She, in turn, woke me and for a moment we lay listening to what can only be described as an excerpt from a Peters Sellers' *Pink Panther* film. From outside and between swear words we heard, 'Get the ***ing thing. No, no, no, swing it round 'dis ***ing way.' Crash! 'Pick it tup! Pick the ***ing ting up! ... Arrr, me foot; it's on me ***ing foot; get it off; get it off, for God's sake! Get it off!'

Eileen and I looked at each other and both said, 'The cement mixer!' Leaping out of bed, naked as a jay bird, I turned the light on and jumped into me hobnail boots. I opened the door and yelled, 'Where's my gun? Come on, Fang,' I said to a pretend guard dog, 'let's get 'em!' By the time I rounded the bungalow I saw a car and trailer disappearing down the road and the cement mixer lying on its side.

Fortunately, I'd chained it to a tree, which couldn't be seen in the dark and this, I believe, was what was causing the would-be thieves problems. Eileen peaked through a crack in the boarded-up window and said I was sight to behold: a vision in pink. Standing stark naked in the moonlight, except for the hobnail boots, waving a piece of four by two.

We lived rough for the first two years; I suppose rough is an understatement. It was more like camping indoors and Eileen wasn't too keen, but the girls thought it was great. Not your normal run-of-the-mill childhood.

Meals at the Gatelodge were fun; the floor was our table and we would all sit in a circle on the floor eating our meals from trays on our laps. When we'd finished Emma, our youngest who was 6 years old, would say to Eileen, 'Please may I leave the floor, Mum?'

Joe, our Dutch friend, came to see what we were doing. He took one look at the way we were living and said to me, 'Dese girls can't live dis vay!' Turning to Eileen, he added, 'You and dese gels get packed, you're coming home mit me!' They declined his offer, but I think there was a little wavering from Sally.

Our first Christmas at the Gatelodge was a little ... what shall we say ... alternative. My eldest sister was on her way to spend Christmas with her friends in Norfolk and she called in to see us and check out our new address. As she sat on the only chair in the 10 foot square room that had become our kitchen, dining and living room, her face was a picture and when water was fetched from the outside standpipe to make her a cup of tea her eyes widened with amazement.

It was 22 December and was very cold outdoors, but our little room was cosy, heated by a paraffin fire. Smelly but very warm. Even so, she declined to remove her hat and coat, insisting that they couldn't stay long as they had to be on their way. She couldn't get out quick enough, but was too polite to say anything.

Many years later she told us what we already knew. She said, 'I thought you were bloody mad moving out of your lovely little house in Kedington to live like that.'

Eileen's Turn

No, I really didn't fancy moving to the Gatelodge, but I realised straightaway that there would be no arguing with Bob; he was an immovable object and I knew that if he didn't get to do this he would regret it forever and I wasn't going to be responsible for that. So the kids and I went along with his dream and we tried to make it as much fun as we could. Looking back, I can hardly remember the building site that was our life but rather the fun things we got to do, like when Bob, in a lull while we were waiting for building materials to arrive, built the kids a little shack out of the old branches and wood from rotten trees we'd chopped down. They called it "their little house on the prairie" and played out there all day.

Then there was the time it snowed really hard and no work could be done, so he made them a sledge, but it was so solid and heavy it could hardly be pulled. We solved that by making a harness and attaching it to our, by now, huge dog Lottie and all three of the girls climbed on while the dog happily and effortlessly pulled them along. Lottie enjoyed this as much as, if not more than, the girls and when the girls got cold and came in to warm up, Lottie sat outside next to the sledge and howled for them to come out and play.

There was an empty Edwardian mansion behind the Gatelodge and the children made this their playground, dancing in the ballroom, exploring the other twenty-seven rooms and generally doing what kids do in empty mansions; we hardly saw them except at mealtimes – no daytime telly for our kids.

In general, the children enjoyed it, but Sally really missed having her friends from the village on hand. We were just that bit too far for them to call round and Sally was too young to walk the 2 miles on her own. So we did as much toing and froing as and when building work allowed and life got even busier.

We grew accustomed to the army of builders that went through our lives at that time. Weekends were the busiest, as Bob had done deals with these guys: they supplied the skills and he supplied the muscle, while I supplied the sandwiches and tea; we wore out three kettles in six months. Life was certainly an adventure. I would go out shopping for a couple of hours and return to find a wall missing or another wall built.

Living in cement and brick dust and all the other paraphernalia that goes with this madness, I had to adopt a certain pioneer mentality. I knew it would be finished eventually and I never ever lost faith in Bob, so I accepted almost anything that life threw at me and waited for normality.

The worst thing was not having a bathroom; we had an old enamel bath but no running water attached to it. A friend had lent us a small electric boiler in which I could heat the water and then bucket it into the bath. The girls would go first, then me and then Bob, but as he reckoned he got out dirtier than he got in, he took to showering in the local sports centre for a while.

The bucket was invaluable, as we also had no water access to the loo, so again, a full bucket of water was always at hand in the toilet and the rule was that "you use it – you bucket it", which worked, although visitors had a bit of a shock. Filling the bucket was an adventure of itself. The hosepipe which Bob had fixed to a tap had to be straddled like riding a horse owing to the pressure as the water came through and if left to its own devices, it would run amok, clattering into everything, including you.

Age No Problem and Animal Antics

After a couple of years at the Gatelodge we became civilised once again: the extension had been built and we now had proper toilets, hot and cold running water and central heating. Our friends and families decided that the Gatelodge wasn't such a bad place after all and even Joe said, 'Boy, didn't I tell you dis vas a great idea?' I had bought an old caravan to use for storage before the extension was finished and it now lay empty, the kids using it as a playroom, even sleeping in it on occasion.

On one summer Sunday in Suffolk, when the only "s" missing was the sun – indeed, it was raining hard – there was a knock on the door and two young teenagers stood there dripping wet: a boy and a girl. The boy spoke in broken English, 'Vee are Danish students on holiday and look for a place to sleep. A barn, a shed, anything.'

'Well of course,' said Eileen, 'the girl can have the spare room and you can sleep in the caravan.'

'No, no!' the girl explained in very fractured English. 'We must stay together, madam; vee are eighteen.'

Eileen shook her head and replied, 'Look, dear, age isn't relevant. It isn't proper; there is no way you are sleeping together in my house! Take it or leave it.'

They gabbled at each other in Danish and then said, 'You have no barn?'

'No, sorry,' she said.

They thanked Eileen very much, got on their pushbikes and rode off down the lane. A few moments later I was looking out of the window and I shouted to Eileen, 'Quick, come and have a look at this!'

There were the two Danes cycling past, followed by the others, all on bikes! Well, sixteen to be precise, making a total of eighteen in all. They meant eighteen people not eighteen years of age.

On Emma's ninth birthday, a so-called friend turned up and asked where Emma was. Without any consultation with us, he called Emma and said, 'Wait there and I'll bring in your birthday present.' He came in carrying a kid goat. We both protested that it wasn't practical, we had nowhere for it to live, we knew nothing of goats, etc., etc., but Emma was in love and John, the perpetrator, said not to worry, he'd build it a pen. I'd already built the kids – children that is – a tree house, but this was a tree house with a difference: it had a downstairs as well as an upstairs. Anyway, John built the pen around it, so the goat could have the downstairs.

The baby goat was a male and it was only a few days old; John had rescued it from being put down, because the breeders only wanted females for milking. Emma christened him Milligan after her beloved Spike Milligan. Because Milligan was so young there was no way it could move into its new home; oh no, it had to live indoors. Naturally, John had also given us an abundance of goat milk, but neither Eileen nor the girls could get him to take it from his bottle. Emma was getting stressed and she feared for his life as Milligan was losing condition.

In the farm next door lived Jim the farm manager, so Eileen sent Emma over to get him. Jim came over, grabbed Milligan by the head, squeezed his lips open and "whop", in went the teat and he was away with it and never looked back. Emma decided that from that day forth, Milligan would be known as Jimmy Milligan after her two heroes. We had already acquired two more dogs, so Jimmy Milligan was bought up with two Rottweilers and a mongrel called Kipper, 'cos he was brown and smelly.

It was a sun-drenched day in the middle of summer. I swung gently in my hammock in the shade of the trees and watched a squirrel come loping tentatively across the garden, its ever watchful eyes darting from side to side, looking vulnerable and ill at ease on the open ground. But as soon as he came to a group of trees he moved with silky smoothness vertically up the trunk. Leaping from bough to bough, he scampered out along a thin branch that overhung the bird table. With astounding expertise, he seemed to fly through the air, landing perfectly among the scraps of food.

For a moment he stood frozen, his eyes taking in the surroundings, and then moving to the edge he hung by his long, bushy tail from the shelf of the table.

I watched motionless and became aware of what the little rascal was up to as he began to gnaw at the bag of nuts that Eileen had tied onto the table for the birds. Within seconds, the bag spewed its contents onto the floor. He was down in a flash and gobbling up his ill-gotten gains.

Bella and Holly, our two Rottweilers, lay snoozing in the shade alongside the hammock. Then the peace was broken as Kipper came onto the scene. Kipper was half the size of the Rotties, but he was more of a guard dog than the two of them put together. Strolling out of the house, he caught sight of the squirrel and like a flash from a canon he was off in pursuit, howling with the pleasure of the chase.

The two Rotties lifted their heads in mild interest. Bella – so named because a more beautiful animal you would never see – lazily got to her feet, went over to the nearest tree and cocked her leg. Then she staggered back and flopped down, snorting and grunting as if everything was too much trouble. Holly – named because we acquired her at Christmas – rolled onto her back and juggled a tennis ball with her front paws and huge jaws.

The sun began to slowly crest the top of trees and Eileen called from the house, 'Come on, Bob; it's time to take the dogs for a walk.' This was the signal for Kipper to go berserk. He knows that word well and his excitement transferred to the Rotties as they both began to show interest.

We were so fortunate to live in a very rural environment. Eileen, born in West Hartlepool, at least had the sea nearby, while I on the other hand was born in London, surrounded by bricks and mortar. We both love living in Suffolk and never tire of watching the beautiful sunsets, the gentle, rolling fields and the changing colours of the seasons; then there were the excellent walks right on our doorstep.

It's just as well there aren't many people about when we take the animals for a walk, because as well as the three dogs, we also had a cat that was raised by Kipper from four days old and he thought he was a dog. Jimmy Milligan the goat also loved its evening constitutional.

As we were about to leave the house, one of our daughters turned up with two of our grandchildren and, of course, they all wanted to come. We lived in a lane and had to walk to the end of it, before turning away from the road to join the country walks. Off we set in convoy, our daughter at the forefront, attempting to hold back the ever eager Kipper; we have to keep them on leads until we reach the relative safety of the footpaths. Following Kipper was Eileen with the two Rotties, lolloping along at a more sedate speed. Then came our eldest grandson with the goat, leaving his younger brother bringing up the rear with the cat – on a piece of string! I had locked the house and looking along at the cavalcade, I wished I had the camera with me.

A police car was parked at the end of the lane and the policeman had his back to the procession. He turned on hearing us and watched with mild interest as my daughter was dragged by Kipper past his car. His interest in the two Rotties, however, increased, especially as big and beautiful Bella "christened" his front wheel. Eileen mouthed, 'Oooh, I'm sorry!' and tried to shift their bulk.

I watched the policeman's eyes following Eileen with, I think, his interest being more in our two gorgeous Rottweilers than her. But it was the goat that caused the greatest reaction. I could see that the corner of his eye had caught the movement as they approached and he only half glanced as his attention was pulled from the dogs. But as his head gently swivelled back, the scene before him registered The policeman's mouth dropped open wider as he looked back along the lay-by to see what else was in store for him and that was when he was greeted with a cat on a piece of string.

Once away from the road, we released the dogs to do their own thing: Holly retrieved her stick with monotonous repetition, while Bella was content to sedately walk with us. Then there was Kipper, our very own lunatic, who runs on ahead chasing anything that moves and the rabbit population is sent scampering in all directions.

The wildlife aside, we always have the footpaths to ourselves. But this time an intruder dared to venture onto our patch, also walking their dog, of course; it was Kipper that caught sight of them first. He turned a corner and came face to face with an elderly couple walking a large black Labrador twice his size; but this was kipper's territory and he was soon in hot pursuit of the interloper.

Its owners were shouting in an attempt to get him back, but they were stunned into silence as we came into sight and the Rotties sniffed around them inquisitively. I reassured them that we only had one crazy animal and he was about 2 miles away by now and with any luck wouldn't come back. Eileen explained that the beefy black bear-like creatures were really just gentle giants and the only danger was that they might sit on your foot. We continued with our walk and left the hapless couple traipsing across the fields in search of their dog, knowing full well that our "shitty" little creature would return in his own good time.

Fawlty Towers

It was a Saturday morning in January 1977, it was 6.00 a.m. and I was tiling the bathroom, when from outside I heard a dull thud and a breaking of glass. There had been a car accident on the road near our house. As I went to render assistance Eileen, having crawled out of bed, could be seen groping her way to the kitchen to the kettle.

Arriving on the scene, I found two cars smashed beyond repair. It was pitch dark, freezing cold and drizzling with rain and several people were milling around trying to direct traffic around the smashed cars. I took one injured guy back home, whose name was Brian and he was built like Geoff Capes; the poor sod must have wished he'd stayed put after I'd pushed and pulled him across the embankment and into the house.

'Cup of tea, luv?' Eileen asked him.

'Yes, please,' he grunted through gritted teeth.

It wasn't so much his chest pains that were bothering him, but more so the two dogs jumping all over him. They do love company, bless 'em. Anyway, Eileen decided to evict the dogs into the garden as two more casualties arrived, Bill and Francis, helped in by a couple of policemen – more tea! Francis, the driver of the vehicle, who was even bigger than Brian, was crying and he was blaming his fate on a fox that had run out in front of them. Eileen, seeing he was upset, offered to put some whisky in his tea.

'No, no, madam,' said the constable choking on his tea. 'Not a good idea!'

Bill, the other passenger, explained that they had been sea-fishing all night – and people think I'm crazy – and they were now on their way home from Yarmouth. Brian's head was bleeding, so Eileen fetched some cotton wool and antiseptic, tripping over my bucket of grout in the process. She hobbled back and, ignoring her own pain and discomfort, applied the antiseptic to Brain's head, to which he lets out a scream like a man possessed, jumps from the chair and rolls over onto the floor. Not bad for a guy with busted ribs, eh! Later, we discovered the antiseptic was really nail-polish remover! Picked up by accident in the dark. Ah well, what's done is done.

The dogs were going mad, so Eileen opened the back door to behold a vision. The doctor had arrived and upon getting no answer at the front door, he'd come round the back. Bad move! He was pinned up against the wall by Bella our Rottweiler bitch. Her front feet were on his chest as she licked his face, while Kipper, our mongrel, ran up and down barking. The doctor was a large, fat man wearing a long raincoat over some very nice stripped pyjamas and a delightful pair of bedroom slippers; he had obviously dressed in a hurry.

The doctor was all red-faced and flustered as Eileen pulled him into the sanctuary of the house. He declined Eileen's offer to take his coat, but accepted a cup of tea. Eileen's diagnosis of cracked ribs was confirmed by the doctor, to which she said, 'Well, it's always best to get a second opinion, I suppose.'

'Cup of tea, luv?' smiled Eileen as the ambulance men arrived on the scene.

'No thanks,' they replied; I reckon the word had got out about the menagerie and they didn't want to stay longer than necessary.

As the police were leaving, one of them turned and said, 'Bye, thanks for the tea, missus,' but the ambulance men, the doctor and Brian weren't too impressed with Eileen's tender nursing skills.

Then Bill and Francis couldn't find their boots, having slipped them off when they came in. We looked everywhere. Then I remembered the dogs! Oh yes – that's exactly where they were; or should I say what was left of them. We forced what was left of their boots onto their feet and off they went. 'Bye, lads, safe journey.'

We found out later that Bill, Brian and Francis were off-duty policemen on leave and even though Eileen had tested Brian's mettle and his pain threshold, they sent her a beautiful bouquet of flowers and a thank-you note.

Brief Encounter

We lived in a very small village. Our house was quite isolated and our nearest neighbours lived in a farmhouse called Hill Top Farm situated about 500 yards away; we became very friendly with Jim and Grace who lived there. Eileen and I had just returned from buying a Christmas tree – she'd insisted when we bought it that it wasn't too big but, as you well know, women and measurements are a tad out of wack. I attempted to fit it in our living room and ended up resorting to my saw and I was in the throes of lopping off several feet from it when Jim and Grace popped in for a chat.

This, of course, was the very excuse I was searching for to give the tree job the elbow and have a cup of tea with our neighbours. As we chatted, the dogs started barking and the doorbell rang. At the door stood a rather large gent, who said, 'Sorry to trouble you, but could you tell me if that is Hill Top Farm down the road?'

As I knew Jim and Grace were sitting in our living room, I retorted with, 'Why do you want to know?' What he thought of me Gawd only knows; Eileen is always telling me to modify my tone.

'I'm looking for a Jim and Grace; it's been a long time since we visited them.'

I continued to cross-examine him. 'Do you know Jim and Grace well, then?' Well, for all I know he might a have been a debt collector.

'Err, well yes, we see them quite often over at our house. But it's been many years since we've visited them.'

'Come in,' I instructed him.

Having made him run the gauntlet with our three dogs, I led him into the living room, where Jim and Grace were sitting enjoying the last of our Bourbon biscuits. A greeting filled with shock and surprise ensued.

Jim went out to the car and bought back the guy's wife, his mother and his daughter. A continual buzz of chatter took place and after a cup of tea and more chat, the guy said, 'Well, we can't stay any longer, we're on our way to Romford.'

'Oh!' I said. 'I have a friend in Romford.' This comment could be compared to the time when I was in Jordan and the bartender asked me if I'd met his brother when I was in London. Romford is a big place. But me being me, I continued with, 'Yes, he lives in Wigton Road.'

Everyone went quiet and they looked at me. 'That's where we're headed,' the guy said.

'Number 24!' I exclaimed.

Penny, the guy's wife looked amazed and said, 'That's my mum and dad's house!'

We were stunned and I replied, 'You're George North's daughter?'

I had known George for many years – he was a chess club stalwart. I had played him at chess (proper), pirate chess and even draughts. Yes, you heard it right: draughts. He was, indeed, a champion draughts' player. I met him and his wife Peg at different get-togethers over many years, but never knew the connection with Penny. Moral of the story: be very careful next time you answer the door.

The Joke's on Me

Several years ago Eileen bought me a bedside telephone-cum-radio/alarm clock. I pretended I was pleased, but to be honest, a telephone at my bedside is my idea of hell. In fact, if I had my way the phone would be disconnected when I went to bed.

Now I was very slow on the uptake, because the truth of the matter was, although it was my birthday, she had applied the old Oliver ploy method. Put simply, on birthdays and Christmases, I think of something I would like and buy it for Eileen; this time, however, the swine had turned the tables on me.

But Bob being Bob put the bloody thing in the cupboard and tried to forget all about it. I say tried to forget, but Eileen wasn't about to let it rest and every few days it was, 'What about your birthday present, Bob! You've never fitted it! It wasn't cheap, you know. Don't you like it?' Then she would give me that whipped-pup look and continue with, 'You hate it, don't you?'

Being the solid-gold gent that I am, I reassured her, saying that it was a beautiful present; I just hadn't had time or the know-how to fit it. I kept promising to find out how to wire it up and make time to do it. Anyway, two years later our regular telephone broke. Now how it got broke is still a mystery, but I have my suspicions. Eileen called the telephone engineer and while he was fixing it she asked him about an extension. He told her not to waste money on an engineer, as a 2 year old could do it blindfolded. That was it; I was done for.

I tried one more ploy, saying that I didn't have the necessary equipment, but Eileen replied, 'Don't worry, love, the engineer told me what to get and that the cheapest place was Woollies.'

That was it; I really was done for and I didn't know who to hate most: the engineer or Woollies. I suppose it had to be the engineer, as he had even given Eileen a booklet explaining how easy it was. Well, you can just imagine Eileen being in possession of that kind of enlightenment. How would "Devious Bob" get out of this one? The simple answer was that he wouldn't; especially when my well-meaning son-in-law offered to give me a hand.

Once I'd accepted defeat and we were out buying the necessary equipment, Eileen decided that it would be nice if we had a second extension in the kitchen. Ever had the feeling that the world was ganging up on you?

The "dictator" gave her instruction as to the precise position of the new phones and I decided the easiest route for the wiring was via the loft. This was fine for the kitchen and we were able to hide most of the cable, but the bedroom was a different story. We looked at several methods, but they all meant exposed wires all over the place. Then I had a great idea: we would come down the chimney! No, no, don't be silly – this is an unused chimney, in the old part of the bungalow; years ago, they had chimneys in nearly every room. A hundred years ago they had a contrasting concept towards building than what they have today and the chimney was the mainstay of any building, so you can image how the old stack was; they certainly didn't intend for it to fall down.

There are four rooms in the old part of the Gatelodge, each with a fireplace, all coming from the main stack. I set my ever-helpful son-in-law the chore of drilling through the stack, pointing out where he should cut the hole. An hour passed and he was still at it. I had completed my task and was wondering why he was taking so long. Climbing into the loft, I was confronted with a vision of sweat and dust. He had drilled a hole and had widened it with hammer and chisel. The hole was about 6 inches in diameter and a good 12 inches deep.

'I don't understand it,' he puffed, 'I should be through by now.'

Surveying the situation I declared, 'It might help if you'd drilled the hole 10 inches this way.'

As the realisation dawned on him that he was cutting through the centre of the stack and wouldn't hit fresh air 'til he came out the side, he let out a scream of anguish and turned on me, snapping, 'You bloody well told me to drill there!'

Smiling, I replied, 'I was only testing your initiative, Richard.'

Can't make out why he had the hump with me; we're all only human, after all is said and done.

We finally got there and having done all the donkey work, we began the task of wiring in the extensions. When we'd connected the first one, Richard tapped in a number, put the receiver down and the phone started ringing. I hadn't seen this before and he explained that it was a test call the telephone engineers use when doing repairs.

I practised this a few times and was quite chuffed at my new-found skill. The possibility of getting Eileen running to and from the phone fired my twisted sense of humour. I couldn't wait 'til she got back from the shops. After the third time of ringing she said, 'Bob, you must have done something wrong with these phones. Every time I pick it up it goes dead.' I could have had her going for months, but Richard squealed on me.

When all the work was done Richard left, still whingeing about the chimney but secretly laughing that he'd dropped me in it with Eileen.

Thinking that I'd earned a rest, I relaxed in front of the box and nodded off; the television is a wonderful vehicle to induce a hypnotic state. I was awakened by the sound of the telephone ringing and I can remember thinking what a clever boy I was.

Eileen answered it and called to me, 'Bob, it's the telephone engineer. He's on about a loop call or something; can you talk to him?'

Still half asleep, I made my way to the phone.

'Hello, Mr Oliver?'

'Yes!'

'Ah, Mr Oliver,' he continued. 'We've received several loop calls through the exchange from your number and as we have no record of an engineer being at your address we wondered what was happening.'

'Loop calls. What's a loop call?' I questioned.

'A loop call is a test call that the engineers use to test telephones.'

'Oh, 174!' I said and started to explain. 'That was me; I fitted a new extension and was testing it.'

He cut me short saying, 'Well, Mr Oliver, loop calls are restricted and are for only engineers' use and not the general public.' He had become extremely officious.

'I'm sorry,' I replied. 'I didn't realise.' I was bumbling.

'There has to be a charge made for these calls,' he snapped.

'OK, OK.' My brain was clearing and I was getting arsey. 'How much?' I barked.

'It's ten pounds a call, there were eleven calls, so that will be a hundred and ten pounds.'

I momentarily choked and then it slowly sank in that I'd been on a hook and was being played for a chump. 'You bastard, Richard, I'll get you for this.'

My ears were pierced by maniacal laughter. 'That'll teach you for getting me to drill in the wrong place,' he managed to say through fits of giggling.

I'm just an innocent at large and if he'd said ten pence a call, he could have milked me for a lot more!

Burgled Again

We'd been burgled in London and once more we were unfortunate enough to get done again. The police did catch the culprits, but it wasn't from any great police work. They were two young lads, apparently from the North East of England, would you believe – Eileen's birth place. They had skipped probation, stolen a van and driven south and were staying with their sister who lived locally. They'd then resumed their thieving in pastures new.

It was pure chance that they were caught. Among their other victims was a shop in town that sold guns, fishing tackle, etc. The shop owner's mother was out walking her dog over farmland and spotted these two criminals with guns shooting pigeons. She became suspicious, because of their age and, of course, she also knew of her son's break-in, so reported the incident to the police.

The police acted quickly and after a chase one was caught and the other escaped, but with one in custody it wasn't long before the other was arrested. Now I will let Eileen explain how she discovered that our house had been broken into and how our trusted Rottweiler guard dog protected our property:

Eileen Continues with the Saga

Well, strictly speaking, it wasn't Lottie's fault. She had been with youngsters since she was a pup and thought they were all welcome visitors; now had they been adults it would have been a different tale! Anyway, I'd returned from work and in a nutshell, realised we had been burgled as soon as I saw the front door smashed. The bedrooms had been ransacked and amongst other things my knicker drawer had been upended in the search for anything valuable. Beth'd had a birthday a few days earlier and the few pounds she'd been sent as a present were gone. I had a few bits of jewellery that I'd inherited and that was also missing, including the jewellery box they were in.

I rang the police and then sat on the floor in the hall and cried. It was then that I realised I couldn't see the dog. I rushed round the house and found her snoring in the kitchen. First, I felt relief and then fury, 'Where were you when we were being burgled?' I screamed; to which she wagged her tail and fell asleep again! After a very short time the police arrived and guess what – Lottie went for them!

Fortunately, the girls were at school while this happened and I worried about their reaction when they came home to find the house full of police. Not a bit of it, they thought it was great and rejoiced that they would have a great tale to tell at school the next day. Beth was upset about her birthday money, but Bob and I replaced it. Sally followed the bobbies round the house asking them to show her their guns and was disappointed to find that they didn't have any. Beth helped me make tea for them and passed the biscuits round and Emma, watching the fingerprint man, had her prints taken as well and they were on her bedroom wall for years.

These yobs were caught, but tried to escape from the prison van as they were escorted from the prison to the court, roughing-up a policeman in the process.

I resisted feeling sorry for them as I watched them being bundled into the court room in handcuffs. Even my slight pangs of sympathy completely vanished when it was revealed that they'd done twenty other similar crimes in our area, plus those committed on their own turf and, of course, skipping their probation. Yet, still they were only given minimum sentences. Who says crime doesn't pay! We were fortunate to be unharmed by them, but there are those who never recover from these types of crimes and if I had my way ... well, it's just as well I don't have my way!

At the time, I truly believe I could cheerfully have killed these intruders who'd violated my home and rifled through our possessions; they were, and probably still are, the bottom feeders of life and it took me a long time to get my sense of security back.

Moving Home

Moving home after nearly thirty is an awesome task. Eileen and I had been married for forty-two years and one can only imagine the stuff we'd accumulated. Because we were moving into Beth's house, I was able to ferry stuff over before the moving date, filling her garage to bulging point. Even her garden shed was overflowing and all our garden furniture filled the garden. Well, the garden is small compared to the Gatelodge – something that Eileen has found hard to come to terms with. Beth had emptied her fitted wardrobes into packing cases and was foolish enough to tell Eileen when I was in earshot.

'Blimey!' I exclaimed. 'I can start putting stuff in there, then.'

Not only were we buying our daughter's house, but Sally was buying our house. Sally and her husband planned to give the Gatelodge a major overhaul and they didn't wait for us to move out before starting work.

We watched in amazement as men and machinery moved in, ripping up the paths in their wake. Though it was when they tore up our beautiful laurel bush that measured 15 foot as broad as it was long that bought a tear to Eileen's eye. But what made her burst into tears was when the 35 foot Christmas tree came crashing down as the JCB attacked it and all this amidst of the sounds of a Kango Drill rattling away into 4 inches of concrete, the compressor buzzing merrily and the vibrator – no not that sort of vibrator – thumping down the hardcore on the new drive. If all that noise wasn't bad enough, Eileen had put up the decibel level with her own howling.

The weather had been kind to the builders, with September being almost totally dry. However, we did have one day of solid rain. I'm not talking drizzle here, either; I'm talking heavy lumps, a real rain. The whole place was turned into Flanders Field and we were marooned in a quagmire. The postman made a delivery and departed 4 inches taller than he'd arrived. The milkman decided he was happy with his height and left the milk stuck on a lump of clay by the front garden. It was as I have always suspected – the postmen are a hardier breed.

The garage wall nearest the bungalow that supports the passage roof had been forcibly removed and the whole of the front of the garage received the same fate; two large windows were cut out and the whole thing was perched on arco props, the plan being to convert the double garage into a kitchen/diner. As if it wasn't big enough already, they were extending it by adding another 10 feet by 22 feet.

Each evening before the builders departed they dragged everything into what was left of the garage and covered the front with a huge tarpaulin. The footings for the extension were dug, the concrete poured and the brick footings built to above site level.

At every opportunity, Eileen insisted we went out to escape the mayhem. When we returned from one such trip we were surprised at the progress that had been made, for the timber-framed extension was now in place.

The next morning, when the foreman arrived with his crew, I told them that they'd done really well and it was looking good. He was pleased by my comments, until I posed him with a question. 'Tell me,' I said. 'No doubt there's a simple answer, but I was wondering, now you have the walls in place, how do you propose to get the compressor out?'

The compressor was the size of a small car, weighing over a ton, and was firmly ensconced. He smiled broadly and shook his head as he realised the predicament.

I went on to say, 'Perhaps if you leave it there, Sally could put a pot plant on it and have it as a feature.' Blimey, I've heard about painting yourself into a corner, but this was a new one on me.

Later in the morning, I watched as they dismantled the front wall and wheeled out the compressor. It's a good job it was a timber frame and not brick, otherwise the air would have been bluer than it was.

With ten days to "M day", the renovation of the Gatelodge moved up a pace in an effort to beat the oncoming winter months. In the meantime, we were bemused by all the activity surrounding our normally tranquil setting. Yes, even the hyper visits of our grandchildren paled into insignificance with the activity now engulfing us.

With October came a dramatic change in the weather, where there were more wet days than dry. It was 5.00 a.m. Saturday 5 October when the alarm rattled in my ears, telling me that I had to go to work. Dragging myself from my pit, I made my way to the kitchen for my life-rendering cup of tea. From the semi haze of sleep I was suddenly propelled into the world of the consciousness as my bare feet trod on something cold and wet; an experience that I had long forgotten since the dogs were pups. At the same time, I stepped under a shower of water on my very vulnerable bald head.

The builders had removed all the tiles from the roof, leaving only felt and batten between us and the elements. A night of torrential rain had proven too much for the flimsy felt and in came the rain. I looked up, to see the rainwater dripping though a light fitting. I turned to switch the light off, but I was too late – it cracked and with a flash, the earth trip was activated and I was plunged into darkness. Even in a place that I had lived for nearly thirty years I was still disorientated and because the night was as black as Newgates Knocker, I was, as they say, in the dark.

I clattered into a chair and stumbled to the floor. Then I sat nursing my shin in complete blackness, listening to the silence, except for the quiet sound of rainwater landing on the dining-room carpet. I found a torch, put buckets under the leaks, left Eileen a note and went to work, where I could have a nice cup of tea.

Eileen wasn't best pleased, but at least it was daylight when she got up. David's men made some temporary repairs to the roof and got the electricity back on. How on earth did our parents get by without electricity?

Moving day arrived and, of course, the rain fell; indeed, it was sheeting down. Conditions were gruesome and I had to lay a temporary path of bits of plywood to enable the removal men access across the sea of mud.

As I'd suspected, unpacking was worse than the packing and the actual move. We'd moved to a smaller house and the old saying of "trying to get a quart into a pint pot" has never meant so much to me; and for Eileen it was even worse. Not only was she leaving her beloved Gatelodge, but she had forty-two years of accumulated rubbish to find a place for. 'Chuck it away!' I said. But oh no, those words weren't part of her vocabulary.

I went into the living room and found Eileen sitting among a sea of boxes, some full and others empty, with a dejected look on her face and tears in her eyes. I'm naturally very sympathetic, so I said, 'Stop snivelling, you silly cow!' But alas she was unable to lift herself from the gloom and used phrases unbecoming of a lady! I pride myself that I'm a tower of strength in such feminine emergencies, so I did what every red-blooded Brit would do: I made a cup of tea and left her to get on with it.

Then came the winds and, of course, when this country experiences a slight breeze, chaos hits the industry that's supposed to supply us with power and all went dark! We were without electricity for about four hours, during which time

Eileen fished out the candles and lit the fire and it got quite cosy. Did I mention that at times like these the birth rate tends to increase? Besides, we couldn't exactly watch telly. But my romantic suggestions were rebuffed.

The next day I went up to the Gatelodge to video the progress. As I stepped inside it took me back fifty odd years. I can remember me and Dutchy in London during the war crawling about the bombed-out buildings and a feeling of déjà vu hit me. But this wasn't wind damage; builders had created this carnage. Think of a house that had taken the brunt of a bomb blast, leaving just the shell standing. The roof had been ripped off, the ceiling had caved in and the whole place was a scene of brick, rubble and splintered timbers.

Eileen wouldn't go near the place until it was rebuilt. Me, I loved it and was there at every opportunity. It was in the garden that I found wind damage. The branch on an old plum tree that had held the kid's garden swing had been torn from the tree, but apart from that, damage was minimal.

Waste Not, Want Not

It must be the times into which I was born that moulded my character. Rationing and shortages were things that shaped my outlook and "nothing wasted, nothing needed" was a paramount motto to us all. We lived in an age of make do and mend and although we tried to pass this attitude onto our kids, we failed miserably. The first ten years of their lives weren't exactly luxurious, but we went without nothing, despite struggling to make ends meet.

In the mid seventies we began to reap the benefits of our hard work and found ourselves able to afford luxuries like holidays (staying with friends or family), a car (albeit an old banger) and a colour telly (although the kids insisted that we were the last people on the planet to acquire a colour set). But that wasn't unusual as, according to them, we were always the last to get everything. Our kids are now grown up with families of their own. One of the girls was moving house and I was drafted in to help. She had boxed up all the stuff no longer wanted and she'd asked me to take it down to the dump or pass it on to the charity shop. You wouldn't believe what she was chucking out. Anyway, we had a field day and very little actually reached the charity shop. Her sisters had a dip, but we bagged the lion's share: clothes, household goods, toiletries and booze.

Some of the beer was out of date and had been stuck in the back of the cupboard for years, but I persevered and managed to get through it. The half full bottles of whisky, brandy, etc. were far more tolerable, although the full bottle of Pernod was vile; no wonder it was full. I managed to force it down, but was glad when it was finished and I knew my mum would have been so proud of me following her waste not, want not code. Eileen scored well with the toiletries, bubble baths and scents, not to mention the moisturisers – oh joy. I had a phone call from David asking me to cut his lawn and while I was at it, could I do his grandma's. At the time, I was sitting in the conservatory reading and every time I looked up my lawn had grown an inch. The phone call was all I needed to spur me into action.

First, I cut his grandma's, then his and mine was last. By the time I'd finished I was shattered and every bone in my broken body ached. A long soak in a bath was what was needed. Running the bath, I noticed a collection of bottles and bubble bath that Eileen had "won" from Beth's chuck-out session. I had a choice of four, but one in particular smelled really nice, although another one's label boasted that it was good for aches and pains, so I threw them both in.

With a cup of tea, my radio and, of course, my chess magazine, I settled in for a nice long soak with the bubbles coming up to my chin. After a few minutes I started to get a tingling feeling in my precious parts. I tried to ignore it, as I was immersed in my reading, but after a short while the tingling became a burning sensation and panic gripped me. I was instantly transformed from a knackered old man into the Incredible Hulk. I'm not sure how I did it from the vertical position I was in, but I leaped into the air, out of the bath and onto the floor, where I quickly scrambled into the shower and sprayed cold water onto the offending parts.

As the burning sensation abated, I became aware of the tingling all over the rest of my body and to my great concern, I found myself to be covered in huge red blotches. Upon investigation, I discovered that the sweet-smelling bubble bath was in fact an oil meant to spice up the potpourri. Well, it certainly spiced mine up, anyway. I did try to dry out my magazine after I'd retrieved it from the bath but, fortunately, Eileen had a spare copy, for which I was grateful, even if she does put the potpourri oil in with her bath oils.

Miscellaneous Stories: All Creatures great and small

Spring is Here

There was a war going on in our garden. Eileen had bought her spring plants from the garden centre, which meant me humping bags of potting compost; my back still bears witness to these awkward and heavy bags of dirt.

She'd carefully laid out the compost into the various size receptacles and had lovingly planted them out. Then she'd situated the plant pots so they got the benefit of the morning sun. There was just one problem – they were in the vicinity of a line of conifers; home of one or two snails. Now how these little buggers can sniff out freshly planted shoots as opposed to all the other greenery is completely beyond me, especially at the speed they travel, but travel they do and straight for Eileen's tender, newly planted plants they went.

The next morning I heard wails and cries of despair coming from the garden. I thought the least she'd done was broken her leg. Rushing to her assistance, I found her jumping up and down, fuming with rage, waving a poor little snail in the air, pointing to what was left of her newly planted pansies and declaring the snail fatherless. Gathering up some of its friends, she plunged them all into a bowl of vinegar and watched them sizzle; I wasn't about to let her use my beer, another anti-snail remedy she'd been advised on. I felt sorry for the little creatures, but beer is beer, after all.

There was a repeat of events the next morning, so a trip back to the garden centre was deemed necessary, where Eileen – at great expense, I might add – stocked up with all manor of anti-snail junk.

'This stuff,' she told me, 'will stop the little blighters!' as she carefully distributed it around the containers.

The next morning there could be heard anguished cries exclaiming, 'I don't bloody believe it!'

Apparently, the snails hadn't read the instructions and had tramped across the anti-snail repellent to feed contentedly on the new shoots. No matter how many she "cures" in her vinegar concoction more appeared, causing her suffering, distress and anguish.

I told her, 'Darling, why don't you shift your pots away from the conifers overnight?'

But I think she was beginning to enjoy the battle and gleaned masochistic pleasure when pickling those poor little beasties.

Gnat Bites

There are several walks near the Gatelodge, but I enjoyed the ones that we could do without retreading our steps. Our circular walk had all but been completed, when I felt a sharp pain on the top of my left ear. As I took hold of my ear I crushed an insect. The little swine had bitten me and drawn blood, but it had paid with its life. It itched for a while but then seemed to be OK.

After dinner the bite steadily became more painful and had swollen considerably. My pain was exacerbated with the ridicule that came from Eileen and things got worse when we went to bed, when I tossed and turned, moaning and groaning, for over an hour.

Eileen finally lost her rag, complaining that she couldn't sleep with my whingeing and whining. Never mind my pain and whether I could sleep; oh no, it was all me, me, me. Anyway, she stormed off into the bathroom saying she had something for insect bites and would soon "fettle my hash". Returning, she grabbed my head and gave me the full blast with an aerosol spray.

Now I wasn't expecting an aerosol, I was expecting a nice cool, soothing cream to relieve the burning, but instead I was blasted and then followed the most excruciating pain, making me squeal like a stuck pig. Sucking in my breath, I inhaled a mouthful of fumes that made me cough and choke. 'Are you trying to kill me, woman?' I howled.

By this time I was out of bed and running around on all fours, making whimpering noises. Eileen in the meantime was having a giggling fit between bouts of hysteria, saying, 'At least it's stopped you moaning about a silly little gnat bite.'

When the pain subsided I asked her what was in that insect spray. Stuttering through bouts of cackling, she confessed all. 'Honest, Bob, I was half asleep. I didn't realise it was fly spray.'

I wouldn't mind if she hadn't got so much pleasure from it. Not to mention the fact that I had to listen to the incident being retold over and over again to all and sundry. I still have my doubts and suspect she isn't the total innocent she professes to be.

One in the Eye

Eileen and I were walking through the village and as we turned to walk along the riverbank, she stopped suddenly and clasped her hand to her eye. Very concerned, I asked what the matter was.

She answered saying, 'Damn midgy flew in my eye!' As I retrieved the little blighter she said, 'Why did it pick me?' I said in a confused manor, 'I dunno, luv, I'm still trying to figure out how the hell it missed your mouth.'

I thought it was a perfectly reasonable question. Eileen didn't, but then again, I've never professed to comprehend the inner workings of the female mind! Women, eh?

Oh, and by the way, the bleeding stopped; but there's a nasty bruise over my left eye.

Animal Magic! How Lucky can One Man Get?

Sally was a brilliant baby; she slept through the night at six weeks, cut her teeth without a grimace and walked at nine months, but then the trouble all began. Ladybirds, flies, worms, you name it and she bought them home to keep as a pet, with always the same story. 'Pleeeese, Dad, let me keep it. I promise to keep it clean and take it for walks.'

Years on, Sally and her two younger sisters were still bringing in the creatures and it seemed to me that every time one of my kids' friends' fathers decided that their own kids' pet had to go, it arrived at the Oliver household. I didn't stand a chance; it was three against one, all with their pleading big, wide eyes. Every one of them could wrap me around their little finger, with Eileen of absolutely no help at all.

With so many pets it was only natural that there were a few bereavements, followed by many tears and a period of mourning. They insisted on proper funerals, with a cross to mark the spot. I did offer them a twenty-one gun salute, but Eileen raised her eyebrows at my facetiousness. Our garden soon began to take on the appearance of Boot Hill.

One day, Sally came home from school full of excitement and proudly announced that she'd won the draw. Her wonderful prize was the great privilege of looking after the school tortoise for the summer holidays. 'Tell me, Sally,' I enquired. 'Just how many of you were in this lucky draw?'

'Well, actually, Dad, it was just between Karen and me and the teacher flipped a coin.'

'Oh, I see, and you won the toss, eh?'

'Well, not exactly,' she answered. 'Karen actually won the toss, but her mean old dad wouldn't let her keep it.'

My word, what luck! And, of course, *I* couldn't be that mean, could I? Anyway, it was to be the longest six weeks of my life. The damn thing escaped five times and every time Sally cried her eyes out and vowed she would never go back to school again. After much searching and lots of anxious beating of the undergrowth, Houdini – the nickname I'd given the wee beastie – was found and re-incarcerated.

But the worst moment came when Sally came in screaming from the garden, 'Bella's eating Houdini!'

I rushed out and rescued the poor thing from Bella's slavering jaws. The dog's face was a picture and she looked accusingly at me as if to say, What's he doing with my crusty pork pie? Poor old Houdini recovered, with only a few teeth marks on his shell, and we heaved a sigh of relief when the school holiday was over and back he went.

After the terrible teens the girls grew up and got married. Sally was the first one to present us with a grandchild. Sam was born in hospital and when we went to see them for the very first time. Sally, looking radiant and holding her newborn in her arms, turned to me and said, 'Dad, if I keep him clean and take him for walks, can I keep him?'

A Good Night's Sleep with All Sorts of Creatures

I've slept in some rough places in my time, including a bench on a Waterloo Railway Station where, incidentally, I was propositioned and offered a bed for the night by a "very nice boy". I declined the offer and preferred the bench.

Then there were the nights I slept in a Standard 8 and that wasn't the only vehicle I've had the misfortune to sleep in. Of course, in my army days there were some really gruesome times, from freezing nights under canvas in Britain, to a freezing night in the desert with all sorts of creatures seeking the warmth of my body. If it's not the wrong sex, it's the wrong species. How lucky can one bloke get?

Before that there was the semi-permanent residence in the air-raid shelter during the war, but we were so young then that we didn't know any difference. I recall a certain bed and breakfast in most definitely not the "posh end" of Blackpool – how Eileen and I suffered two nights in that place is beyond comprehension.

But when I think of sleeping rough, my first thoughts are of the most recent experience. It was a several years ago now, but it still burns clearly in my mind. Sally had her Russian sister-in-law staying with her for a couple of weeks. They lived for a long time in Czechoslovakia, where their eldest daughter was born. Are you still with me? Please do try to keep up. They've also lived in Bulgaria, where their second daughter was born, and, more recently, France. Anna, who was 10 years old at the time, could speak Russian, Bulgarian, Czechoslovakian, French and English. It makes my attempts to learn Italian rather pathetic.

During their stay, Anna and my eldest grandson became great friends and they were like shadows, never leaving each other's side. When they visited us, Sam and Anna asked if they could fix up a tent in the garden and stay the night in it and all the grandchildren mucked in to erect it. I say "tent", but in actual fact it was a large sheet of tent-like material, loads of rope and broom handles to support the said structure.

They were all set and as the sun began to disappear on the horizon, Sam and Anna pleaded with Beth to come out to the tent and read them ghost stories – something Beth is renowned for. Out they went with torches, sweets and bottles of fizz and after about half an hour I thought I would have a game with them. The Gatelodge was very isolated, without any immediate neighbours. There were large trees and spooky corners with an abundance of wildlife: owls, foxes, bats and rats with, of course, rabbits and squirrels by the thousands. Like a Navajo Indian, I belly crept towards the makeshift tent and although I was 60 at the time, I was still acting like a 6 year old.

I listened for a while to Beth reading from a book of ghost stories, their torches shining on the roof of the tent; the scene was perfectly set. I could feel the tension oozing out as the kids were breathlessly silent and only Beth's voice, full of mystery and suspense, filled the air. I began my act, making noises of a tormented soul and casting distorted shadows, like the Hunchback of Notre Dame.

Beth's voice stopped and there was a whimper of apprehension as she pulled back the flap to investigate. My coat was pulled up over my head, when the light from the torch picked out my cavorting shape. She let out a scream that frightened me and those in the tent erupted into mass hysteria. As soon as Beth realised who it was she threw the book at me, followed by a quantity of verbal abuse. I told her she shouldn't talk to her dad like that, but it made little difference. After the fright, Anna decided not to sleep in the garden, but Sam was adamant and wouldn't be put off by daft old grandad playing the fool.

This presented a problem, 'cos when Eileen found out what I had been up to and what was going on, she gave me the ear-bashing of my life and told me that there was no way that Sam was staying out in the garden on his own and I would have to go out and fetch him in. This really hung a guilt trip on me, 'cos if I had to drag Sam in it would ruin his adventure, and all because Grandad had been acting the goat.

Eileen was insistent and wouldn't budge an inch. There was only one thing I could do to make amends, but I still can't believe I said it. The words were echoing in my brain as if someone else was saying them. 'OK, OK, I'll sleep in the garden with him.' Of course, as soon as I'd offered myself up for ridicule, scorn and a night of hell and purgatory, Anna's eyes lit up and she decided that as a grown-up was going to be present then she, too, would win back some of her courage.

We settled down for the night and although it was a hot summer's night, there was a draught whistling around my neck and while those two sods slept on like dormice, I heard every noise imaginable. Yes, even the fox made an appearance. My heart stopped beating following a piecing scream of some poor animal that had met its executioner. The kids were blissfully unaware of the teeming wildlife going about their nocturnal business, so I steadied my nerves and peered out of the flap into the moonlit night. The full moon was half nestled behind a cloud that was scurrying across the sky, with the stars sparkling in competition. A sudden movement attracted my attention. It was, indeed, the fox, loping nonchalantly across the bottom of the garden with something hanging from its mouth.

I closed my eyes, trying to shut out the garden noises. The breeze rustled the leaves in the trees and an owl hooted. 'This I can live with,' I told myself. I was, of course, telling myself a lie and couldn't live with it or sleep with it.

The night went on and on and on, the lumps in the rock-hard ground penetrating my personage – I was feeling every year of my ageing body. I began to lecture myself about opening my mouth before the brain was in gear and scolding myself that I would never, ever be as stupid again. Just as these thoughts were buzzing my mind, I suddenly had a feeling of a presence close by. My eyes were closed and I could feel the hair on the back of my neck begin to bristle and every part of my body locked with tension. It was only for a few seconds, but seemed endless.

The chilly draft from the night breeze on my neck suddenly became warm and then wet. At this sensation, I shot bolt upright with my heart pumping blood through my veins fit to bust. My face was inches from an awesome shape with bright, gleaming eyes. It was Holly, my Rottweiler! She'd been disturbed, possibly by the fox, and had whimpered and whined until Eileen was forced from her nice comfortable bed, poor thing, whereupon she kicked her out into the garden to join us happy campers.

I lay back clasping my heart in an attempt to slow it down, while Holly tried to lick my face. I grumbled at her – and, of course, Eileen; Eileen because she had let the dog out and for being tucked up in a nice warm bed and Holly for being almost as stupid as me. I turned and looked at the kids. Not a movement, sleeping as soundly as logs. After our nocturnal adventure my bones ached for a week, my neck was stiff for a fortnight and God only knows what damage was done to my nervous system and my poor old heart. Never, and I really mean *never*, again!

A Horse, a Horse, my Kingdom for a Horse!

When our kids were young, one of the many crazes they went through was the desire to own a horse. I stuck out! No bleeding way was I going to buy a horse. We had cats, dogs, hamsters, chickens, gerbils, birds, tortoises and even a goat that a well-meaning, so-called friend landed me with, but I drew the line at horses.

Sally was 14 years old, Beth 12 and Emma 10 at the time and you can well imagine the hassle in the household because I'd point-blank refused to allow them to own their own horse. In my wildest dreams I could never believe that *everyone* at school had their own horse and that my kids were the only deprived children in the world. Gullible I might be, but even I found that old carrot hard to chew; after all, their school was some distance from Rhodene.

One day, while I was at work and Eileen was cooking dinner for the girls, there was a knock at the door.

'Your horse is loose and roaming the main road,' the stranger said.

'Quick, Sally, the horse is loose; go and get it!' Eileen hollered as Sally dashed out. 'Wait a minute!' Eileen explained, 'We don't have a horse.'

Nevertheless, Sally returned with a beautiful white pony and took it to the back of the house where she, Beth and Emma took turns riding their new-found friend around the garden. It was love at first sight and they were all begging Eileen to keep him. The horse obviously belonged to someone and she told the girls that they had to find out who the owner was.

Eileen rang the police and the copper also begged Eileen to keep it; at least until they could find out who it belonged to. He explained, 'We've just moved into a brand new station and we aren't equipped to stable horses.'

Yippee! The kids were over the moon. 'Perhaps they won't find the owner,' Sally said hopefully.

I was completely oblivious to the events of their exciting day and when I returned from work, tired after a particularly hard day, I wasn't in the best of moods. Of course, riding a pushbike uphill against the wind did nothing for my disposition. It was 10.30 p.m., the night was as dark and dirty as a miner's helmet, the wind gusted the rain into my face and every step was an effort. Pushing the side gate open, I wheeled my bike into the back garden and into the garden shed.

As I turned off the lamps, I was plunged into complete darkness and at that moment, in the silence of the shed, with only the gentle sound of the wind as it rustled through the trees, I could feel the hairs on the back of my neck begin to bristle as I became aware of a presence. Sucking in my breath, I listened intently and could hear what sounded like a man's heavy and laboured breathing. In seconds, I snatched up my stainless steel bicycle pump and in one movement I spun round, wielding my trusty weapon.

The curious horse that had come over to see me reared back startled, but not as startled as me, for in the dark all I could see was a ghostly white form standing 10 foot high and snorting smoke from his nostrils. Stepping back in fright, I tripped over the bike and fell arse over tit; the phantom ghost just stood there snorting and watching.

My heart was doing its level best to burst through my coat and if I could have made a sound, I would have screamed the place down. After what seemed an eternity my eyes became adjusted to the dark and the ghost was slowly transformed into a bleeding great horse! This was all I needed on top of a bad day: a heart attack, a bruised leg, a sore elbow and trousers that were extremely close to being soiled; I was not a happy chappie.

Bursting into the house, I demanded, 'What's that bleeding 'orse doing in the garden?'

Eileen, with a perfectly straight face, replied, 'It was a snip, Bob; it was so cheap I couldn't turn it down.'

'What?' I shouted. 'I don't care how cheap it was; it's going back! There's absolutely no way we're having a horse!'

Whenever we recall the saga, Eileen says that it wasn't a planned wind-up; it was my reaction that fired it, but it was no more than I deserved and it was just a little payback for all the times I'd wound her up. She had, indeed, pushed me to the very limits.

Sally mimics me when I'm angry. She says that my lips turn thin and white, my eyes come out on sticks and I stand with my hands on hips, my teeth clenched and my chin jutting out.

The horse? Oh yes, the horse. It had escaped from a riding stable some 10 miles away, would you believe. When they came to pick it up they told us that they'd been frantic, thinking it had been stolen because it was worth a fortune. Reward? No such luck – the silly sod only wanted to sell it to us.

Bob Oliver

Are Cats Really Intelligent Creatures?

Some people say that cats are intelligent creatures, but I say they're thick. Dogs are intelligent: they will sit, roll over, beg or fetch the stick no matter how many times you throw it; now that's intelligent. A cat will just look at you as if you're mad if you ask it to get your slippers for you; they come and go as they choose and still expect to be fed. Thick or what? They're even vicious killers; OK, this can be beneficial, as it keeps the vermin down, but why do they have to bring home their prey, half eat it and leave the rest on the carpet? This just compounds my theory that they're thick.

One day one of my grandchildren called me, saying, 'Grandad, I've found a mouse's bum!' Sure enough, there lay the remains of the poor creature; just its back legs with its curly little toes and a long, thin tail, with a small amount bum fluff and little else!

Someone released a white rabbit once and it used to frequent our garden. We nicknamed it Wellard, 'cos it put the wild rabbits in their place, although it used to scoot when the dog gave chase – and who wouldn't? It completely ignored the cat and, in fact, we even watched it have a go at it and much to the cat's disgust, he had to give way to Wellard. Maybe they do have a little bit of sense – or is it just self-preservation?

I bought one of these old-fashioned fly catchers home once. You know the type – you pull the tab and it uncoils a strip of brown sticky paper that the flies are attracted to. Eileen said, 'I'm not having that thing in the house.' So waste not, want not, I hung it in the coal house. As it danced in the breeze the cat thought it was something to kill and jumped up at it, dragging it to the floor. Before I'd had time to put my toe in a suitable place, he rolled over violently and the fly paper completely engulfed him. He was trapped and I was tempted to walk away, but Eileen insisted I freed the bloody animal. However, I was unable to pull it off, as it was stuck rigidly to its fur. My only option was a pair of scissors: have you ever seen a punk cat? I could swear Wellard chuckled every time he walked by!

The Mating Game

Eileen decided it would be nice to have a litter of pups from our Rottweiler bitch Bella. A friend of ours knew a guy who had dog Rottie and he offered to drive me and Bella to get "laid"; not me, just Bella. This was particularly brave and selfless act on behalf of John, considering he's terrified of Rottweilers; he did lay down certain rules, though. Bella had to wear her chain and lead, I had to sit in the back with her and when I took Bella in to be introduced to her blind date, he would wait in the car. John was visibly shaking when we pulled off the drive and we had only travelled half a mile when Bella decided to put her tongue in John's ear.

Well, to say we're all extremely lucky to be alive is putting it mildly. The car violently swerved across the road towards the oncoming traffic, I tried to grab the steering wheel to pull us back, Bella thought we were playing and jumped on John's back and then John let out a scream and disappeared beneath the dashboard. By this time, we had miraculously avoided a head-on collision with an articulated lorry and were now careering through some poor old dear's front garden. Still don't quite understand where John found the inspiration to jam on the brakes, but I suspect it was more by accident. Fortunately, not a lot of damage was done. Mrs Coote – the lovely old lady whose garden we had, by chance, discovered – gave me a cuppa, John a sedative and Bella a drink of water and then she waved us on on our journey.

John relaxed a little as he began to understand that Bella was just playful and not in any way vicious and so he began to tell me about a friend of his and his dog. This dog, he told me, wasn't a bit like Bella. This dog was evil and there was no way he was going to assist with the mating game on this occasion. When one is attempting to mate big animals they sometimes need assistance, so you can imagine what went through my mind when John told me his friend only has one arm. A vicious Rottie, a nervous friend and a one-armed assistant – what had Eileen got me in to?

I can't go into too much detail of the attempted mating, because Eileen won't let me. So I will merely state that it was the best laugh I've had in years. The male Rottie turned out to be too young, inexperienced and far too eager for his own good. Bella was very willing, but far too strong for her new-found boyfriend. On the way home we called in to see Mrs Coote and this time it was Bella's turn for a sedative.

Passing the Buck

Our neighbours in the farmhouse had just acquired a Labrador pup. It kept escaping and, of course, its first aim was to make for the Oliver household, often making its escape when it heard the kids about. Indeed, it spent more time with us than our neighbour and when it made its entrance the kids went mad.

They, of course, loved the bloody thing. All except for George, that is. He was frightened of it because it used to jump up. He thought it was attacking him rather than just wanting to play.

I scooped George up and sat him on the safety of the kitchen table. Then he looked at me with his big, beautiful eyes and said, 'You're my hero, Grandad.'

The pup in the mean time was running around causing havoc, chasing the kids and scaring the cat. I could hear George shouting to Grandma, 'Grandma! He's eating the cat's food!' and 'Grandma, he's eating the table!' Actually, the pup was eating food under the table that the kids had dropped. Then it got hold of Eileen's slipper and George lost no time in informing us as he shouted at the top of his voice, 'Grandma! He's eating your slipper!'

Grandma told him not to worry as, 'Pups will eat anything.'

'Will he eat this, Grandma?'

Grandma went over to inspect what George was holding. 'What's that?' she enquired.

'A bogie!' he explained.

As I soon as I bunged up one gap in the fence it would find another weakness in my defences. Finally, after weeks of plugging holes, I managed to become dog proof.

Eileen, hair still in rollers, had just emerged from her bed at seven thirty one morning and was sipping the tea that I'd just placed in her hand when there was a knock on the door. Still only semi conscious, she fumbled with the bolts on the door. Finally opening it, she was confronted with an irate woman holding the neighbour's dog shouting, 'Your dog was out on the main road, you should take more care. It'll get killed.'

All this time her husband, who was sitting in the car, was shouting at his missus, 'Come on, we're going to be late for work. We ain't got time for messing about with that bloody dog.'

'But, but, but,' Eileen protested, 'the dog doesn't live here, it belongs next door!'

Of course, it didn't help that the dog was all over Eileen licking her legs, as if she was its mother. Then it roared in the house as if it was home. The woman, needless to say, wasn't convinced and went off threatening us with the RSPCA.

The dog knew exactly where the cat's food was and made short work of it. Then she stuck her foot in the water bowl, tipping it all over the kitchen floor. Thinking this was all good fun, she proceeded to jump up and down in the water.

Eileen came in still shell-shocked from her ordeal and gave me what for, for not answering the door. But I'd had more important things to do: I was writing an email. Eileen then opened my office door and the dog raced in, giving me the benefit of her soaking-wet paws. She did that on purpose, you know.

We rang the neighbour and she came scurrying over in her night attire, flustered and apologetic. As she left, she told Eileen that if anyone asks, she would tell them who it's true owner was. Eileen said that because everyone was denying ownership of the creature she should rename it Snot, 'cos everyone keeps saying, "Snot my dog."

Adventure in the Far East!

The 'Inlaws' of Hartlepool.

Eileen's sister Lemmie was sixteen years older than her and Lem's six kids were more like her brothers and sisters than Nephews and Nieces to Eileen. Because they still lived in the 'The Far East' of England (Hartlepool) Eileen, who has always had strong links to them, still has the desire to return home for a visit. I was in the army when our courtship began, so when I was demobbed in 1958, Eileen insisted we visit her sister and meet the family.

In those early days we always drove a state-of-the-art motor vehicle and as always, the 250 mile journey was an adventure; with a huge question mark as to "if" rather than "when" we'd arrive at her sister's.

We travelled through the night to avoid traffic; the trip was longer in those days – in distance and time. Towns weren't bypassed and it was in the days before motorways. About 10 miles south of Stockton, in the early hours of the morning, our old banger took on the sound of a racing car with a straight-through exhaust pipe. Eileen was very worried and wanted me to stop to see what the problem was, but I wasn't in the stopping business and my motto was always to keep going as long as the engine moved the wheels.

Luck was on our side and we avoided contact with the old bill, arriving at our sunshine resort –13 Brunswick Grove, West Hartlepool – at four in the morning. Entry to the holiday apartment was quite simple and the back door, as usual, was open; locked doors in those days were unheard of, although a later incident was to force Alfie into fitting a lock, as one morning Lemmie entered the kitchen to find a thief breaking into the coin-operated electric meter. Lemmie being Lemmie attacked the "feeving get" and copped a black eye for her troubles, but the intruder was recognised and later chastised for the incident. No police were involved – it wasn't necessary.

Anyway, the couch was unoccupied, so we snuck in, curled up and snatched a couple of hours sleep, before daylight came and we were invaded by the kids; all six of them. Thus it was that I met Eileen's family. Lemmie, hearing the kids' excited yelling, came downstairs and without batting an eyelid she put the kettle on. I'd already met Lemmie at Eileen's mum's house in North London and some of the kids, but Eileen wanted me to pass muster with the rest of the family before the wedding.

During a slap-up breakfast I met Alfie, who had been out on the local beach gathering sea-coal and had to work according to the tides. When we got round to discussing our journey down I told them about the exhaust, so we went out to check the damage. The exhaust had, of course, blown a bleeding great hole, so the ever-resourceful Lemmie supplied the means for me to make the necessary repairs: an old Oxo tin, two jubilee clips and some chewing gum.

The area they lived in has long since been pulled down and the car we drove always seemed to blend in nicely with the surroundings and was thereby safe from vandalism, as it looked as if the job had already been done. I recall that once, I came out to find a kid trying to nick the car aerial. Well, it wasn't a real aerial; just an old metal coat hanger and I suppose it was the only thing worth nicking. Lemmie's kids were aged from about 3 to 12 and I was somewhat of a novelty to these young north-easterners with my cockney accent, but they were smashing kids and they soon warmed to me as I did them. It's marvellous what a packet of sweets can do and, of course, having the car enabled us to take them on adventures.

One such adventure was a trip to Middlesbrough via the Transporter – a floating bridge over the River Tees into the borough. As we motored through Seaton Crew and along the coast road I said, 'Right, kids, has everyone got their passports?'

The older kids knew I was having them on, but little Danny Boy, with wide-eyed amazement, declared, 'No, Bob, I haven't a passport.'

As we approached The River Tees and the Transporter I said, 'Right, kids, those of you without passports keep down and the policeman won't see you. How the hell Danny got under the seat was truly magical. Danny is now soon to be a grandad, but I still don't feel safe and I expect him to get his own back at any time. Mary wasn't a good traveller and was feeling the worse for wear when we returned from one of our excursions. I think it might have been the fish 'n' chips from the chippy or the roller coaster afterwards that did for her. Either way, she hadn't touched her bag of sweets, while the others had scoffed theirs. Give Mary her due, it wasn't until we'd stopped and she'd got out of the car that she parted company with the fish 'n' chips. Thank goodness it was the pavement that got the benefit and not the inside of the car.

Danny Boy must have been concerned about the welfare of his big sister, because as I was carrying Mary into the house he kept saying, 'Bob, Bob, Bob!' as he tugged on my jacket.

'In a minute, Dan. In a minute. She'll be OK, don't worry,' I said.

But he was persistent, saying, 'But Bob. But Bob, she's left her sweets in the car.'

Eileen and I were courting at the time and thought we would like to spend a little time on our own, so I suggested we went to the pictures. The kids obviously overheard our whispering and before we'd time to put our coats on they were lined up at the door, booted and coated, waiting for us.

The holiday over, we set off for home. The long journey back to the Smoke was uneventful and for once, we didn't have to use the RAC's expertise to get us home. A year later, almost to the day, we'd been visiting friends in London, when the exhaust burst into a roar once again. We laughed and joked about getting Lemmie to send us another Oxo tin.

The next day I investigated the damage and was gobsmacked. The whole exhaust pipe had vanished – even the Oxo tin – and all that was left was a small piece sticking out of the manifold. I was left imagining what hazards I'd left on the queen's highway.

Sea Coaling

Our next trip to Hartlepool was a couple of years later, when the kids were a little older and we looked forward to our visit. Although I'd been accepted, they still considered me to be a soft Southerner and no amount of my tales in the Paras would convince them otherwise.

Along the North East Coast are some fine beaches, though there are, of course, some problems that hinder the Tourist Board in their quest to promote it as another Bournemouth. First, there are the north-east winds that can cut you in two, so that even in the height of summer the locals still wear long johns and vests. But the temperature is only a minor problem compared with the coal that's washed up on the beaches; the canny locals collect these for their fires. Then there are the banks of sea coal that appear after high tide. I've heard two theories about where the coal comes from: one, that there's an undersea coal mine and the tides wash it up; the other supposition is that the offshore dumping of slag and waste from the local pits is rejected by the sea, washed and given back to the land. The banks of fine black sand-like coal are something else that the locals capitalise on, for they collect it and sell it to the power station to burn and convert into electricity.

Alfie "Jack the Lad" Hutchinson had an old army lorry that he'd bought for fifty quid and he used it for collecting the sea coal. Snooky – number three child – said, 'Hey, Bob, how about coming sea-coaling with us tomorrow?' expecting me to decline the offer.

I, of course, volunteered to help. Silly boy!

Pat said, 'We have to be up at three, Bob, to catch the first tide,' thinking that it would dampen my enthusiasm.

Little did they know that I'm a lark and always up before God. Indeed, they were a little surprised to see that I was first up and dragging them from their pits with a cheery smile and a, 'Come on, lads, we have to catch the early tide.'

And I thought I heard Snooky say to his brothers, 'Let's see what he's like with the shovel.'

There was Alfie, me and the three eldest boys and we drove down to the seafront in the old army lorry, with no seat belts and Alfie at the wheel, with us four crammed in beside him. As we came across the spoils, Alfie dropped us off in pairs, to heap the coal into mounds. He, of course, took the eldest and the strongest boy – no flies on Alfie. Being the odd fellow, I was left on my own to be tested.

When he and Pat had collected their heap, he drove back down the beach picking us all up. It was hard work using massive miners' shovels to chuck the coal dust up into a heap. Alfie told me later that the boys were giving me some stick, suggesting that they would have to do the job for me. But they were pleased and surprised when they saw me leaning on my shovel with the biggest pile they'd collected thus far. I was very young, fit and fresh from the army in those days.

I now felt accepted, especially when they said I must have lied about being a Southerner and that I was really a Northerner. I had a glorious week of catching the early tides, to take advantage of the super sands of Blackhall, and furthering the existence of the local power station; not to mention Eileen's brother-in-law's beer money.

Alfie could always earn a shilling or two. I remember one occasion in particular that typified his entrepreneur skills. After doing a sea-coal run at three in the morning, we returned home at 8.00 a.m. for breakfast; bread and butter and boiled potatoes. I came from a large family and was used to seeing food being demolished, but we had nothing on the hungry Hutchinsons.

Lemmie would butter two loaves of bread, boil 10 lb of spuds and put them in the middle of the table. They had the same philosophy as us Oliver hordes; he who eats fastest gets the most. I would grab a couple of slices of bread and as many spuds as I could get my hands on in one go, find a corner and sit and watch in awe as the food vanished before my eyes.

After breakfast, Alfie said, 'I've got a little job to do, Bob; do you want to give me a hand?'

Before the job, he took me to The Brunswick Arms for a drink. It was 9.00 a.m. and I couldn't believe what I was seeing. We gained entrance to the pub via the back door and as we entered, my mouth gaped in amazement. It was packed with people and the atmosphere was heavy with smoke. The buzz of conversation ceased and all eyes were on the stranger in their midst. I felt like Richard Pryor and Gene Wilder when they were in prison in *Stir Crazy*. Act tough, no shit! No shit!

Alfie bought me a beer and then vanished into the smoke; I could just about see him wheeling and dealing in the corners of the bar with a few of the customers. Not used to drinking at nine in the morning I felt quite heady as we left the Brunnie Arms and drove off in the 3 ton ex-army vehicle.

The job was to shift 10 ton of hard core for a guy who wanted shot of it. After we'd sweated cobs loading, I saw money change hands; to Alfie, of course, not from! Then we took the hard core to the other side of West Hartlepool and unloaded it onto the drive of another guy, who also paid Alfie. The fifty quid lorry was most definitely not in debt to him. This took us late into the afternoon and we had a mad dash to the Job Centre; he had to sign on before four o'clock.

That evening saw an incident that, many years later, had apparently scarred Snooky for life. I'd been teaching them the basic moves in chess and after some time, when I could see that they'd enough, we got into the boys-will-be-boys mode. You know, wrestling. Them jumping on me and me being as rough, without hurting them, as I could.

It was then that the infamous incident occurred. I grabbed Snooky's foot and in the scrum, I pulled off his sock. His foot was as black as Newgates Knocker. I, of course, played it down by saying, 'You dirty git', or as they say up t'North, "dirty get". 'Look at the state of your feet!'

Snooky, protesting his innocence, declared, 'I've been sea-coaling, Bob. I bet your feet are dirty, too!' I removed my socks to reveal snowy white feet.

Lemmie said, 'Bob, take him upstairs and bath him.'

This I did, much to his disgust, and as he told me many, many years later it was a moment that has haunted him for the rest of his life. Sorry, Snook; I know I'm a Southern bastard.

One of our other visits was to Pat's wedding, when Tommy came home from the stag night pissed out of his head. While most of us crammed into Brunnie Grove that night were attempting to sleep, he explained, in a very loud voice, that he'd had this absolutely fantastic Indian meal at the local tandoori restaurant and then proceeded to enter the bathroom and chuck it all down the toilet. The sounds coming from the bathroom were quite indescribable.

But it didn't end there, for as he went to exit the said room, the door handle came off and Tommy was securely locked in. His predicament was heard three blocks away between expletives. Apparently, the door, the bathroom, the house and some other things that have been lost in the fullness of time were parentless. Oh yes, of course, the tandoori restaurant had also lost its allure.

Eileen's sister Lem came down from Hartlepool for Beth's Christening to stand as God mother and she enquired as to when we were coming up to see them again. It seemed a good idea at the time, when I replied, 'We can come up over the Whitsun weekend on the 650 Panther and sidecar!'

Eileen was a little apprehensive at the thought of two adults, a two and a half year old and a baby of just five weeks old, not to mention all the paraphernalia that goes with it, travelling on a motorbike, but I was able to convince her that all would be well. In those days, she used to believe what I told her.

The 250 mile journey took a lot longer to complete in those days, as every town en route had to be driven through; bypasses and motorways had yet to be built. It was I who suffered most as it was very cold and as I froze, the three of them were snug and warm, tucked up with all the luggage in the "super deluxe" sidecar. Some eight hours and twenty-five minutes later we trundled into Hartlepool, where it was even colder. I now realised a day out to Clacton might have been a better option.

After a bath, a heap of mint-flavoured boiled potatoes and a night's sleep, the world began to look a better place. The sleeping arrangements were interesting to say the least. There were four of us, Lemmie, her husband and their *six*, yes *six*, kids; twelve of us in total in a small three-bedroomed maisonette.

Eileen, her niece and Lemmie slept in the double bed, with Sally in a cot and Beth in a pram, all in the one room. The rest of us grabbed a bed if one was available; otherwise, it was the floor. Alfie, Lemmie's husband, always laid claim to the couch; well, seniority must carry some privileges.

All in all, as always with our trips to Hartlepool, we had a great time with loads of fun.

Our plan was to travel back on the Tuesday, to miss the Bank Holiday traffic. With a possible nine hour journey ahead of us, I really needed an early start, so I got up at 5.00 a.m., packed everything up around the sleeping forms of Eileen and the girls and an hour later I tiptoed into the bedroom and attempted to wake Eileen. She was in the middle and was difficult to communicate with. By using a broom handle, or brush as they say up t'North, I managed to jab her in the shoulder. She knocked the handle away, bouncing it off Lemmie's head, and buried her head under the pillow. Lemmie grunted, but didn't wake.

Right! I thought. I'll drag her out of bed. Lifting the bedding at the foot of the bed, I grabbed her leg and pulled ... I was horrified to see Lemmie vanish beneath the blankets. After repeating the operation on Eileen's niece, I finally got hold of the right legs and Eileen fell giggling from the bed while the other two slept on.

At long last at 7.30 a.m. the Panther roared into life and we chugged out of Brunswick Grove, Hartlepool. A mile down the road there was a crack and we were bought unceremoniously to a halt. The chain had snapped. I told Eileen not to eat so much breakfast next time.

What we looked like walking back carrying two kids, one can only imagine. The looks we had from all the workers on their way to work varied from amazement to pity. They must have thought we were doing a moonlight flit.

We had to wait for the shops to open before I could buy a chain link and effect repairs. As insurance I bought two links, in case of a repeat occurrence. I still have that spare link, but I have long since grown out of any desire to drive a motorbike ever again.

Moonlight Capers

Eileen's sister moved to a small village just outside Hartlepool called Greatham. The locals pronounce it Gree-th-m, while outsiders and cockneys like me call it Great Ham, much to their disgust.

Anyway, we were up there visiting one year and we were coming home from one of the clubs in Hartlepool in the early hours of the morning, when I spotted something in the road.

I say road, it was actually a very narrow lane, and there in the middle were two copulating kitties.

The headlights on the car didn't seem to bother them and they were completely oblivious to our presence. I gave them the old full beam and a blast on the hooter. I think she might have moved, but there was no way he was about to let go and his rhythm didn't miss a beat. Winding down the window, I asked if they wouldn't mind shifting, as it was late and we did rather want to go home to bed.

But all my efforts to distract them and no amount of flashing lights, honking hooters and screaming abuse had any effect on them. I had two choices: I could either run them over or drive onto the grass verge and try to get round them. As Eileen wouldn't let me do the former, I had to attempt the latter. Not an easy manoeuvre, as the grass verge rose up steeply from the lane.

After a few anxious moments we made it and drove off, leaving the happy copulating couple behind.

I said to Eileen, 'What's the betting when we come back in the morning they'll be lying on the grass verge smoking a cigarette.'

Suffering with a Smile

Penance

When I was sixteen I broke my arm. I never did tell the truth about the accident, but my mum summed it up when she said, 'I bet you were up to no good, you little git!' Of course, she was spot on. Dare I reveal my teenage criminal activities now? Ah well, what the hell, I'm in my seventies, so I doubt there'll be recriminations for my petty crime.

A friend of mine who shall remain nameless had this wonderful idea concerning how we could get our hands on some cash. He knew a dodgy scrap dealer who wouldn't ask questions, the idea being that we would break into a scrapyard, relieve them of some of their scrap metal and flog it to the other dealer. Though, the dogs were a problem and had to be avoided at all cost.

It was ten o'clock at night and it was dark apart from the occasional dim street light. We had to scale this 15 foot high fence, fill our sacks and make good our escape, scampering through the backstreets of London, carrying our ill-gotten gains. I still can't understand how we got away with it, but fortune favours the brave and the first mission went well. What's more, we got seven pounds ten shillings for our efforts at retrieving the copper and the dodgy dealer indicated it was good stuff and that he would be interested if we had any more.

This convinced us to have another go, but the second attempted robbery didn't run quite as smoothly. We were in the yard gathering the loot when two rather large Alsatians appeared. I was first to the fence. Like a shot from a gun, I clambered to the top. Just as I was about to descend, my companion in crime hit the fence with the Alsatians' slavering jaws inches from his arse. The fence shook and sent me head first towards the unwelcoming ground on the other side, snapping my arm in two. My forearm was folded, with my fist touching my inner elbow. My buddy dragged me to my feet and we sped off like the wind.

Nearer than the North Middlesex Hospital was a police station. Can you believe the audacity of us? We went into the police station, told the desk sergeant that I'd tripped over and broken my arm and could they get me to the hospital. This they did and they also informed Mum, who wasn't best pleased at that time of the night.

The break was a particularly bad one and the hospital surgeon had to cut open both sides of my forearm and piece together the two shattered bones. I was in a cast and out of work for six months. My share of the seven pounds ten shillings didn't last long and left me reflecting on whether crime is a paying game or not. I suppose I was lucky that it was my right arm, as I'm left-handed.

I started to get some excruciating pains in my right shoulder thirty years later and it began to affect my sleep pattern, so after several weeks of discomfort I went to the doctors for advice. I explained about my broken arm that had happened when I was sixteen, leaving out the how and when, and suggested that it might have something to do with the aggravation I was experiencing with my shoulder.

I don't think doctors are comfortable with patients giving medical advice and this one went down like a lead balloon as he pooh-poohed the idea, saying that this was a common ailment with people of my age and the right shoulder was prone to a condition called frozen shoulder. He completely ignored me when I explained that I was left-handed and he put me on a course of painkillers. I was very naive in those days and did exactly as the doctor ordered. After a few days of taking these painkillers I began to get horrendous headaches.

On a return visit to the doctor he told me in a very casual way, 'Oh, yes, those particular tablets do have this side affect, just cut down the dose.'

Needless to say, I didn't take any more of those pills that were supposed to do away with pain, instead only serving to transfer the pain to another part of my body; this for me was not an option.

My third visit to the doctors instigated him into more drastic measures in the form of cortisone injections. They worked for about six weeks, but then the pain slowly increased again. I was going to go back to see if I could have some more, but Eileen had read up on this treatment and she told me that too much of that stuff and I would become a soprano instead of a base. So this time, the doctor suggested that physiotherapy might be the answer.

Thus far, I'd had painkillers that moved the pain from my shoulder to my head and cortisone injections that would make me light on my feet, so I figured that I had nothing to lose by trying physiotherapy. After a year the physiotherapist gave up on me, saying that there wasn't anything else she could do.

By this time I'd taken things into my own hands by prescribing cod liver oil and I swear it did better than the pills, the injections and the physiotherapy put together, but it was never comfortable and I'd completely given up on getting any help from the doctor.

In the summer of 1999, while the grandkids were on school holiday, they had me running round the garden like a man possessed. During a game of football I fell heavily, landing on my right elbow, jarring my shoulder severely. The pain was excruciating, but not wanting to appear a softie in front of the kids, I carried on. Even the cod liver oil couldn't ease my suffering this time and Eileen suggested I consult a chiropractor, so I gave them the benefit of my shoulder, to see if they could do anything for me.

This guy was on the ball; I should have consulted him first. He gave me the once over, looked at my shoulder, got me to walk up and down and afterwards said, 'There's an obvious problem there, Mr Oliver, but before we do anything we'll X-ray the shoulder, which'll tell me what the problem is.'

On my next visit, the chiro showed me the X-ray and told me that when I'd broken my arm forty-five years earlier, I'd also fractured my shoulder and chipped the collarbone. This injury had been missed by the hospital and had been allowed to heal on its own; although he did say that they'd performed wonders with the broken arm. Apart from suggesting exercises there was little he could do but recommend that I have surgery at a hospital to remove the lose chip. According to the man, unfortunately, with the injury being so old, it was probably something I would have to live with; I think it was a nice way of saying that I was too old.

The good news is that I have for some time now been taking glucosamine, omega plus chondroitin tablets. Eileen researched this product, which is for joint care, and the improvement in my joints, especially my shoulder, is great. OK, it's not perfect, but when folks reach their seventies one is no longer immune from aches and pains.

I've a lot of time for hospitals owing to personal experience with treatment received by me, Eileen, friends and family. I also have faith in the chiropractic field, but don't talk to me about doctors and physiotherapists. I know, I know. It's been said many times: don't blame the doctors and the physiotherapist, blame your criminal past. Bleeding fair, ain't it?

Smoke -filled Room!

I always thought that thirteen was my lucky number; until, that is, Wednesday 13 June in the 1980s. In those days, Eileen worked in the mornings and I was on 2.00 p.m. to 10.00 p.m. I was young and fit and had been busy doing my chores, but the morning was disappearing fast and it was time for a bite to eat. After rummaging through the fridge, I decided to do myself some cheese on toast.

Eileen was always nagging me about taking the rubbish out, as if I didn't have enough to do and as if she couldn't carry out this simple task. Weighing up all the pros and cons, I decided that it would be preferable if I did it, as the alternative – severe earache – was unthinkable and, after all, the plastic bag in the bin was a tad overfull. Never being one to waste time and energy, I decided to make the trip worthwhile and take out the empty milk bottles; another of Eileen's jobs.

With my arms full of milk bottles and the bulging bag of rubbish, I kicked open the back door. I was doing fine until the youngest of our three dogs caught sight of a rabbit at the bottom of the garden. Now, she might well have been the youngest, but she was a fully grown Rott, weighing over 5 stone and as strong as a bull. Although I can't really blame the dog, as she's normally as gentle as a lamb and doesn't know her own strength, but seeing the rabbit she must have thought it's play time! and launched herself through the door.

It mattered little that I was in the way and fortunately, I landed on the grass and not on the concrete path. Unfortunately, the milk bottles didn't and three out of the four bottles smashed into a million shards. The bag of rubbish, like a dart player's belly, bulged and as it hit the ground, it burst and disgorged its contents over the lawn.

One doesn't think too much about the disgusting things we put plastic bags destined for the dump; out of sight, out of mind. But a nasty reminder came to me, as I was covered in the most obnoxious array of items you could ever hope to image. Returning to the house to get a dustpan and brush, I was shocked to find the back door was locked.

I was amazed, because it wasn't possible to lock the door without a key. I pushed, pulled and kicked at the door, all to no avail. We kept a spare key with our neighbours and their farmhouse was about 100 yards away and I did it in less than a minute, losing no time explaining my predicament to the neighbour, as I'd remembered my cheese on toast still under the grill.

Gasping for breath, I attempted to get the key into the lock. My attempt was in vain, as the key on the inside was blocking the way. Running around the bungalow, I searched for a way in. Nothing – the place was battened down like Fort Knox.

Panicking, I peered through the kitchen window, watching on helplessly as black smoke filled the room, my brain buzzing with possibilities of how to break in with the least damage, which was rather difficult in my frantic state.

On the back of the house was a conservatory, inside of which was a patio door. Eileen was always forgetting to lock this door and I was always nagging her about it, telling her that anyone could easily remove the glass from the conservatory and if she didn't lock the patio door, anyone could walk in. Now was my chance to prove it. Having built the conservatory myself it was easy for me to gain access. I held my breath as I grabbed the handle of the patio door. It was locked. The silly moo had locked it. To plan "C".

I climbed up on the roof, removed some tiles, tore the felt aside and clambered into the loft space. I was in and I could smell the smoke. I knew the loft like the back of my hand, so I moved swiftly to the trap door. "Crack!" Blast, I'd forgotten about that beam. I swung down from the loft, ignoring the pain and the blood oozing from my poor old battered bald head and found the cheese on toast cooked to perfection; well, maybe a tad overdone.

I blasted open all the doors and windows to get rid of the smoke before the guv'nor returned. She would have no sympathy for my split head but would certainly have scored a few points on my carelessness. How that back door locked itself is still a mystery.

Decorating! 'Hoi, Del Boy, Come and Have a Look at This!'

For Christmas I got a new computer. What a machine! I'm on the Net, I'm on the fax, I got this scanner; can't use it yet, but I got one. Hopefully, Richard would get time over the Christmas holidays to show me how it worked.

It has this little paper clip on the screen with eyes – the user's friend – which shakes its head whenever I do anything wrong, changing shape into a square, with its eyes dodging everywhere as if to be looking for the answer to correct me. The bloody thing produces a dictionary and thumbs the pages when I misspell. Then, when I'm in the "help" pages and can't understand what it's telling me, it raises its eyes to the heavens and shakes its head in disgust. I feel quite inadequate, but I'll beat the illegitimate metal image of modern technology if it's the second last thing I do. It even has the cheek to wag its tail if I do something right.

My dream of spending hours with my Christmas present was terminated when Eileen decided that it was time to paint the kitchen and dining-room areas; my least favourite pastime.

We'd renovated the Gatelodge and doubled it in size by building a huge extension and I'd loved the challenge and revelled in the work, but when it comes to the finishing touches like wallpapering and painting I just hate it. But Eileen can certainly put the pressure on when she'd got the bit between her teeth.

I had for some time put off this chore, because we were in the throes of building a small extension that involved putting a new door through the wall of the dining area and I'd convinced her that to decorate would be a complete waste of time. OK, so it took two years to make the final decision to go ahead with my plans for the extension. That aside, I kept telling her to wash the grandchildren's' grubby handprints of the walls and it wouldn't look so bad.

After we'd decided to go for it, I had to plan the event. I wasn't exactly in a hurry, invariably delaying the inevitable, but there was a great deal to consider – money for starters – but after a great deal of humming and harring, she gave me an ultimatum: build the extension or get the paintbrush out.

David had agreed to arrange the necessary skilled tradesmen to do their bit to get the extension under way. I'd made whisperings that there was no rush and that he could take his time, but Eileen's influence was greater and with his inbuilt industrious nature it was done in no time. Fortunately, there wasn't any wallpapering involved – if there's anything I hate worse than painting it's wallpapering – and stashed in my garage I had more paint left over from previous jobs than B & Q. However, I found it nigh on impossible to persuade Eileen we could save a few bob and use what we had when the time came to it.

On the new extension I'd initially used this nice pastel yellow – my helpful son-in-law had described it as Sellafield Silt – but I later decided it wouldn't pass muster so found a better shade. Actually, I mixed some white with it, painted it again and redeemed myself, but she wouldn't let me use it in the kitchen and dining room. She was on the verge of going to buy some, when I found a gallon and a half of soft peach, which was reluctantly deemed acceptable. Boy is she picky!

The dining room came up a treat and to my great relief she liked it. I'd left the kitchen till last, being a right "pig" to do, and there was just enough paint to go round. Finally, it was done and hopefully I'd now have a little respite during which I could sit down, write some letters and play with my new computer.

The following day Eileen called me into the kitchen. 'Hoi, Del Boy, come and have a look at this!'

No, no, it wasn't luminous. The half tin clearly said soft peach, exactly the same as the full one, so how was I to know it would dry a slightly different shade? I tried to convince Eileen that the patchiness could catch on and might well be the in thing. But, alas, I feared a trip to B & Q was inescapable.

It only seems like five minutes after it was finally completed that Eileen decided that it was time for yet more decorating. Even though we still had a wonderful selection of perfectly good paint in the garage, she insisted on fresh paint this time; none of the old garage stuff after last time.

I told her I would make a start after Christmas and I then promised that I would definitely make a start after we'd got back from our winter break in Spain. And I would have, if half term hadn't followed swiftly on the heels of our holiday, during which we had a week of grandkids. It was all very traumatic.

I was going to make a start after that, but I had another excuse lined up. 'Eileen,' I exclaimed, 'I can't start now, Cathy and John are coming next week.'

Our American friends were just about due to arrive, when we received an email telling us their flight had been postponed till Sunday. What a shame, for this just didn't give me enough time for decorating, or so I said.

A real Bargain.

We've always insisted that any house we own has to have a real fire, but the fireplace in our living room was just a hole in the chimney breast; very 1980's, but the smoke from the fire makes a hell of a mess of the chimney breast, so for some time Eileen had yearned for a proper mantelpiece. You know, a wooden, marble or stone structure above and around a fireplace. Eileen was out, so Richard showed me several that were for sale on the Internet and I took it upon myself, without the ever-watchful eye of Eileen, to choose one that was, as far as I could see, something she might approve of and was the right size for our chimney breast.

We put a bid in for it and I was gobsmacked when it won. I know it was a little more than what I intended to pay, but what the hell – it's only money! And if Eileen didn't like it, for five pounds and ten pence I could always smash it up and use it as firewood. Richard arranged to get it shipped down at a cost of fifteen pounds; I did offer to pay, but was easily persuaded to the contrary.

The surround arrived and I positioned it in place for Eileen to make the final decision. Once more, I was absolutely gobsmacked – she actually liked it. So much so that while I was out of the room, she decided to place lighted candles on it (just to see what it looked like. You will note: this was long before I'd had the chance to fix it to the wall, which would have been fine if she hadn't stood it upright.

I walked into the living room just as she had stood back to admire her handiwork. I won't say I was once more gobsmacked, as three times in one story is a little over the top, so I'll just say I was stunned, because as I stepped through the door the wooden fireplace surround, as if in slow motion, fell and came crashing down, spewing candle grease everywhere, ruining the carpet and the settee. This of course meant a new carpet *and* a new settee. The five quid wooden fireplace surround was proving to be a tad more costly. But that wasn't the end of the saga.

I then had to tear up the old hearth that was too small to accommodate the surround, lay a base and, of course, fit some very expensive slabs of granite; nothing but the best for her bleeding Ladyship. Hold on, boy ... and there's more. The inside of the surround had to be tiled and let me tell you: they don't give them away, matey. The result was the five-pound bargain put paid to any holidays that year and possibly the next as well!

One of Those Days That Went From Bad to Worst

It was one of those days. An absolute shocker; or, as Dad would say, 'A right mare.' Nothing went right. After a virtually sleepless night, I got out of bed only to crack my knee on the bedside cabinet. Naturally, it was Eileen's fault. She'd moved it the day before while doing one of her mega clean-ups. That was my high point – from then on it was all downhill.

An unavoidable shopping trip to Cambridge loomed over me like a black cloud; as you well know, shopping isn't my most favourite pastime. We were going to a wedding that evening and Eileen just had to get another outfit, because she, "positively had nothing to wear".

Cambridge is a great city with bags of atmosphere, full of students, foreign tourists, *Big Issue* sellers, buskers and, of course, the universities. The buskers are top class and I normally sit and watch while Eileen does her thing in the shops, but Saturday in Cambridge is a nightmare, absolutely heaving. The city has a serious traffic problem and the later you venture in, the worse it becomes. It was getting late and I was decidedly irritable.

After Eileen had changed her mind three times about what clothes to wear – well, one has to be confident about the way one looks – we finally got out of the house. Then the car wouldn't start; it was the battery – flat as a pancake.

Yes, it was Eileen's fault; well, I certainly wouldn't have left the sidelights on all night. In the pouring rain we managed to bump-start it at the third attempt. There was an inordinate amount of bad language, because Eileen wouldn't use the correct second gear in a push-start scenario, no matter how often I told her.

Halfway to Cambridge, the car's rear end swerved violently and for a brief moment we were on the wrong side of the road.

Memoirs of a Working Man

Fortunately, there was a break in the oncoming traffic and I was able to get us to safety. I changed the punctured wheel in the still pouring rain and climbed back in the car, my hands now filthy from mud and grease and my knuckles dripping with blood. As I pulled away my heart sank, as I could feel the metal rim of the wheel on the road. Thinking the spare must have been duff, I got out to investigate. To my surprise, the spare was good. I felt a brief moment of joy. Then, circling the car, my joy was turned to despair as my eyes saw the other rear tyre was flat. Was this some sort of record? I asked myself.

Walking nearly a half a mile to find a telephone box, at a time before mobile phones, I rang the RAC and bless them, they were there in twenty minutes. He shook his head in dismay when he saw my threadbare tyres; it was at a time before the MOT was introduced and one never changes a tyre until the canvas was showing. He took the two offending wheels away, returning later with remoulds; I couldn't afford new ones. So it was home again, showered, changed, bandaged knuckles and off once more.

It was chaos in the city; solid traffic and parking near impossible, in the days before park-and-ride. The overcrowded shops heaved with people, but we survived and all things being equal, it was only to be expected that Eileen wasn't speaking to me by the time we got home. After she'd had her hair done and was all dressed up in her new outfit and I'd told her how gorgeous she looked, we were able to resume diplomatic relations. How could the poor girl resist me? I'm such a silver-tongued swine.

Bob Oliver

The wedding we were going to was a work colleague of Eileen's and was at the same hotel we were at the previous week. I wouldn't mind, but it was the second wedding in two weeks. We were only attending the evening do and not the church ceremony, which had been followed by lunch for close friends and relatives. I didn't know a soul and Eileen only knew the bride, but she can have a conversation in an empty room, so she wasn't at all fazed by not knowing anyone. Unlike me; I hate these situations and find it difficult to mingle.

By the time we arrived – late, of course – the party was in full swing and a drunk met us at the door. 'Hello, darlings.' He pushed a champagne and brandy punch into our hands – it tasted like fizzy orange, but was as deadly as neat whisky – and we began to mingle. Eileen bubbled and soon knew several people and their life history. I chatted to a bloke at the bar about the day's football results and he took the punch from me and handed me a pint of best bitter saying, 'You're not enjoying that crap, are you?'

After about half an hour my new-found friend went to the toilet and I managed to corner Eileen and ask as to the whereabouts of the bride. She told me that she was getting changed to make their exit and would be making an appearance shortly. Eileen went on to explain who she'd met and what connection they had with Karen the bride.

As she chatted a cheer went up as the young couple made their entrance. Eileen's face went white and her hand tightened on mine.

'What's up?' I said.

'The bride!' she replied. 'She's not Karen from work – we're at the wrong wedding!'

'What!' I said, choking on a pickled onion. 'The wrong wedding?'

We shook hands with the groom and kissed the bride, wishing them a long and happy life together. They thanked us for the lovely present and I told them, 'It was nothing, really!'

Edging towards the door we were waylaid by Auntie Maud, who was crying because she was so happy, her huge floral hat perched on the back of her head. Finally, we managed to offload Auntie Maud on some poor bloke who was on his way to the toilet, but she was in full flow and was completely oblivious to his pleas to excuse him.

As we attempted to slip quietly out of the door, the guy I'd been talking to earlier grabbed hold of my arm and said, 'You're not going yet; you're the only one I can talk to out of this toffee-nosed lot!'

He literally dragged me back to the bar. 'Look, mate!' I tried to speak quietly among the hubbub of the surrounding noise. 'Just between you and me, we've come to the wrong wedding. My wife got the venue wrong; we should be at another wedding!'

As I explained he broke into hysterical laughter. Trying desperately to quiet him and wishing the ground would swallow us up, Eileen whispered through gritted teeth, 'Fat mouth!'

Then, stifling his giggling, he called out loudly, 'Karen; come over here, Karen!'

Strewth, he was only calling the bride over! I looked round for Eileen, but she'd disappeared. Then I spotted her hiding behind Auntie Maud's hat.

Karen came over and said, 'What do you want, Dad?'

Oh my Gawd – he's the bride's father!

When it was obvious that we were welcome uninvited guests and not about to be slung out, Eileen reappeared and I thanked her for her support in my hour of need. The hallmark of true love! We spent another hour with them, but eventually we had to leave and find the other wedding. Yes, it was Eileen's fault again. She hadn't read the invitation correctly and wrongly assumed it was being held at the same venue.

Woe, Woe, a Thousand Times Woe!

Whenever Eileen and I are out and we meet someone, the question is always posed, 'How you doing?' My answer is always the same, 'Struggling, mate; under pressure.'

After one of these encounters Eileen said to me, 'Why do you always do that? Why do you always say you're under pressure and struggling, when it's obvious to all and sundry that you're living like a fighting cock and having the life of Riley? Why do you do it?' All this was said in an agitated voice, without any due consideration for my feelings.

I had to explain that when I was a young man living in London, way back in the early 1950s, I used to ask this Old Jewish barrow boy – I use the word boy very loosely – who sold his wares in Walthamstow High Street and whom I had become friendly with – how he was. 'Solly, my friend,' I would say in my best Jewish accent. 'How's business; how you doing, then?'

His reply was predictable; always the same. 'Terrible, my son, just terrible. Don't know how I'm going to make ends meet. Business is shocking, no one is spending and my wife wants money, my kids want money and then there's my cousin Ira. My God, my cousin Ira is worse than useless already. I tell you, he's useless.'

Cousin Ira looked at him from across the other side of the market stall, slapped his forehead with the palm of his hand and looked to the sky for celestial guidance.

Solly continued, 'Every week I pray to god to win the football pools. Nothing – not a thing! I spoke to the rabbi. You know what he told me? He said, "Solly, give God some assistance; spend half a crown and send Littlewoods the football coupon." My God, he wants me to do everything!'

Then I reminded Eileen of the time she worked for a guy named Siddy Bacon, whose brother Maxie Bacon was a then famous band leader. Siddy also yearned to be in show business, but their father insisted that one of them carry on the family business and Siddy drew the short straw.

I got to know Siddy quite well and both Eileen and I took casual jobs with other companies during our annual holidays. We couldn't afford to go on holiday, so this was a good way to earn some extra cash. Eileen would do secretarial work with an agency and I would drive Siddy's 1953 beaten-up old 3 ton lorry around the streets of London delivering his goods; it was an old banger even in 1961, but that's another story.

I experienced similar conversations with Sid that I'd had with Solly a few years earlier, especially when it came to paying me.

'Oh dear, Bobby boy, my son, the import business is going down the pan. The taxes are killing me already. I've never known times like it; I'm really struggling. You wouldn't believe the pressure.'

Then, of course, just like Solly, he would climb into his Rolls-Royce and drive off to his six-bedroom detached house in the posh part of North West London. We knew his house, because Eileen and I used to babysit for him and his missus. Blimey, I should struggle like that at the drop of a hat – if only.

Then there was Lew Rose, another Walthamstow market trader, except he was more upmarket than Solly; he had a shop – tailor's shop to be more precise. He was a true craftsman, crafting the best handmade suits you could get anywhere in London. Not only that, but for just five shillings down (that's 25 pence in today's money) and two and six a week (that's twelve and a half pence) you could have the very best Teddy-boy outfit and it wasn't too difficult on the pocket. But you had to put up with the same old hard-luck stories: the price of material, the rent, the taxes, the wife, the kids and, to top it all, 'No one wants a bespoke tailor any more. It's all off der peg now, my son,' he said.

When Eileen and I moved from London to the wilds of Suffolk I got to know a few farmers. Now if you think that the barrow boys, shop owners and businessmen can tell a hard-luck story then you should listen to the farmers' plight. With the most horrendous hangdog look, they shake their heads and say,

'Bad! Very bad! It's too wet, can't get the crops in; it's too dry, the ground's as hard as rock, I can tell you; it's too windy; it's too hot; the rain isn't wet enough!' Can you believe that? 'It's not the right sort of rain; those late frosts have ruined everything. Bad, bad; doom and gloom.' Gordon Bennett, I should shoot myself. Is it any wonder I'm struggling and under pressure? I've been brainwashed!

An Aversion to Queues

There's something that's always puzzled me: why do pensioners queue up long before the post office opens? Is it a social thing? I have often wondered. Being a queue-hater myself, it's always been far beyond my comprehension.

My old-age pension is paid straight into the bank, so Eileen can spend it as quickly as it comes in. Most of our bills are paid by standing order and if I need cash, I just stick my little bit of plastic in the hole in the wall and out pops the money. If there are more than two people waiting at the cashpoint machine, in my opinion that's a queue – my signal to walk on by. But there are times, much to my displeasure, when I'm forced to queue.

I had a package for posting one day and Gordon Bennett! you should have seen the queue. It snaked through the partitioned area that resembled a cattle pen and out onto the street. There were sixty-two people – not counting the kids – in front of me. I know there were sixty-two, 'cos I had plenty of time to count them. It wasn't easy, as I had to stand on tippy-toes peering through the window, but it helped pass the time.

The one redeeming feature about the queue was that it was only one queue; unlike the bad old days of the multi-queue system. If you haven't experienced multi-queues you've never lived on the edge. Entering the premises, you quickly scan and assess the best option. Naturally, you leap on the back of the smallest, where you wait with resignation and then you wait and wait some more. But what's this? you ask yourself – your small queue hasn't moved. After what seems an eternity, you begin to realise why this is the smallest queue and your calm endurance begins to fray at the edges as you watch people in other queues enter after you and exit the building having being served.

All the while the guy in the front of your queue continues to produce documents, bags of coins and wads of notes. The clerk who is dealing with the said customer has the look of a cross between an absent-minded professor and Mr Magoo and is completely oblivious to the growing tension that lies in front of him.

Anxiously looking around, with one's calm endurance completely destroyed, your eyes dart from queue to queue, seeking out a better alternative. A couple of old ladies enter and head for a queue that's being dealt with by a very competent and efficient cashier. Quick as a flash, you bundle the two old dears out of the way and triumphantly take your place in the queue, while the two ladies join the next one.

You queue slowly, but steadily it dissolves and now there are only three people between you and your goal. You start to unwind and your calm endurance begins to return. Suddenly, the cashier stops serving and calls for the manager. We all look on with baited breath, while a discussion between them takes place; then, without explanation, a "closed" sign goes up.

Those in the rest of my queue vanish before my eyes, while I stand, gobsmacked, mouth agape in disbelief.

Someone was giggling! Spinning round, I saw the two old ladies that I'd pushed in front of chuckling as they walked out after being served. Life's a bitch! Thankfully, those days are long gone and thank goodness for the introduction of the single queue system, where you know exactly where you stand.

Anyway, I stood in the single queue with my package neatly wrapped and clearly addressed. While the queue was long, with all those serving points I was confident that it wouldn't take too long to be seen to. My eyes began to scan the serving points and I slowly began to realise that only two were actually manned. Little wonder there was such a queue. I also became aware of the agitation that was being generated – people were shuffling and mumbling. One woman in particular was becoming extremely upset and her comments grew louder, until she shouted at the top of her voice, 'Are there any more serving points that can be opened or are we expected to stand here all day?'

There were yells of "hear hear!" and "well said!" and the effect was remarkable. A clerk who was sitting at a desk in the rear stood up, took off his glasses, looked round at the disturbance, grunted something and then sat down and continued with his crossword.

Without the worry of what queue I should or shouldn't be in, I was quite even tempered and so I amused myself by studying the different characters around me. I kept telling myself that it was all part of life's rich tapestry and rather than fight it, I should just relax and try to get some enjoyment out of the experience. It mattered little that Eileen was waiting in the car park and in another ten minutes she would have to put another ticket on, if that "Little Hitler" who patrols the car park with Germanic efficiency wasn't to slap a fine on us. At least, I hope she was waiting in the car for me; otherwise, it would be a very expensive package to post.

Slowly, my position in the queue improved and I gradually approached the front. This is the point when the adrenaline begins to course through your veins as your eyes dart from serving point to serving point, debating in your mind which one will be free first. Naturally, you're looking in the wrong direction when a position becomes vacant and that annoying voice announces, 'Cashier number twenty-eight, please.' Then the retard behind you digs you in the ribs while you momentarily hesitate and says, 'There you go; there you go.' Oow how I hate that!

At long last I was at the counter. The clerk took the package from me, gave it a casual glance, saw it was postage paid and slung it unceremoniously on top of a heap in the corner.

'Err, excuse me.' I hesitated and thought twice before asking, 'Do you think I might have a receipt?'

He views me with distaste, releases a huge sigh, drags himself from his chair and retrieves the package. He hands it back with a form and says, 'Fill this in.'

Like the toff I am, I step aside to fill it in, so as not to hold up the queue. Then I wait for the person now being served to clear the serving point and give him the form and the package. Once again, I get a look as he screws up my form. Handing me another, he says, condescendingly, 'Not *your* address, sir!'

How the bleeding hell was I to know? And besides, I didn't have my glasses with me! I returned to the dunce's corner and started again. When I returned to my very own personal counter clerk, he was attending to a very attractive young lady. I couldn't believe my eyes! He was filling in one of these forms for her! She glanced at me and smiled. I could read her thoughts; they were saying, "You're using the wrong perfume, matie". I watched in awe as she not only got him to fill in two of these forms for her two packages, but he also stuck the stamps on for her.

Back in the car park I told Eileen about my tale of woe. All she said was, 'Did you get my stamps?'

Oh dear me; I knew there was something else.

April in Paris

When Eileen told me we were going to see *April in Paris* it conjured up thoughts of romance, singing and dancing and my expectations were immediately of the delicious Leslie Caron with legs up to her armpits and the suave toe-tapping Gene Kelly, dancing and loving their way around Paris. I'd never been to Paris in April or any other month come to think of it. It was a show billed as a comedy, without reference to the old musical, but somehow I couldn't relate it to the local town hall where it was being staged. Eileen's friend, who had seen the show, explained that it wasn't a musical, but a modern comedy; with a cast of only two and little or no scenery, but, apparently, it was really well performed.

Whenever we go to a show we like to go to the afternoon performance, so we can have a meal afterwards, yet still get home early, have our hot chocolate and go to bed at a reasonable time. They don't call us the swinging Olivers for nothing.

It was a bright sunny day, so when we arrived our vision was severely impaired when we were plunged into a dimly lit theatre. Stumbling to our seats, I discovered an old lady sitting in one of them. At first I thought I had the wrong row, so we shuffled back to the gangway, treading on toes and cracking knees. After double-checking, we braved the abuse of several old dears and I gently tapped the one in my seat on the shoulder, saying, 'Excuse me, dear, but I think you're in my seat.'

She completely blanked me. I was just planning my next approach, when the old lady in the row behind shouted, 'Beattie, Beattie; I told you you're in the wrong seat.'

By this time my eyes were becoming adjusted to the darkness and I could see Beattie's expression – and it wasn't very nice. If looks could kill I would've been well and truly dead. With great huffs, puffs and sighs, she gathered her belongings – four carrier bags, a handbag, a walking stick and an umbrella – and crashed down the row grumbling and grunting as she went.

Beattie finally got settled in her own seat; unfortunately, it was the one directly behind mine and I knew then I was going to suffer for making her move. Gradually, our eyes focused in the dimness and we became aware that we were seated amidst a sea of grunting grannies. Just after the show had started, there was an unbelievable commotion as the second wave of the Over 60s Club made an untimely entrance.

Over the rising voices of the actors on stage, we heard Beattie's mate explaining why they were late. Apparently, Mrs

Murdock's boyfriend'd had a heart attack and she'd had to wait 'til the ambulance had carted him off, before she could get on the coach to come to the theatre. The chat finally stopped; then the rustling of sweet papers, crisp packets and the like began.

The show must go on and our gallant actors did their best to conjure up the illusion of romance in Paris, but Beattie and her cronies weren't to be won over. "Ere, Lilly, this ain't no musical. When they gonna start dancing, then? What a bleeding load of old rubbish ... Don't you shush me, mate, I paid for my ticket.'

Mercifully, the interval came. If they'd been teenagers they would've been chucked out after ten minutes. As it was, a mob of them stormed out to the foyer and demanded to see the manager. The poor young man didn't know what had hit him and because they were causing such a rumpus, he refunded their money and gave them a free bar of chocolate. However, instead of leaving quietly, they all trooped back in.

The chocolate did shut them up, but then we had to contend with more paper rustling and champing, after which there was the bragging of how they'd got their money back. I couldn't believe their cheek. Don't tell me about harmless old ladies! They're formidable, especially *en bloc*.

Then it went strangely quiet. I was beginning to think it was because they'd got a free night's entertainment and the play was now more acceptable to their dispositions, particularly as the price was right. But the reason was soon very obvious as the chat and the rustling was replaced by some gentle, and some not so gentle, snoring.

Spring Water

Several years ago Eileen and I were at the Ideal Home Exhibition. At that time Eileen had a thing about drinking spring water, which was being sold on one of the exhibits. The guy on the stall had a great sales patter and one of his boasts was that his company would deliver anywhere in the UK to your house within twenty-four hours of the order being placed. I can't for the life of me remember where he said the water came from; probably The Sweet Water Canal in Egypt or maybe the coolant tower at Sellafield.

Eileen had the taste for it and her teeth didn't dissolve, so she wanted to order some. The salesman could see that I wasn't too keen and was far from convinced, so he then turned his attention on me. 'Do you drink whisky, sir?' he inquired.

Now how he knew that was a mystery; perhaps it was the hangdog look or the bags under my eyes that gave him the clue. I told him modestly that I did partake of a little on occasion, purely for medicinal purposes, you understand, but never with anything added, especially water. With the guile of Paddy Flanagan, my Irish friend, he convinced me that by adding this spring water to my whisky, it would double the quantity without losing any strength or flavour. Not only that, but it would also enhance even blended whiskies and what it does to single malt was beyond praise. That did it – I was sold and he promised delivery by Monday evening.

On Monday the phone rang. 'This is Spring Water Limited. Our driver's having difficulty finding your address; I wonder if you could give me directions, so I can relay them to him on his mobile.' This was in the days before satnav.

An hour passed and I was getting excited at the thought of consuming double the rationing of my favourite brew. I poured a smallish double and placed it on the side while I waited in anticipation.

The phone rang again. 'He's still having problems, sir!' the voice said. 'At the moment he's on the industrial estate.'

'Ah well,' I said. 'He's almost here!' I then proceeded to give directions. 'It's only ten minutes away,' I assured him.

Another hour went by. It was now half past eleven, way past my bedtime and Eileen, losing interest, said, 'Goodnight, I'm off to bed.'

I walked up and down outside looking in vain for the "water" man and as I went back into the house the phone was ringing. Now I wonder who that could be at this time of the night.

'I'm sorry, sir, but he still can't find you. I wonder, if I gave you his mobile number, would you be so kind as to ring him and talk him in.'

I was tempted to tell him to put the spring water where the sun don't shine, but looking at my waterless whisky on the side and the fact that he was, after all, so close I could taste it, I agreed.

'Hello; hello, is that the spring-water man? Right, then tell me exactly where you are.'

The driver started to babble on about his problems and how he was hoping to get home because his kid wasn't well and it was his birthday and he was only doing this run as a favour for his mate; on and on and on he rambled.

I was forced to be a little harsh and was quite unsympathetic, saying, 'Look, mate; just tell me where you are and you'll be on your way home in no time and I can go to bed.'

'I can't get home tonight; I'm almost out of time on my tachograph. I'll have to park up and sleep in the cab.' He was almost in tears, so I had to let him bend my ear some more.

'Look, mate, are you still near the industrial estate?'

'Yes, yes!' the driver said. 'I'm parked up on the A1214 just outside of Ipswich.'

Ipswich is about 50 miles from our house in Little Wratting. I drank the whisky and jumped, freezing cold, into bed. Eileen wasn't best pleased, but whose bloody idea was it in the first place?

An Old Man and his Fantasies!

I went shopping with Eileen and came out of the shop leaving Eileen to pay, while I made my way to the car with the trolley. I'd parked the car under some trees and as I opened the door I ducked, to avoid some overhanging branches, and in doing so head-butted the corner of the car door. I exclaimed, 'Well bless my soul, isn't that just a nuisance and a little painful to-boot!' Or words to that effect! As I rummaged in the glove compartment for the first-aid kit with blood streaming down my face, Eileen entered stage left and said, with not a little agitation in her voice, 'What the hell has happened?'

I explained, 'There were these three muggers who tried to rob me. As I fought them off, I drop-kicked one of them and broke the second one's nose with a forearm smash, but the

Memoirs of a Working Man

third caught me with his flick-knife. I broke his arm and they all ran away!'

'Oh yeah!' Eileen exclaimed with eyebrows raised. 'An old man and his fantasies! I can just imagine how they wanted to rob you of the rubbish you've just bought from the "shit shop"!'

'Rubbish, rubbish, rubbish! Let me tell you, girl; there's some good gear there. Just look at this pen knife; you can actually get stones out of horse's shoes with it!'

Oh, the cut on my bonce? Well, it looked a lot worse than it was and a visit to the A&E where Eileen wanted to take me wasn't really necessary.

Under Pressure

It was in April 2008 that I was really under pressure. There wasn't a minute to spare and I thought retirement would mean a life of leisure and ease. As soon as the sun shines, Eileen begins to notice things in the garden that require my attention. First, it was decorating and then it was the garden. Mind you, the garden had to wait, as I was in the throes of ripping our bathroom to pieces. Because the shower in the bathroom is on the same level as the hot-water tank and because it's not a power shower, the pressure has never been that great. It was installed when the house was built way back in ancient times when showers were a new innovation to houses and en-suites were unheard of.

I'd had a shower unit fitted downstairs when we'd first moved into the Gower House, so the shower upstairs wasn't used for a considerable time. Not, that is, until we had visitors. Whenever we get visitors we give up our downstairs bedrooms, so they have all the facilities, while we move upstairs. It all came to a head when one evening Eileen burst into the bedroom, where I'd been sleeping soundly, and loudly declared, so that my dream with Doris Day was rudely interrupted, 'That bloody shower will have to go! I stood there in my all-together trying in vain to get wet.'

So it came to pass that my next project, as soon as the visitors had departed, was to have a new shower.

'While you're at it, you can replace that silly little corner bath with one I can lay down in. And!' she continued, 'that shower could be a little roomier. I'm sure whoever installed it wasn't aware that there are people over 5 foot tall and a wee bit more bulky than Twiggy.'

Well there you have it, at the tender age of 70 and a bit I was instructed to once again indulge in physical activities. Because the guv'nor wanted a larger shower, this meant a partitioned wall had to come down and be replaced with another, creating a larger area. But the sink was in the way, which meant it had to be relocated, but not until the bath was replaced. My throat was on fire from breathing in all that dust. Yes, yes, I know, I should have used a mask. I had to bag up and handball everything downstairs; the window was not an option.

Half the ceiling came down when I ripped out the stubborn partition wall, I repeatedly cracked my knuckles with the club hammer, I cut myself in all sorts of places and my back ached from humping heavy bags of rubble downstairs. If I made one trip I made a thousand. I kept telling myself as I choked on the dust, 'It's all good exercise, Bob; it's all good exercise.'

You wouldn't believe the shower tray; and I use the word "tray" very loosely. It was more like something from the Stone Age. At 3 inches thick and weighing a ton. I had to take my sledgehammer to it; even my son-in-law Richard, who is well known for his strength, wouldn't have been able to lift that beauty, I can tell you. Every bone in my body was in trauma; every muscle was dull with pain.

My only salvation and diversion from the stresses and strain of the demands placed upon my personage was my office, where I could sneak off to play with my computer and do things I enjoy, like my 'Natcorian Chess Secretaries' duties.

Days Gone By

When is a billet not a billet?

A friend of mine once told me that when he was a lad, he'd had his collar felt behind the bike shed with something else in his hand other than a fag. Now there's a funny thing. When I was a lad, a fag was a cigarette and you didn't smoke joints, you ate them on Sunday with spuds. Then there were the sliced, fried spuds which were called chips; you ask a kid today what a chip is and they will only think of computers.

When the kids were young, I told them we had gas lighting in the streets and houses; one of them even asked if the televisions were gas-powered, to which one of the others said, 'Don't be silly, they didn't have televisions in those days; it was the radios that were powered with gas!' And when I told them we washed and reused nappies, you should have seen their faces.

I can remember when being called gay meant you were happy-go-lucky, grass was something that grew between the cracks in the pavement, coke was kept in the coal house if the tin bath was full and a "big mac" kept you dry when it rained. Even though words lose and change their meanings as time passes, the English language is full of words that confuse the English, let alone a foreigner attempting to conquer our native tongue.

I was working at Richard's factory and one of his managers asked me to go to the saw and pick up the billets. 'Er, listen, mate, a billet was something I slept in when I was in the army,' I said; far too big for me to pick up!

He took me over to the saw and explained to me that a billet was their jargon for cuts of metal. I looked it up when I got home: a billet is an accommodation, a barracks, a lodging, quarters, a berth, a thick piece of firewood, a small piece of metal, a short roll inserted at intervals in hollow moulding. Confused? Me, too, but that's the English language for you

Technology

We bought Jim, who was eighty-seven, and Grace, who was eighty-four at the time, a DVD player and went to great pains to show them how to use it. A few weeks later I asked Grace if she'd watched any of the films we'd got for them.

She said in her wonderful Scottish accent, 'Oh no, Bob, we were going to watch *Pride and Prejudice*, but Jim couldn't get it to work. He put it in but it wouldn't play.'

I asked her for the disc and she told me it was still in the machine. I opened the tray: no disc. After searching in vain, she and Jim insisted they hadn't taken it out, so I came to the only conclusion that the disappearing disc was still in the machine. After stripping the machine, I managed to find the said disc. Instead of opening the tray and inserting the disc, Jim in his wisdom had inserted it underneath the tray into the actual works of the machine.

Gracie was well pleased that it wasn't she who'd done the deed and now she won't let him near the thing. I then went step-by-step through the procedure of how to operate the machine with Gracie, while Eileen wrote down the instructions.

We normally visit them a couple of times a week and we have a great laugh as I insist Gracie gets out her DVD instructions and goes through the procedure. She's slowly coming to grips with it and she tells me they've watched a couple of films, but without Jim's help.

Into the New Millennium (The Year 2000)

I don't normally stay up to greet the New Year. It's just another day as far as I'm concerned, but Eileen convinced me that this year was a little special and so we saw the new century in with the kids and grandchildren. The grandkids thought it wonderful to be able to stay up so late; even 2-year-old Sonny managed to stay awake. It was a toss-up who would go first – him or me! But I did manage to get my second wind and with the help of my son-in-law's whisky, I lasted 'til 2.00 a.m.

The party was great; so, too, the food and the fireworks – London eat your heart out. Did I mention the booze? It was all a bit of a haze. Sally, Beth and Emma lived in Kedington just a few hundred yards from each other and at that time we lived in Little Wratting a couple of miles away. All of the kids offered to put us up for what was left of the night, but crazy Eileen decided we'd walk home. From Kedington to Little Wratting there's a path avoiding the main road and Eileen was emphatic that, in her opinion, the best route to take, even though it had been raining, was this muddy bridle path across farmland.

I should have argued, but I knows me place. She hadn't wanted to take the main road for fear of getting knocked over, but at that time of day on the morning of the New Millennium, the likelihood of seeing a car, let alone getting struck by one, was extremely remote, but I followed obediently nonetheless.

As we trod wearily up the initial steep incline it began to rain and the already muddy surface got stickier. The night was as black as Newgates Knocker but, fortunately, our son-in-law had lent us a large torch, enabling me to see exactly where I was after slipping over and landing in the adjacent ploughed field.

Eileen took to a fit of the giggles and thought it highly amusing. Fortunately, I was under the influence and beyond caring. I was caked in mud, but the lashing rain was washing it away. We slipped, slithered and slid the rest of the way home and my New Year's resolution was to be a man and to put my foot down whenever she came up with dumb ideas. My other resolution was never to see another new year in! Showered and changed, we crept into bed at 3.45 and were soon fast asleep; all was right with the world. Welcome to the year 2000. The New Millennium – big deal!

Posh

I was born in London and the name of the road where I came in kicking and screaming into this world was called Derby Road. Now I know exactly how you have pronounced that. You pronounced it Darby, with an emphasis on the "ar". Well, in that road where I was born in the depths of winter, February 1938, we had a posh end and the people who lived there pronounced it just like what you did, but us what lived down at the poor end pronounced it with the emphasis on the "er" as in "berserk"; no cracks, please! Just resist the temptation.

Posh in those early days was when you took your annual holiday in Southend and not going hop-picking in the fields of Kent. Then, of course, there were those of us who stayed in D-er-by Road and holidays were only a figment of our imagination. Posh has many meanings; posh was:

1. If you were an only child, like my mate Les! My mum had ten kids);
2. When you have a table cloth; we reached for newspaper when we were expecting company;
3. Having a change of underwear for Sundays;
4. Having a front room that's only used for guests who think you're posh;
5. When you have more than one room heated in your house;
6. When you use toilet paper instead of newspaper;
7. Eating your fish and chips off a plate;
8. Using a napkin and not your sleeve;
9. Using three fingers to get the pickled onion out of the jar;
10. Reading *The Observer* and not *The Sun*;
11. When you have a freezer where the food's rotated;
12. Having a car that passes the MOT – legitimately;
13. Thinking that some of the hotels in Blackpool aren't up to scratch. OK, OK, I plead guilty to that one!

The Da Vinci Code

We'd read *The Da Vinci Code* – or should I say we'd listened to the talking book – and I found it very good and enjoyed it. Eileen is a Catholic and I'm an atheist, so we had two very different viewpoints. While I saw it as a good story about a very influential man who lived 2,000 years ago and left an amazing legacy, Eileen viewed it from her religious beliefs.

We'd heard all the critics giving the film a lambasting, but after experiencing the book we were determined to see the film, ignoring the critics and judging for ourselves. Most of these so-called critics probably spend their lives with their heads where the sun don't shine, so we went to the cinema with a completely open mind.

Needless to say, we both thoroughly enjoyed the film, even though our religious beliefs are as different as chalk and cheese. It was very close to the book, apart from one item near the end – in the film there wasn't any mention of her brother still being alive as the book had stated. Contrary to what some of the critics said, we thought the acting was superb and the film well worth seeing. Not sure if I would advise people to read the book before or after seeing the film, though.

We saw the early showing, which was poorly attended, with only about twenty people present. We sat right at the back and two rows in front was an elderly woman, who was motionless throughout the film, and I remember thinking how engrossed she was.

At the end we got up and made for the exit. However, the woman still sat motionless. At the bottom of the steps we stopped and looked back, but she hadn't moved. Our guess was that she was either asleep or dead. We didn't stop to find out and I said to Eileen if she was asleep, she must have disagreed with us about how interesting the film was, or could she have died from boredom? On the other hand, she could have been a critic. Well, we still thought it was a good film. Next up was the sequel, *Angels and Demons.*, another excellent film. There aren't many films I can see more than once, but these two are definitely on my list.

Smoking Can Seriously Damage your Health

At the factory where I used to work was a workmate named Fred. He was a short, stocky guy with a straight back that exaggerated his broad shoulders. His walk, or should I say "waddle", resembled a cross between Bat Man's great adversary the Penguin and Charlie Chaplin.

Fred would join me every tea break and he once sat down in front of me, took a deep breath and, with a look of great satisfaction, exhaled with a deliberate emphasis on his breathing. His movement was calculated, inspecting his tea closely before taking a sip. Moving his head from side to side as if to check his audience, he then opened a bag of crisps. With chest bulging in front of his ramrod back and an elbow jutting out parallel with his shoulders, he plucked a crisp from the packet and munched on it with relish. 'How's it going, Fred?' I was trying to be polite and asking the question that he'd been begging for.

'Bob,' he replied, 'I've never felt better! I packed up smoking last week, well two days ago, but do you know something, mate? I feel magnificent.' Pausing, full of self-esteem, he snatched another crisp. Waving it in the air and gesturing towards the door he continued, 'And do you know something else, Bob? I came up those stairs and didn't even get out of breath. What do you think of that, then?'

What could I say, except gasp in amazement and adulation? That was on the Monday. By the Tuesday tea break Fred went into detail of how his breathing had vastly improved and what a new man he was since giving up the accursed weed. On Wednesday, he told me how he was exercising and tuning up his muscles. By Thursday it was getting a little bit boring, but I did so love to see Fred strutting across the canteen floor, with his flat feet at right-angles to his body and his chest stuck out like Arnie Schwarzenegger. Friday was the closest I came to telling him to change the record, but who was I to deny him his moment of glory and, after all, it was Friday and I had the weekend away from him.

Well how was I to know he would be in on overtime on Saturday morning? I almost choked on my buttered roll when he waltzed into the canteen. 'I just ran up the stairs, Bob; look, not even out of breath!' he declared with vigour. His neck was beetroot red and the veins on his forehead protruded, but he was able to control his breathing to a steady gasp. The following Monday, Fred's walk wasn't quite so jaunty and as he sat down his shoulders dipped slightly. I watched him closely, but he didn't even acknowledge my presence. After sitting in silence while he drank his tea and munched on his packet of crisps, he pulled out a tobacco tin from his pocket and began to roll a cigarette. I folded my arms, leaned back in my chair and sat there quietly watching him. His eyes slowly came up to meet mine. 'Oh Bob!' he whimpered – a cry from the heart. 'I did feel so bad!' Poor old Fred went on to tell me about his pounding head, his aching and how the craving for a fag was worse after a packet of crisps.

A Waking Experience!

I was only working one day a week. I have two alarm clocks: one driven by electricity and one battery, just in case there's a power cut. Having said that, I can't remember the last time I ever slept on to allow the alarms to wake me, but it's a safety blanket and I can rest easy without worrying about oversleeping.

I'd been suffering with a stiff back for some time and Eileen wanted me to take the day off work on Sunday, but the stubborn old git – that's the term of endearment that Eileen refers to me as – wouldn't listen and I made my normal Saturday evening preparation: laying out my work clothes, making my sandwiches, setting the alarm clocks and at 9.00 p.m. kissing Eileen goodnight and off to bed. Eileen, full of sympathy, made a passing comment as I made my way to bed. 'You're like *Marley's Ghost.*'

Richard usually picked me up at 6.00 a.m., so I set the alarm for five. I woke at half four and lay there for a few minutes waiting for the fog to clear, but as I turned a sharp pain engulfed my lower back. Resisting the urge to scream in agony for fear of waking Eileen and suffering verbal abuse as well as the physical pain, I rolled out of bed onto my knees and stayed there for a moment in the praying position, with gritted teeth, waiting and hoping for the pain to subside. At that moment I discovered religion and whispered under my breath for some divine assistance.

Dragging my distressed, racked body from the bedroom, I went into my office and strapped on my support belt. After a couple of cups of life-resuscitating brew, I began to feel human again and the back pain became bearable, movement improving as I gently exercised and got some mobility going.

As I was having a shave I thought I could hear a noise, so I turned off my electric razor and listened. Nothing – total silence. A few minutes later as I dabbed Old Spice on my face I began to hear a beep ... beep ... beep ... beep! Then the realisation dawned: the alarm clocks. I dashed at the speed of light – and in my condition that was quite an achievement – out of the bathroom and headed for the bedroom. Standing outside the bedroom door with the alarm sounding behind her was Eileen, not looking best pleased. As I scurried past she snapped, 'That's the second one that's gone off.'

'Ah!' I replied. 'It's just as well you're up then!'

A Woman's Logic

Understanding Women!

It really is incredible and I will never understand a woman's logic. My familiarity with women is vast and no one can dispute the extent of my experience, but they never cease to baffle me. My mother was one, most of my five sisters fall into that category, I have three daughters and, of course, there's Eileen. With over forty-four years' association at the time of going to print, she is without any doubt the woman to whom I owe the most, regarding my acquired knowledge of the species.

At a very early age, I suspected that females were strange and unpredictable creatures. My mum always insisted that I washed behind my ears. Now I ask you – where on earth is the reasoning behind that? No one can see behind your ears, can they? And why was it that Dad never once hit my sisters, while I had to learn to duck before I could run? I know now that it's because they have immunity and only those who desire to burn in hell dare raise a hand to the fairer sex. Is it just Eileen? Or do all women demand 98 per cent of the bed, while I sleep with one arm and one leg on the floor, with the fingers of the other hand clinging on for dear life.

Women's fixation on the unimportant defies deduction. All that fuss she created over a few hedge trimmings.

You wouldn't believe the earbashing I got over something so trivial. While focusing on the inconsequential, they totally ignore the serious things in life that agitate and annoy. What's more irritating than toilet paper being placed on the roller the wrong way round? And while we're on the subject of the loo, why can't men put the lid down afterwards? Women seem to get annoyed at all sorts; sometimes there's just no pleasing them.

In our argument over the hedge trimmings, I only mentioned her inability to rotate the contents of the freezer because I know well the theory of straight and crooked thinking. Unfortunately, some years ago, I stupidly explained it to Eileen and she can no longer be distracted from the main point of the discussion with diversion tactics, but it did throw her for a brief moment.

The Art of Conversation!

Talk! my missus can talk the hind legs off a donkey, the telephone bill is enormous and I dread going shopping with her. Apart from hating the whole process of shopping, I know that the whole procedure should take only half an hour, but this is trebled because of the people we meet and, of course, all of these people represent a long chat. Eileen says that I'm the most unsociable bugger on the face of the earth.

After forty-five years I'm getting better. I know what to expect and I resign myself to at least a two-hour session and use this time to observe the masses. It's still not my favourite pastime, but at least I'm not going home in a foul temper and I've found that I actually enjoy watching folk.

It was just before Christmas and everyone and his wife was in Sainsbury's buying everything in sight; it was rather like being in the clock end at Highbury when they were at home to Tottenham Hotspurs. Amidst this chaos, Eileen met an old friend and a conversation ensued, causing a bit of congestion, but the girls were oblivious to the confusion and carried on yakking.

I pulled over to one side and sunk into my normal position of lolling over the trolley with a look of abject misery and boredom on my face. It was then that I witnessed my first case of trolley rage. This poor guy had obviously had enough. He was going against the flow of traffic for whatever reason – I wasn't about to enquire – he was pushing an overloaded trolley while dragging along two kids, who were hanging onto his coat for dear life, with distinct orders to the effect that if they let go they would be lost forever. With one hand on the trolley, he used his other to cast aside anything and everything that got in the way of his goal – whatever that was.

One old man was thrust aside in the wake and landed on top of me, tipping his entire basket into my trolley, and was only saved from serious injury by my catlike reactions, grabbing him by his lapels before he vanished into the freezer with the frozen peas.

The old man looked at me with appreciation and we both turned our attention to the perpetrator as he continued to leave more casualties in his stride – and all this as the carols on the loudspeakers screamed "peace to all men" and "joy to the world"; the irony didn't escape us. I looked across to Eileen, who was still talking, with her friend joining in when she could, until they parted at last and we moved on to the next aisle.

In the car on the way home I posed a question that had been bothering me for years. 'Tell me, luv, when did you master the art of breathing though your ears, so that you can carry on talking without taking a breath.'

She hit me – why?

There's a Time When all Rules are Null and Void

I suppose most homes have rules and the Oliver household is no exception. Most of these rules are unwritten, but written or not they must be observed in the interest of a quiet life. The first rule of the day is to introduce Eileen to the day with a nice cup of tea; to ignore this rule is fatal and would set the mood for the rest of the day. I have a great deal of experience with women, my own mother was one and then there were the hordes of older sisters, Eileen, three daughters and three granddaughters, so I have earned my spurs, chum, I can tell you. My daughters gave me my greatest insight into the female species and I watched with sheer amazement as they negotiated their teenage years, moved into adulthood and now have children of their own.

The second rule is that the female is never wrong; she knows all the rules by heart and if it looks like the male is catching up then the goalposts must be moved.

Our daughters' teens were a particularly harrowing time for us both; Eileen had this idiotic idea that if she used reason and common sense all would be well. I, on the other hand, would never enter into a debate or a discussion. I took the stand that I would affirm the rules of the house and there was nothing else to be said. No doubt psychiatrists would say that I scarred my children for life, but all I know is that I had far less aggravation and heartache than Eileen did.

Rule three: in the unlikely event that the female is proved wrong then the male should still apologise for causing a misunderstanding. I think it's the changes that women have to go through that makes them so difficult to understand. What blokes must try to understand is that women, from twelve onwards, are slaves to their hormones.

Rule four: if the female is aged between 13 and 19, all rules are null and void. Of course, there are many more rules, but they can only be overcome by trial and error; though a bit of mind-reading wouldn't go amiss.

Never get involved in an argument with them. You cannot win, but if you do happen to find yourself in this situation, you could save yourself a lot of aggro by apologising for being a male chauvinist pig and a unfeeling swine, 'cos the chances are that you are!

Ice Cream

Eileen always tells me that I could pick a fight in an empty room, but it was her who caused a fight over an ice cream. Her first day as a volunteer in an old peoples' home was quite memorable and things were going well as she bustled about serving tea and chatting with the old dears. There were mostly women in the home; not many men make it to the "super senior status".

Anyway, one old boy was sat in the corner on his own; he must have been pushing a ton if he was a day. He beckoned to Eileen and whispered, 'Don't trust her, she's a troublemaker.' He was pointing to a sweet little old lady who looked as if butter wouldn't melt in her mouth. Was it the smile on his face that gave her the impression that he was having her on or was it that he was groping her as her attention was being diverted?

The cup of tea Eileen was holding went clattering to the floor as she jerked forwards in shock and amazement. The warden gave her some sound advice. 'Hold their hands, it's safer.' From outside, the sound of an ice-cream van filled the air. Mabel, a sweet old dear clearly in her nineties, caught hold of Eileen and, giving her a pound coin, told her to pop out and buy her a Cornetto.

On returning, Eileen was distracted and gave the Cornetto to Elsie, who didn't decline the offer and got stuck in. Mabel, witnessing her Cornetto being consumed by Elsie, leapt to her feet, brandishing her walking stick and shouting abuse at her.

'She gave it to me, it's mine,' said Else defiantly.

'I paid for it, it's mine!' came the stark reply.

Eileen, fearing for her very existence, intervened. Wrestling Mabel back into her chair, she promised to go out and buy another one. Unfortunately, the ice-cream van had departed, so Eileen decided to slip quietly away, with only her imagination to recall that which she'd left behind.

Do This, Do That Syndrome

I think most husbands are subjected to this syndrome. After years and years of, "Bob, do this; Bob, do that," I just accept it and do as I'm bid, but the thing that really gets on my nerves is when Eileen asks me to get her reading glasses. They're never near where she is at the time and it must happen at least four times every day.

I gave her the post the other day and as always it was, 'Oh, Bob, pass me my glasses, they're in the bedroom.'

Right, matie! I thought to myself. I'll fettle her hash! So I got her glasses and carefully put sellotape on the lenses. After I gave them to her I left the room, but stood just outside the door waiting for the explosion. A couple of minutes passed and nothing happened, so I walked back in the room, where she was busily opening her letters and reading them; she hadn't yet realised that her vision wasn't quite what it should be. I left the room and returned to my computer, thinking it was just a matter of time.

An hour lapsed and I finished what I was doing and then went back into the living room, to find Eileen reading her book completely oblivious to her impaired vision. I took the glasses from her and said, 'Well, it's obvious it didn't work.'

She sat there, mouth agape, wondering what was going on and then watched in total amazement as I removed the sellotape.

She put the glasses back on and said, 'Ah yes, that's better; thank you, darling.'

Struck out again!

Working Hard

Eileen truly believes that I'm enjoying myself when I'm on my computer. What she doesn't realise is that I'm working hard and the pressure is enormous. Yes, it's true, it corrects my spelling with the spellchecker, it gives me a choice of words with the thesaurus, it centralises and aligns text and it allows me to put words in bold or colour if I want to emphasise a word or words. Indeed, there are a thousand and one other facilities at my fingertips, a far cry from an ink well and pen nib.

Because I'm dyslexic, reading and writing has never come easy, but my love for the written word spurs me on, even though it's hard work. So you can imagine my glee at finding the following on a round-robin email:

> Aoccdrnig to a rscheearch at an Elingsh uinervtisy, it deosn't mttaer in waht oredr the ltteers in a wrod are, the olny iprmoetnt tihng is taht frist and lsat ltteer is at the rghit pclae. The rset can be a toatl mses and you can sitll raed it wouthit porbelm. Tihs is bcuseae we do not raed ervey lteter by it slef but the wrod as a wlohe. Ceehiro.

One day, I was busy at my computer saving, for posterity, a bit of our history for the kids to read after we've shuffled off this mortal coil. Anyway, while I was hard at it, Eileen was enjoying herself in the garden doing a bit of weeding, planting out her spring flowers and generally pottering about and having a good time.

The sun was shining, so I decided to give the computer a rest and go into the garden and have a look at my chess games. Setting myself up in the shade, I attempted to get my brain in chess gear. It was very hard work, as my opponent was making things very difficult for me.

'Eileen!' I called out lovingly.

'What?' she replied, rather caustically, I thought. It was obvious that I was interrupting her enjoyment.

'Time's getting on, darling!' I replied. 'Don't you think you should be getting the lunch?'

Well, her reply was something else and blimey, I didn't even know she knew words like that. She's busy? Anyone would think I wasn't!

After she'd calmed down, she said, 'If I wasn't here, you'd have to get your own food. Just pretend I'm not here and go and cook the lunch.'

I dragged myself from my more important tasks and rustled up some grub. I was just sitting down and getting stuck into my culinary delights, when Eileen came in and said, 'Where's mine, then?'

'But, sweetheart, you told me to pretend you weren't here.'

Teenage Daughters

I saw three daughters through their teens and there were times when they were all suffering from that dreaded affliction that descends upon the female species each month and that included Eileen. Can you imagine *four* women in one house and all in that condition? Even the cat was a she and the three dogs were bitches and I swear they'd join in the monthly celebration. What I really want to know is if it was them who were suffering or was it me suffering from them?

Of course, the bathroom was another problem. Both were always occupied and I can remember pacing the passage between them, shouting to the greater being, 'Please hasten the day that three idiots come and take them off my hands!'

When those wonderful guys did finally whisk my daughters away, I tried to give them some sound advice, but the blank look on their faces was an obvious indication to their view that the old fool was talking through his backside. Time has told them a different story.

Family Capers

The Fun of Camping!

My memories of camping are deeply rooted in my mind and they're definitely not pleasurable. My experiences of living under canvas were gained in the 1950s when I was serving in the army for Her Majesty the Queen.

It was hard; very hard. Sometimes it was in freezing cold weather, other times in the pouring rain; never in the warm English summer sunshine. The Middle East under canvas experience wasn't any better, either: blazing heat during the day and freezing cold at night.

When Eileen and I got married, we spent our honeymoon in a caravan. This was in 1960, when facilities on caravan sites were, to put it mildly, a little primitive, so caravan, like camping holidays, have never been high on our list of desirable vacations. A couple of our daughters have taken to the camping lark like ducks to water, though, and they always come back with stories of great enjoyment. With my appalling memories, I take some convincing of the dubious delights of living rough under canvas. I have to admit to being impressed with the equipment they have, though. The tents are more advanced than those old army bivouacs and, most importantly, they never, ever venture out in the wintertime.

One particular year Beth had booked into a camp site in Sheringham, North Norfolk. It was only just over two hours' drive from us, so Eileen suggested we drive up and pay them a visit. Our plan was to get to the campsite, spend some time with them and then find a B & B.

We were mightily impressed with Kelling Heath Campsite and after turning off the main Holt to Sheringham road, we drove for a couple of miles along a narrow, thickly wooded lane with the sunlight sparkling through the trees. The site itself is situated in miles and miles of unspoilt countryside, with walks and cycle paths aplenty, well away from the hurly-burly of our traffic-choked roads.

It was nothing like any sites I've ever experienced. Indeed, our honeymoon caravan park was hardly what one would call a park – it was a muddy field with a block of ten crude, filthy loos servicing fifty vans and Gawd only knows how many people. The one and only outside water tap regularly froze overnight, so if you hadn't forward planned, you couldn't start the day with a brew.

This campsite, however, was a revelation. Each plot had a post providing electric points, with an immaculately clean toilet block, showers, a laundry and washing-up facilities. There was also swimming pools, indoor and out, a bar, restaurants, shops and evening entertainment laid on. Indeed, some of the tents were mini bungalows with separate rooms – a regular home from home. These people were professional, seasoned campers and the equipment they had was mind-boggling.

Beth, on the other hand, only had a small tent; she also had an extra tent that was even smaller than the one she'd taken with her, for when husband Richard joined them at the weekend. She suggested that rather than a B & B, we could use the other tent. Mine and Eileen's first reaction was, 'No bleeding way!' But after Beth had made us a cup of tea and we'd sat on her camp chairs, chatting and enjoying the peace of the countryside, we began to warm to the idea and Eileen, much to my surprise, said, 'What do think, Bob? Do you fancy a night in a tent?'

I replied, 'If you're game, I'm game!'

So that was settled; we would stay the night.

That afternoon we walked through the woods for about half a mile to the railway station. This short stretch of railway that Beeching didn't get his hands on is called the North Norfolk Railway and the steam trains run from High Kelling to Sheringham. The station that we walked to is called Weybourne and it's like stepping back in time.

Unfortunately, as we arrived at the station, the steam train was just pulling out, but it wasn't a hardship to wait the forty minutes for the next train, as there was quite a bit to see and we could have a cup of tea and a home-made cake and sit in the old-fashioned waiting room with all its pictures and memorabilia. But what was disappointing was that the next train wasn't steam; it was diesel. Not wanting to wait for the next steam train, we hopped on the diesel to Sheringham. I asked the porter for a refund, as we had missed a steam-train ride, but he was having none of it.

Sheringham is nice; we found a great little fish and chip shop, took our meal to the seafront and enjoyed the food sitting on the stones. The tide was in, with not a grain of sand in sight. The kids went for a swim and the only way we could get them out was to bribe them with an ice cream.

We meandered back into town, browsed the shops and then it was back to the station, arriving just in time to watch a steam train pulling out. Yes, you guessed it – the next one was a diesel. Well, at least we saw the steam trains, even if we didn't get a ride on one. And I've always got the postcards.

As we walked through the woods from the railway station dark clouds loomed overhead, with flashes of lightening turning the black sky bright, followed closely by the crashes of thunder. Our pace quickened from a stroll into a power walk and we arrived back at the campsite just in time, before the heavens opened and the clouds emptied their contents in an unholy deluge. Typically British, it didn't stop us from putting the kettle on and in no time Beth had made us a cup of tea and we sat in the tents watching on as the rain hammered, the lightening cracked and the thunder erupted. It only lasted a short while and the storm moved on, leaving crisp blue skies in its wake.

That evening we had pizza, I had beer – too much – and the girls had wine – far too much. It was a balmy evening following the storm and all was at peace with the world while we ate our fill and slowly got drunk. The grandkids were exhausted and were asleep by nine. Just after nine thirty I decided to make an attempt to cross the threshold into the tent and onto the air bed. Now I always thought that an air bed sounds so nice and oh so comfortable. Well, let me tell you, if you've never experienced the delights of an air bed that it ain't nice and it ain't comfortable; in fact, it's bloody awful and was a real struggle to get in.

After unzipping the tent flap and squeezing into the small outer tent area, zipping up the tent flap, unzipping the outer insect flap and then the inner insect flap came the real test of endurance. To clamber across an air bed that seemed to fight you every inch of the way, chucking you in the opposite direction to which you intended, is quite a challenge, I can tell you. But succeed I did. Finally!

My head was spinning from too much beer as I lay wobbling on the bed that wouldn't stay still, listening to the girls outside chatting and giggling. Actually, it was more giggling than chat. Slowly, I became aware that too much beer was having an adverse effect on my bladder. Not fancying the trip to the loo with all that it entailed, I tried to erase it from my mind.

Cursing, I finally had to give way to nature, wishing I hadn't drunk that last beer. As you might imagine, it took quite a while to exit the tent and as I emerged from the tent like a baby coming into the world, the girls' giggles turned into roars of laughter. And as I disappeared into the dusk I could hear Eileen shouting, 'Bob, put something on. You can't go to the loo in your underpants.' Tell the world why don't you! But I was beyond caring.

Relieved, in both senses of the word, I returned to face the mission of clambering back into the tent. Head still spinning from the effects of the alcohol, I settled down once more on the wibbly-wobbly mattress.

Eileen, seriously under the influence, made her entrance a while later. Now this was worth seeing and that picture will forever stay in my mind's eye. Finally, I had to lend a hand, an elbow, a knee and a foot. There were shrieks, giggles and all sorts of noises coming from Eileen, while I made all sorts of loud comments that to the passer-by could easily have been misinterpreted. And all this while Beth was outside loudly proclaiming that we didn't belong to her.

Eileen made the final plunge at the air bed and as she made contact I was propelled skywards. But as the tent is only 3 foot 6 inches high at the apex, I didn't travel into orbit and was pinned momentarily to the canvas roof, returning to bounce Eileen back through the opening. Her next attempt was more of a belly crawl, accompanied by more ribald comments from me.

We finally settled and listened to the other campers walking by on the gravel path as they made their way to and from the toilet block. After midnight things quietened for a while; then, in the distance, we heard a slight rumble. No, it wasn't from the loo; it was further away than that. As we held our breath and listened intently, the tent was lit by a flash of lightening. We counted to six before the crack of thunder, indicative of how many miles away the storm was. Now I'm not sure how fast the storm was travelling, but it made that 6 miles in about four seconds flat as the rain started to hammer our little canvas abode. Once again, we were in the middle of a violent thunderstorm.

I turned to Eileen and said, 'I need to go to the toilet,' knowing full well that by the time I'd exited it would be 10 miles away. Well, it wasn't quite 10 miles, but it was moving steadily across the sky and the rain had eased. It was a truly spectacular sight and I watched for a while before I had to scurry to the loo to get rid of some more beer.

Wondering if I was ever going to get any sleep I settled once again. After a while, the realisation that the air bed was slowly deflating became apparent. At first I thought good, we might not be such a movable feat and every time Eileen moves I won't be catapulted. But as I gradually sank lower, my left buttock came into contact with the floor and progressively started to freeze. I spent the rest of the night alternating my left cheek with my right and massaging life back into the frozen side. I refused to go to the toilet again, ignoring the pleas from my bladder. It just had to wait. I've never known a night like it.

Relief came as the sun came creeping over the horizon and warmth gradually engulfed the tent, when I could finally clamber from the hell hole and scurry to the loo. We gazed with envy at our neighbours on the next pitch, who had a luxury caravan with an awning, real beds, even a barbecue thingy, a real home from home – but Beth and other "proper" campers frown on such opulence.

Even though the eggs and bacon Beth cooked were delicious, I have to say, "Never, ever again!" If we ever do venture into the world of camping it'll be in the comfort of a caravan or something similar, because having sampled the nicer side of the camping fraternity we quite warmed to the casual life, the fresh air and the relaxing atmosphere. But air beds are most definitely not for us.

Our second trip to the North Norfolk Coast was a fortnight later. This time it was to visit Emma, who was doing her camping bit; are my daughters mad? But her tent wasn't for us; oh no, once was enough, even though she insisted that her tent and her air bed was much bigger and better than Beth's. Beth is a minimalist; she'll take only what's necessary. Emma, on the other hand, is a maximalist; she'd take the kitchen sink if she could. Whereas Sally doesn't do tents.

No, this time we were determined not to sleep in a tent; besides, we had a better offer. One of our friends had a caravan up there and as far as we were concerned, caravan holidaying must have improved since 1960, when we spent our honeymoon in one. Indeed, it was no tale of woe this time. The caravan was first class: mains drainage, hot and cold running water, gas cooking in the compact kitchen, electricity and all the mod cons, including TV, video/DVD, shower with separate toilet and hand basins and, best of all, real beds. The caravan site overlooks the North Norfolk Coast; it only has one small shop. No club, no bar, no swimming pool; just peace and quiet.

The site at Mundesley is known as Kiln Cliffs, as it still has the ancient kiln once used to make bricks. The building now being used as a shop was where the bricks were taken for cooling and is largely set below ground. Mundesley is about 6 miles east of Cromer. Emma had originally planned to camp at Wells-next-the-Sea, but because the site at Wells was flooded, she'd opted for one just outside of Cromer. This meant we didn't have so far to go for our visits; but Emma says that the campsite at Wells is a lot better – apart from being prone to flooding that is.

We met Emma and the kids and had a look round Cromer. It rained for most of the day, that drizzly stuff that seeps through your clothing and gets on your wick, but it didn't dampen anyone's spirits – except mine, so I went back to the car for a snooze and left them mooching around the shops and the cosy backstreets that make up the little town. Women don't seem to notice rain as long as there are shops to browse and they all spent a happy hour or so wandering around and came back to the car with some lovely home-made cakes found in the local bakery. We then went back to Emma's for coffee – all very civilised – and sat inside the tent listening to the rain pattering on the canopy while we munched our squelchy cakes and drank coffee out of plastic mugs.

The kids seem to revel in this outdoor life. They can break all the normal rules by getting muddy, running out in the rain in their pyjamas, having their meals while sitting on the floor and basically roughing it. But then they have advantages that we never had back then, like running water, hot showers in the shower block and flushing toilets; a few yards away, granted, but still better than digging a hole in the ground. Emma thinks it's good for them to get away from televisions and computers, filling their time with long, healthy walks and beach games, so that they're shattered at night and sleep like logs.

After this Enid Blyton experience we said goodnight and headed back to our civilised loaned caravan and opened a bottle of wine. Roughing it? Nah, no way, not us.

The next day Emma and her mob visited us at the caravan site. Beth and her lot also came up and we packed a picnic and climbed the steep path down the cliff to the beach. No mean feat this with six kids, two dogs – oh yes, Emma's dogs came, too – a packed lunch that would choke a horse and all the stuff kids need: buckets and spades, shrimp nets, blow-up balls, etc.

I'm sure they're trying to kill me off. But once there we spent a lovely morning watching the kids in the sea, trawling the rock pools and eating sandy sandwiches.

Baby Oliver was only a year old, so this was his first experience of the beach and he loved it. He sat in his little striped vest-top looking like an Edwardian bather; all he needed was a handlebar moustache.

The day ended with us all trekking back up the steep cliff path lugging our paraphernalia, including Emma's geriatric dog that, exhausted by then, had to be carried. Guess by whom...

Accident Prone?

Des married my sister Lily. I big, quiet man, you would never guess that he'd been a sergeant in the Paras, a foreman in a furniture factory and finished his working career as a bailiff in London. He always reminded me of Michael Cain's portray of Carter in the film *Get Carter*. I could imagine him when he was a bailiff, confronting a large, violent debtor on his doorstep and saying in a quiet, controlled voice, 'You're a big man, but you're out of condition.' Des is quiet and gentle, but he can be tough when pressed. My dad used to call him Lightening, because of his slow and methodical manner.

Lily and Des had a cat that was 14 years old and its name was Buster. Buster hadn't been very well, his eyes were puffed and he had discharge oozing from his ears and when Lily noticed a lump on his chest, she asked Des to take him to the vets. A thorough examination showed he had more hidden problems and had already used up eight of his nine lives.

Treatment for his eyes and ears, and an operation to remove the lump, also pills for a liver complaint, cost a small fortune, but nothing was too much for the beloved Buster. It took time, but his eyes, ears and chest finally cleared. The liver complaint, however, was taking a deal longer. Des was convinced that the vet was getting a rake off from the company manufacturing the liver pills and he cursed every time he was given the unenviable task of getting the blasted pill into the sodding cat. Even though Buster was drugged up to and beyond his long grey whiskers, he was still able to put up stern resistance, with jaws firmly locked. Des still carries the scars.

One evening, Lily and Des were going out and they were, as usual, running late. Rushing out of the house, they jumped into the car and as they backed off the drive they heard a piercing scream. Leaping out of the car, they saw Buster giving a great impression of John Cleese doing one of his funny walks. Buster had been sleeping peacefully under the car. Lily ran in and phoned the vet, who agreed to open the surgery especially for them, which meant cancelling their dinner date.

After a two-hour tear-jerking wait in the waiting room, the vet finally appeared and had some good news and some bad. Apparently, the infected liver had cleared up nicely, but the bad news was that Buster had a broken back and had to be put down. The vet's fee was enormous.

This was the beginning of a critical time for Des. It hadn't been too good for the cat, either. Des was seventy when all this was going on and he could have well done without all this trauma, but life goes on; and so did his problems. You'd have thought at his age he would have known better than to go clambering about in his loft looking for his old cine camera. Should I have been surprised when Lily rang and told me he had fallen, broken his finger and torn the ligaments in his ankle? 'What about the camera?' I asked.

The next problem Des encountered was a leak in his bathroom. Unable to stop it himself, he called in the "experts"; ninety-eight quid's worth of experts, for twenty minutes' work. When Des asked why so much, the plumber replied, 'Eight pounds for putting the spanner on the nut and ninety pounds for knowing which way to turn it.' So Lily gave Des what for, for not knowing which way to turn it!

Meanwhile, they'd been busy arranging a surprise get-together for my eldest sister May, who was seventy and was also celebrating her golden wedding anniversary. May might well have been 70 years old, but that didn't deter her from cycling to work on her pushbike. She never did have my thirst for retirement and they had to prise her out of her job with a shoehorn.

The day of the party arrived; we were all gathered round the tables and the food was delicious, but then disaster struck for poor old Des. We were all sitting eating our dinner and catching up with all the family gossip. I hadn't noticed anything was wrong and even when he stood up and moved away from the table I thought nothing of it, owing to all the noise and chatter going on.

It was hawk-eye Eileen who noticed something afoot; she has an uncanny knack of being able to multitask; she can read a book, watch telly, listen to the radio and hold a conversation all at the same time. Anyway, Eileen was in deep conversation, while passing the salt and eating her dinner, but she still managed to spot that something was amiss with Des. She called out to me, 'Quick, Bob, Des' choking!' He had a piece of meat stuck in his windpipe. Luckily, I'd recently completed a first-aid course and one of the subjects covered was clearing airways and included the Heimlich manoeuvre.

Des is 6 foot 2, weighs 17 stone and by the time I reached him he was on the verge of passing out. If he'd gone down my task would have been impossible, but because he's as strong as a horse and remained on his feet, I was able to carry out the manoeuvre.

To my amazement it worked with ease, with the piece of meat shooting out like a bullet. He recovered well and after a while was able to return to the table and finish his dinner. Unlike his wife, who was so badly shaken she was unable to eat another thing.

When we got home, Eileen was concerned, so she rang Lily to see if they were OK. Des answered the phone and assured Eileen that they were fine, adding, 'Do you remember that plumber who cost us ninety-eight quid? Well, I'm going to kill him. When we got home the bathroom was flooded.'

But Des has never lost his sense of humour and had us in stitches with this next particular story. He's always been a public-spirited sort of bloke and does his bit for the community. He was once doing a survey to find out how many old folk lived in the area and if they needed help or wanted meals on wheels; he and another volunteer would also give advice on benefits to the elderly. Anyway, they had difficulty with one particular old lady in her late eighties, but she was quite sprightly and used to threaten them with her walking stick and a vicious mongrel.

After some tense moments, they convinced her that their intention wasn't dodgy and all their credentials were in order. She agreed to answer his questions, but only through a part-open window.

He was halfway through the questionnaire when he asked if she'd ever been bedridden. The old lady paused and her eyes glazed over as her mind flicked through the pages of time. Finally, smiling privately, she nodded saying, 'Bedridden? Cor, not arf, luv, and I've been table-topped a few times as well.'

A Great Dutchman

When we moved from London to Suffolk in 1965, one of the many new friends we made was a Dutchman called Joe Van Bergan, otherwise known as Yopey and was an unbelievably larger-than-life character. He met his wife during the Second World War; he was a sailor – and you know what sailors are?

Married to an English girl, they settled in England and in the early 1960s they moved to Suffolk, where we made their acquaintance. Our three daughters were just kids when we first met Joe and every time he popped in, and that was most days, he would bring the kids sweets.

Eileen lectured Joe saying, 'Yopey, you mustn't keep bringing sweets, they'll come to expect it.'

The next day Joe's massive frame blocked out the daylight in the doorway and his booming voice declared, 'You!' He pointed at the kids, 'You mustn't ask for sweets!' He paused before continuing, 'I mustn't give sweets!' The kids looked sad and dejected. Then, quietly and gently, he whispered, 'But, if someone was to look, they might find some in my pocket!'

Eileen was thwarted and the kids continued to get their sweets. It was always Milky Ways; always, that is, until Emma, who was invariably the first into Joe's jacket pocket, said, 'Yopey, can't you think of anything else except Milky Ways?'

Eileen scolded Emma for being cheeky, but Joe protested the scolding, saying in his thick Dutch accent, 'No, no, the kid's right; I'm a stupid old Dutchman!'

When Joe's wife died he decided to move back to Holland to Nijmegen, of *A Bridge Too Far*, and we kept in touch with letters and the occasional phone call.

The girls all grew up and I finally found three idiots to take them off my hands. The dust had barely settled on the last of the daughters' weddings, when the phone rang and a Dutch voice declared, 'I'm coming to stay with you for a couple of weeks.' He'd been gone for fifteen years and had continually invited us to go to Holland, but for all our good intentions, we'd thus far been unable to make it.

Joe was eighty and had decided to show us how easy it was to skip across the water for a visit. It was like turning the clock back; we played cribbage and shouted and screamed at each other. Eileen told me off, repeating what she'd said all those years before, 'Bob, Joe's an old man; watch his blood pressure.' But I was the innocent one and as usual was being wrongly accused.

One of his old neighbours also came for a visit and as we sat chatting, she casually asked Joe if they were his own teeth. Joe protested that of course they were and quickly changed the subject. But this woman wouldn't let it rest and continued to press the subject. As with most conversations with Joe, they ended up in a shouting match and he exploded, 'Of course they're my own teeth. They cost me a fortune, but if you want them so bad here, take them!' At this, he removed his teeth and offered them to her. She leapt from the chair and ran screaming from the room.

When we told our daughters he was coming, they made arrangements so they could all come to see him at the same time and, of course, mobbed the poor old boy, rifling through his pockets looking for sweets. Naturally, he loved every minute of it.

We'd always known him as Yopey Van Bergen, so I asked him what his full name was. He told me, 'Johannus Wilhelmus Antonious Van Bergen.'

'In English!' I scoffed. 'That would be Joe, Pete, Bill, Tony. Cor! what a name to hang your coat on.

Joe returned home to Nijmegen and we fulfilled a promise to visit him in Holland the following year. I was so glad we did, as about a year after our visit we had a letter from his nephew telling us that he'd sadly passed away in his sleep. He was a huge man in so many ways and it was a privilege for us to have known and loved him.

'He's Lying!'

My daughters' husbands were to look after the kids while the girls had a day out with Eileen at the Ideal Home Exhibition and I had a peaceful day on my own with my word processor. They'd been planning it for some time and all the husbands were told in know uncertain terms that they would be having a rest from work while they spent some "quality time" with their children.

Richard pretended it wasn't going to happen and that it was too far in the future to deserve even a second thought, but you know as well as I that time has this annoying habit of inching its way on and on. Richard is like the absent-minded professor and although his brain is full of all sorts of things that are way beyond my understanding, he's unable to retain anything he considers as trivia and domestic arrangements are very far removed from his perception of reality. Richard considers me to be his PA and he depends on me to keep him on the straight and narrow, so two days before the event I reminded him. His face was a picture as the sudden realisation that he would actually have to take a day off from work began to find space in that overcrowded brain of his.

'I can't do it, Bob,' he gasped. 'I've got an important meeting; why didn't you remind me earlier?' There! I just knew I'd get the blame! It was pointless me telling him that he'd known for three months and that if I'd reminded him any sooner it would have seeped out of his ears quicker than it had entered. 'How does fifty quid sound to you, Bob?'

I consider that even though my education isn't what it might be, I'm high on common sense and I didn't have to have a university degree to deduce that I was being bribed. So not only did I get a nice little earner, but I spent a lovely day with two of my grandchildren. Little did he know that I'd already foreseen the situation, but I wanted him to suffer a little; after all, things shouldn't come too easily and many years ago an old soldier had taught me never to volunteer, so it never entered the equation.

Emily who was 6 and George who was 3 years old were a pleasure to have and we did the normal things like drawing and fortunately, Eileen has a multitude of kiddies' things about the place, so the rain that had confined us to the house wasn't a great problem.

When I was fixing dinner there was a hell of a commotion in the living room and I thought that at the very least, the third world war had began. I rushed in to see what was up and George sobbed out, pointing at Emily, 'Ish-er lota gota whata lota doa!' and loads of other words that were equally as indecipherable. I looked at Emily questioningly, who looked at her feet and said, 'He's lying!'

Later, when we were playing, or should I say running round like lunatics, the noise was obviously getting too much for George. He grabbed my face, placed a finger to his lips and with his head shaking, he told me to, 'Stop noise-in!' I think he wanted me to be quiet. I wouldn't admit it to Eileen, Beth or any other female, but I was knackered by the time they got home.

Watch your Back, it's Payback Time

Emma got married in 1989, but didn't have anywhere to live, so they bought a caravan and asked if it could be sited in my garden. I, of course, had the job of connecting it to the drains and running water and electricity to it. Digging the drain run was a mission, for it had been a hot, dry summer, the ground was like granite and most of the digging had to be done beneath the caravan. Just my luck to have the mains drain on the other side of the van. Water was easier, especially with all the new fittings they have nowadays.

When it came to the wiring, I laid the cable from the bungalow, through the garage and underground to the caravan. It was all set and merely needed to be connected up. My eyes aren't as good as they used to be, so I waited for one of the son-in-laws. Richard was the first one to show, so I explained that I was in need of his eyes and that I would talk him through it. We went into the caravan and I explained that we had to make the connection through the earth trip. 'We'll take one wire at a time,' I told him. 'This wire goes into that terminal.' I gave him the screwdriver and just as he was about to make contact, I said, 'Do you think I should disconnect it first?'

Richard's face was a picture; his hands retracted at the speed of light as he screamed, 'What?' Then giving me a look to kill, he continued, 'You're not telling me this is live!?'

'Don't worry,' I tried to reassure him. 'As long as you don't touch more than one wire at a time, you won't get a shock.' To demonstrate, I took each wire in turn, saying, 'Look, you can take hold of these wires on their own and there isn't any danger. But what you mustn't do is to touch two together!' I emphasised the point by pretending to touch two of the wires and screaming in pain.

He wasn't convinced and as he made several tentative approaches, I whispered in an attempt to make him more nervous, 'Careful now, careful!' It wasn't necessary – his hands were already twitching with nerves and my boyish sense of humour was amusing only me.

Eileen often tells me that it isn't funny unless all parties can take part, but his little practical joke on me was still fresh in my mind and I was savouring every moment.

Finally, he said, 'No, no way; I'm not doing that live. Oh no, no bloody fear – you'll have to disconnect it first.'

I couldn't convince him that I was only kidding and there wasn't any power in those wires; even after I'd touched the wires together, he still thought it was a trick and that I had the means to turn it on. I finally put his mind to rest by showing him the other end of the wire that had yet to be connected. It's funny how some people are afraid of the unknowns of electricity. Anyway, I take solace in the thought that my evil little prank was just reward for Richard, who had previously wound me up to bursting point.

Paul Kelly and his Love of Beer

When Emma, Paul – her husband – and their four kids were having an extension to their house built, they moved in with us. 'It'll only be for a couple of weeks, Dad!' Emma stated. Seven months later they moved out. But we made the best of it and had some good laughs, mostly at Paul's expense. It's a good thing he's an easy-going kinda guy. He loves his beer and always had a goodly selection of all the bitters you could imagine in the fridge.

I, being the wicked swine that I am, would drink a bottle of his beer, refill it with brown tea, replace the top and strategically place it behind the second available bottle; I knew he was at least a three-bottle man. He would come home from work and after a bath and his dinner, he would settle down to sample his favourite brews. When he came to the doctored bottle his face was a picture as he took a large swig. You could see him allowing the well-chilled tea to pass over his taste buds and down his gullet. He held the glass up to the light and peered at it through squinted eyes as his mouth was still examining the unusual flavour. His gaze was then transferred to me as he said, 'Tastes a bit like tea, Bob.'

'Is it too strong? Do you want some milk and sugar, Paul?' I replied.

His answer is unprintable.

It was his birthday six months later and Eileen bought him a nice selection of beers. The only problem was that there was an odd number and I told her there was no way you could give him an odd number. Do you think I could convince her that an odd number was totally unacceptable? She just didn't understand, but after some devious manoeuvres I was able to hold one back.

You can guess what I did with that "odd" bottle of beer. But my problem lay in how I could get it to him without arousing his suspicion. Eileen had told Paul and Emma that I'd refused to let him have the odd bottle and they also couldn't understand why it had to be even. It never ceases to amaze me how so many people are so illogical. Is it me? Is it really me? I ask myself.

My problem was solved when Joe, their eldest, was sent round to pick some stuff up. I popped the bottle of beer in his rucksack and told him to make sure he gave it to Paul and to tell him that Grandma had sent it round. At ten o'clock that night I received a phone call. Apparently, my fatherhood was in question and accompanying this information came some words I was unfamiliar with. Well, he is a Manchester United supporter and what more can be expected from those uncouth youths?

I couldn't believe it worked again and I only wished I'd been a fly on the wall to witness it.

Facts of Life! Not a Lot of People Know That!

Sam, our eldest grandson, was a teenager and he was very much into reading. Like music and languages, reading is always something I'm going to enjoy doing; at least, it is when I get time – it's always "when I get time". So it was very gratifying for me to see Sam taking time off from television and computer games to read and he seems always to have his nose stuck in a book. Eileen asked him what he was reading.

His eyes beamed with excitement as he explained the plot. 'Listen to this, Grandma, I just love this paragraph!' He started to read and the word "masturbation" came into a sentence.

Jack, his younger brother who was nine at the time, looked at Grandma and said, 'What's marster-baton, Grandma?'

She thought for a little while as to how she could best explain the whys and wherefores of this action. Having brought up three kids and everything that goes with it, she gave the only answer a well-seasoned, experienced veteran could give. She said, 'Ask your mother!'

Jack look over at his mum, but before he could open his mouth, Sally snapped, 'It's a place in Macedonia!'

Later, it was left to his dad to explain and give the kid the real truth. He did it quite beautifully. He told him that it was a form of martial arts and not a lot of people know that – including me.

The Good Old Days

When I was a kid we didn't have a refrigerator; all we had was a biscuit tin that measured about 10 inches cubed and the old man dug a hole in the garden and sunk it in the ground. Milk and lard was the staple food stored in the sunken tin and it did a grand job, except for the fact that my poor old mum had to dig it up every mealtime. Do you think I could convince Eileen that that was all we needed for our refrigeration requirements? Not a chance! Where Eileen was raised, they didn't even have a biscuit tin. Well, even in the height of summer the temperature never gets above plus 5 degrees in West Hartlepool.

Our very first brand new Fridge was in the early 1960s. The previous one I'd built out of spare parts and although there was nothing wrong with it, you know women – it had to go. I must admit we'd got our money's worth out of the new one and it lasted for twenty years. When it finally clapped out I tried the old tin in the garden ploy, but Eileen was having none of it.

Bob Oliver

We started to look for a replacement and the prices frightened the life out of me. I was already working all the hours God sent to pay off the mortgage and didn't relish any more debt. Then, like a bolt out of the blue, I was saved. A friend of Eileen's, who knew she was always collecting and passing things onto the church and charities, told us she was chucking out some stuff and could we find a deserving home for it.

Now I normally wince when this happens, because it always means I get the job of picking up all sorts of junk and distributing it – as if I didn't have enough to do – but this time my ears tweaked and my eyes sparkled at the mention of an old refrigerator. Like a rat up a drainpipe I was there and in no time at all our garden was full of all sorts of stuff waiting for me to deliver it to the charity shop. But in our kitchen stood a brand new, second-hand fridge. OK, so it was slightly soiled and quite a lot of rust was in evidence, but the mechanics were perfect. Eileen stood looking at it, shaking her head.

I could see what she was thinking and I began to panic. 'Look! If we clean it up it'll be just like new!' I attempted to convince her. But she was running her fingers over the rust spots and I was going to have my work cut out if I was going to save myself a few bob on a new one. I told her I could get some special paint to cover the rust spots, but in the meantime I stuck some of the kids' drawings over the front. The kids loved to see their efforts on display, but Eileen wasn't sure.

A week passed and I was just beginning to congratulate myself on my financial coup, when Eileen put her foot down, saying it was an eyesore in the kitchen and it just wouldn't do.

Once again I was saved when my daughter told me she was giving the elbow to her old fridge, which it was small but mechanically sound. Eileen was less than enthusiastic and commented that, 'Uh, now I'm reduced to me own daughter's chuck outs!'

It was still going strong after eighteen months, but with constant reminders that "it was too small", I finally buckled under the pressure and agreed to price up a new one. The one Eileen picked out at the local electricity showroom was a fridge-freezer and they promised delivery within the week as this was a stock item.

A couple of weeks later and still with no sign of the fridge, Eileen was becoming upset, especially as she'd been bragging to the neighbours about our forthcoming happy event. A fridge-freezer for us was a luxury.

She telephoned them to vent her fury. First, she spoke to a young sales assistant who, after being verbally cut to shreds, passed her on to a senior sales assistant, who also fell victim to her ranting and she in turn passed her on to the manager's secretary. After ten minutes of Eileen's badinage, the secretary promised to get the manager to ring her back when he came back from his meeting.

An hour later the manager rang, pacified Eileen and promised to deal with her order personally.

'Look,' said Eileen, 'I don't want you to forget my call as soon as you put this phone down.'

'Your name, Mrs Oliver, is etched into my memory,' he replied. 'When I came in my sales assistants were jumping up and down saying Mrs Oliver, Mrs Oliver; my secretary was also shaking saying Mrs Oliver, Mrs Oliver. Believe me – I'll never forget you.'

When I got home from work the manager had been in touch and he'd explained that they'd had to order one from the manufacturer. In the meantime, as we'd already disposed of our fridge, they would lend us one until ours was delivered.

'But,' I declared, 'we haven't got rid of our old fridge.'

She looked at me with disbelief, 'I know that,' she said. 'But if we borrow one of theirs, they'll be more inclined to rush our order, you plonker.'

I was amazed at her deviousness, especially knowing she was normally so boringly honest. Of course, I had the job of disposing of the evidence, which I did by hiding our fridge under the stairs. The next day, our temporary fridge came and sat like a trophy in the kitchen. The following day I was relating this story to a friend of mine at work and his eyes sparkled with mischief.

'We can have a good laugh at Eileen's expense,' he said and the plot was hatched. We'd arranged for him to ring on Saturday morning. I answered the phone and called to Eileen to pick up the extension, telling her it was the manager of the electric showroom. She was thrilled, thinking it was the early delivery of her fridge-freezer. Then I sat back with my hand over the mouthpiece and listened.

'Ah, Mrs Oliver, my name's Brent and I'm the manager of the showrooms and I'm afraid there's been a mix up. Unfortunately, that fridge was delivered to you by mistake and should have gone to another customer, so we'll have to come and pick it up.'

'And what about another one?' asked Eileen.

'Er, no, I'm sorry; we're out of stock.'

'Well, there's no way that fridge is leaving these premises without a replacement!' she howled, going into the history of the purchase and the people she'd spoken to.

John was brilliant. 'Mrs Oliver, I'm sympathetic to your case, but we have another customer waiting for that fridge.'

'Well that's tough and I'm a customer who needs this fridge,' she screamed.

'Now, now, Mrs Oliver,' he answered. 'You really don't need that fridge, do you? We know you have one hidden under the stairs.'

Time stood still and for the first time in her life she was speechless and stuttering, until she saw me peeping round the corner grinning.

The penny dropped, 'OK, who is this?' she blurted.

Having delivered the punchline, John lost control and cracked up. 'See Eileen, even little white lies have a habit of coming back to visit you.'

'John Smith,' she said, 'I'll get you for this if it's the last thing I do!'

'You'll have to be quick. I'm off to Australia in three weeks,' he said.

Well, women have long memories and they don't forgive easily and thirty years later, she extracted her revenge.

Bob Oliver

Eileen's Revenge:
Came the Time, Came the Moment

I received a phone call from a friend advising me that John Smith was back in England from Australia for a visit and asking if I'd moved house and if so where. He told me that he'd given John and his wife directions and that they'd be here in half an hour; it was to be a flying visit, as they had lots of people to see, but I looked forward to catching up on their lives.

Eileen was at work so would miss them, but I rang her to tell her the news and that if she was to get her revenge she only had half an hour to do so.

They arrived twenty minutes later and we had a great time catching up on old times, although I did feel sorry for his wife, who couldn't get a word in edgeways. Time was running out for Eileen and I was beginning to think that she'd missed her chance. I gave John a sealed envelope and told him not to open it until he was on his way home to Tasmania. It was the story of how he'd wound Eileen up about the fridge-freezer.

'Well, Bob, we have to go,' he said; he was still speaking the words when the telephone rang.

Is this Eileen with the wind up? I wondered. Picking up the phone, I heard our daughter's voice. 'Could I speak to Mr Smith, please?'

I called John to the phone and told him it was for him. 'Who the heck knows I'm here?' he said and like a lamb to the slaughter, he picked up the phone.

Sally, who was an avid fan of Aussie soaps and has an ear for accents, began the wind up. She convinced John that she was from the Tasmanian fire service and that there had been a fire in his home. She said she'd been chasing him all over England and had tracked him down. Naming some of the contacts I'd given Eileen, he was absolutely hooked.

I sat in the living room with his wife and we could overhear the conversation. 'Don't worry,' I said. 'It's my daughter Sally pulling his leg.'

She looked only half convinced, because we could hear the rising panic in John's voice while Sally told John how irresponsible he'd been to leave the house unattended with an electrical appliance switched on under the stairs.

John pleaded his innocence and continued to protest loudly. It had been a lot of years since he'd caught Eileen with his prank and he obviously still hadn't yet made the connection. I began to get embarrassed, as Sally seemed to be going too far, but his wife chuckled and said, 'It's about time he got some of his own back.'

But I couldn't let it go any further, so I went to the phone and said, 'John, it's a wind up; it's Sally pulling your leg.'

John was having none of it and he pushed me away, saying, 'No, Bob, this is serious, really serious,' and then he turned his attention back to the phone. 'What about my daughter and son-in-law who were in the house?' he yelled.

Sally assured him that no one had been injured, as the house was empty, but had burned to the ground. Again, she reiterated that it was because of this phantom electrical appliance under the stairs.

'There *is* no appliance under the stairs,' he screamed, 'only a few cables.'

I went back to his wife and said, 'He won't listen to me.' She, by now, was also looking anxious and was considering the possibility that the situation was real and I could see that the prank was going too far. I ran back to the phone and over John's shoulder, yelled, 'Sally, that's enough!' Once again, John pushed me away; he was very agitated and he was sweating and needed to sit down.

'But there is no fridge under the stairs,' I heard him reiterate.

I knew it was Sally, but the hapless John was convinced that he was homeless. He was scribbling notes nervously when Sally finally let him off the hook. Dropping her Australian accent, she said, 'This serves you right, John Smith, for what you did to my mother twenty years ago.' John took it really well considering the pathos he'd been through, even laughing and complimenting her on her accent and acting skills, although when he recovered he called us lots of rather nasty names.

Sally rang her mum at work to fill her in and Eileen in turn rang John, just so that she could say, 'Gotcha, Smithy. Gotcha!' The Smiths returned to Aussie land, but the Olivers are on alert for their counter-revenge.

Wash-day Blues

When our ancient washing machine sprang a leak I was faced with the daunting thought of coughing up for a new washing machine. The old one leaked and flooded the utility room, soaking everything, including the already rusty fridge. I managed to affect a repair of sorts on the washing machine, but it still leaked, though a strategically placed bowl caught most drips and a towel wrapped round the base dealt with the rest.

All was well, 'til one of the kids borrowed the bowl and once again Mum had to do a mop-up job. She wasn't best pleased and I was on the wrong end of an earbashing.

While Eileen was out shopping one day, I had an ingenious idea: I drilled holes though the outside walls, dragged the washing machine onto the patio and plumbed it in outside. That way, we could water the lawn at the same time. At first Eileen was speechless; or was it that she wasn't speaking to me?

After a few weeks, during a particularly rainy spell I plucked up enough courage to ask her how she was getting on with my unpatented brainwave. It was a taboo subject but, through gritted teeth, she growled, 'I must be the only woman in the world who does her washing in wellington boots with an umbrella.' It lasted six months before it gave up the ghost in a blaze of flashing sparks and I was forced to buy a new machine. The things I do for that woman.

A Smashing Time?

Beth and Richard went to America on holiday, leaving us to house and grandkid-sit, along with leaving me a list of things to do. You know the scenario? 'Oh, Bob, and if you can do this … do that … blah-de-blah, etc., etc.'

Apart from all that, the school runs and everything else that goes with temporarily moving house and looking after the kids.

Beth was getting rid of her old greenhouse and Emma had jumped at it. So it was, 'Dad, any chance you could dismantle the greenhouse and put it in my garden?' Sounds dead easy, dun' it? If you say it quick, that is.

Of course, there's the little business of preparing the ground and laying a base, before even tackling the arduous task of taking the ageing greenhouse to pieces that has, after all, seen better days. And you can well imagine the challenge that the rusted, moss-covered monster had to offer.

Anyway, the base was dug and laid and the greenhouse dismantled and it would have made you laugh fit to burst if you could have witnessed the transporting of the sections of the said monster from one garden to the other. I had to enlist the assistance of Eileen to carry out this particular part of the operation. We manoeuvred a couple of sections on the back of Richard's pick-up truck and because it slightly overhung, Eileen had to sit in the back holding on for grim death.

We only had to repeat the journey three times before I had to sit Eileen down in a darkened room with a G & T! I, of course, had to continue with smaller bits and pieces. With mission accomplished, I then had the unenviable task of reassembling it. Every bone in my body ached and it's at times like these that the realisation that old Father Time is laying heavy on my shoulders crept over me.

Once the greenhouse was up and functional, I told my Emma, 'No more jobs, please!' But I know I'm whistling in the wind. Emma had a smiley face and bought me a crate of my favourite beers; no, not lager, real English ales to be drunk at room temperature, not chilled – well that's my preference, anyway.

Believe me, I'm never without things to do, but I prefer doing what I enjoy, not the little jobs that Eileen and the girls keep pushing in my direction.

'Big trouble, Grandad!'

The things that kids get you doing are nobody's business. First it was my own and now it's the grandkids. I was building a rockery for my eldest daughter, with her second son helping me out. He was 5 years old at the time and was of the firm belief that his grandad was next in line for the throne, was a field marshal in the SAS and there isn't a thing he couldn't do.

This kind of help is always more like a hindrance and I could well have done without it, but Eileen keeps reminding me that, 'These are quality moments, make the most of them!' Of course, she's right and I do get more enjoyment and it well outweighs the hold-ups.

Requiring a few moments to complete a tricky manoeuvre, I told him to ask Mum to make us a cup of tea. He disappeared into the house, but before I could complete the job, I heard him calling, 'Grandad, come here, Grandad.' Naturally, I did as I was bid and followed the direction from where the voice was coming. He was in the outhouse where they had an outside toilet.

He looked up at me with his big brown eyes wide with dismay and explained in a voice that was so serious, 'Big trouble, Grandad!' He took my hand and led me into the toilet and, pointing down the pan, he continued, 'I was doing a wee and I dropped my car down there ...'

Of course, it was I who had to perform the deadly deed and plunge my hand where they should never be. As I washed the toy car, and my hand, I explained to Jack that in future, when he does a wee, he should put the car down, as it's extremely difficult to hold two very important things at the same time. Naturally, his mum was nowhere to be found when such tasks are to be carried out.

A short while after the incident, Jack was playing with the said car, when his big brother Sam came on the scene. Catching sight of Jack, he starts to run towards him, shouting, 'Jack, I've told you not to play with that. It's my favourite car.' I didn't like to tell Sam what his brother had been doing with it and where it had been.

On Manoeuvres

Looking after the grandchildren certainly gave us a goodly share of laughs. Eileen told Sonny, our 5-year-old grandson, that he could play with the box of soldiers as long as he packed them away after he'd finished with them.

A couple of hours later, the soldiers were strategically placed all over the dinning room floor, the sideboard and the table and chairs, while Sonny was in the living room watching *Scooby Do*. Grandma, with her cross look, confronted Sonny.

'Sonny, you haven't packed away your soldiers.'

'I'm still playing with them, Grandma,' he replied, holding up his hand, palm forwards as if to fend off the offending remarks.

'No you're not, you're watching the television,' Eileen replied with hands on hips.

'But, Grandma, you don't understand; they're on manoeuvres!'

Sweet Revenge

We had a right laugh the other day. We were at Beth's House for lunch and the kids were playing out in the garden. Richard called them in when the grub was ready and they all came in laughing and messing around. All except George, that is, who had a face like thunder and he sat at the table starring down. I put my arm round his shoulder and asked him what the matter was. First of all, he just shook his head, but after I said for him to whisper to me his problem, he told me his big sister had been horrible to him. I told him not to let it upset him, as big sisters do that sort of thing.

As everyone began to eat, big sister Emily picked up the sauce bottle and proceeded to apply a little to her dinner. Much to her shock and horror, 80 per cent of the bottle spewed onto her plate. George's face was an absolute picture as his frowns turned to joy. His eyes widened as sheer delight spread across his features and with clenched fist, he declared his pleasure with one word, 'Yes!' Revenge was sweet.

Armistice Day (Offer it Up, Bob, Offer it Up)!

We'd had a busy day on Armistice Sunday: Eileen went to eight o'clock mass, leaving me with the vacuum cleaner. I didn't quite know what to do with it, so I put it back in the cupboard. As soon as she returned from mass we had to go and pick our number eight grandson up, but not before some not-so-gentle earbashing about the vacuuming. I told her that she should be in a state of grace after just coming from church and that she should be exercising calm endurance of all provocation and to offer it up.

That day we were supposed to be looking after our youngest grandson, while Sally led her troop of Cubs, or is it Beavers, through the streets in the Armistice parade. We followed the parade to the church and watched, at a distance, the Remembrance service at the cenotaph.

Sonny was only two and was, of course, very noisy and fidgety, which is why we stood at a distance. Not only could he see his mum, all dressed up in her Akela's outfit, but his brothers and cousins were also all in attendance and he couldn't quite understand why he wasn't allowed to play with them and run amok among the gravestones. I tried to keep him quiet by sitting him on my shoulders and it worked for a while, especially when an old man fainted, cracked his head on a tombstone and began to bleed. This interested him immensely, particularly when the ambulance roared up with lights flashing and siren blaring.

The proceedings continued and Sonny stuck his fingers in my ears and up my nose as he pulled my face this way and that. I strained to hear what was being said and while in deep concentration, I suddenly became aware that Sonny's fingers were pushing things in my mouth. No, no, no, it wasn't that bad; it was, in fact, leaves that he was pulling from the overhanging branches, but it did give me a nasty turn, I can tell you.

Sally had told her little standard bearer to follow the lead of the Scout standard bearer, not realising he was a right dopey dollop. A loud voice boomed, 'Standard bearers fall out!' This they did, except, of course, the dopey dollop, who didn't move and stood there studying his woggle. Because he didn't move, neither did Sally's standard bearer. Sally moved swiftly to his side and said, 'Would you mind awfully falling out.' Next year, the Scouts will be following the lead of the Brownies.

After the church service we handed back Sonny and dashed off to London for another memorial; this time it was for my sister-in-law Doreen, who died the January before. The service went on and on and on. Eileen was in her element – church three times in one day –but for me, not being of a religious persuasion, it was all a little traumatic. Doreen was a lovely lady with a great sense of humour and if there is an after life, she would be watching and laughing her head off at my suffering and no doubt saying, 'Offer it up, Bob, offer it up!' After the family get-together we returned home thoroughly exhausted. Yes, Armistice Sunday was a busy day.

Bob Packs up Smoking

I had many attempts to quit smoking while I was in the army and had lasted nearly three weeks when I was posted to Jordan, where we used to receive free-issue cigarettes. Well, how much

Bob Oliver

can one man stand? Yes – I capitulated. Demob came, free issue went and I was back on the trail to quit once more.

All of my early efforts failed miserably. Then a friend who'd witnessed my feeble endeavours to kick the habit told me, 'Oliver, you'll never succeed; you're too hooked on the weed!' And to back up his statement he placed two bob (ten whole pence) on the table by way of a wager. I remember it well; it was eighteen days before Christmas and that was the deadline for the bet.

This was years ago, long before England first won the World Cup. Unbelievably, I won the bet and it gave me great pleasure to lift the big money wager. But my fag-free days weren't to be, for my flesh was too weak and I was soon back on them again.

Failure followed failure. Once, I lasted three weeks and four days. My failure was down to Eileen and my mum, who both said, 'For God's sake, start smoking again and stop snapping everyone's head off, you miserable git.'

I was 25 years old when I finally cracked it. After several more failures, I was almost resigned to the fact that the weed was part of my life, when Eileen told me she was pregnant. I decided there was no way I would pollute my baby's air with smoke and after watching my father, who was a chain smoker, dying very slowly over a long period of time, it became an added incentive to summon the willpower and overcome that most horrible addiction.

Of course, I suffered and I felt terrible and it took me a year before I really knew that I'd finally rid my body of the craving and put the habit behind me. In those days we didn't have the benefits of nicotine patches, Nicorette chewing gum, hypnotherapy and all the other aids smokers have today.

During that period of cleansing, I can remember waking from a dream and trying desperately to clear my mind of the question burning inside me as to whether or not I'd started smoking again. The dream had been so real and the relief was immense when I realised it had only been a dream and this spurred on my resolve to quit.

Being an ex-smoker makes me ten times worse than a non-smoker and at every opportunity, I show my disapproval and lecture the smoker about the evils of the awful habit. This was enhanced by the fact that we have other close friends and relatives going the way of my father.

Wheels in motion

The Cinquecento

David's parents live in Italy and for some time he'd been pestering his dad to purchase an old Fiat 500 cc, otherwise known as a Cinquecento. He really loved these tiny cars and the best place to get one was Italy, where they're still widely used in the more out-of-the-way towns and villages.

After a couple months Mario, David's dad, phoned to tell him he'd found one in reasonable condition, but getting it to England was another problem. Several options were explored, but were all mega expensive. I suggested to David that we fly out and drive it back. 'Listen, Bob,' he condescendingly explained. 'It's a 30-year-old car, with only two cylinders and a top speed of 50 miles an hour downhill with a tail wind. Not to mention the fact that it's been laid up in some old farmer's barn for God knows how long!' He continued with, 'The drive from Mum and Dad's house is 1,200 miles through five countries and there's the little matter of the Swiss Alps to negotiate.' I explained that Hannibal did it with elephants, but he wouldn't wear it.

A long time had passed and I'd forgotten all about the Cinquecento, when David rang me and said, 'How do you and Eileen fancy a few days in Italy?'

'You betcha!' I replied without hesitation.

'Hang on, Bob, it's short notice.'

'We can be ready in an hour,' I told him.

We had a little longer than an hour; we had a week to get ready. Apparently, David wanted to see his parents. Well, that's what he told us, but if he were honest he'd admit that it was the Cinquecento he really wanted to see.

Sally had declined after her recent experience in Tenerife; an ear infection causing a delay on her flight home. The short notice was because he'd got a deal on the flights at £31.00 return. It was the same old, same old at the airport. We were late arriving and then there was a mad rush through to the departure lounge, only to be told that there was an hour delay. Mind you, I reckon the pilot must have put his foot down, because he cut our flight time by nearly half an hour.

Normally, we would be discussing what we were looking forward to, like the home-made wine, the home-gown artichokes, tomatoes, fresh fruit and, of course, the pasta. Not to mention the winter sun and being able to just bum around and relax. But this time the talk was of – yes, you guessed it – the Cinquecento. David told us that his dad had cleaned it up and put new tyres and a battery on.

'So it's ready for us to drive back is it, David?' I said with a glint in my eye.

'No bloody way, not on your life!' he declared.

Mario picked us up from the airport and told David that the Cinquecento was the absolute bee's knees. It was night when we arrived, but David insisted his dad open the garage and show him the car. If he wasn't in love before, he was definitely in love then. Never mind his wife, kids or parents, this was the real thing. I have to admit it was in fantastic condition for a 30-year-old tin can on wheels. It was bright red and Eileen remarked, 'All it needs is a few spots and you have a ladybird!'

Over dinner Mario said, 'How d'you fancy driving back to England with me, Bob?'

'Can I eat my dinner before we leave?'

He couldn't believe I was up for it, but insisted we not only finish our dinner, but enjoy the holiday first while we planned our epic journey. Jean, David's mum, Eileen and David told us we had to be crazy. A crusty old heavy-smoking Italian, with an even crustier old anti-smoking Englishman.

'Do you think you'll be speaking by the time you reach England?' they mocked us.

After our holiday we put Eileen and David on the plane, bade them "bon voyage", loaded the Cinquecento until it bulged at the seams and cracked off at an incredible pace.

I've often wondered what it was like driving on the inside lane; never fancied it, just wondered. And certainly never dreamt I would drive 1,200 miles on the inside lane. Anyway, we drove from halfway down the Calf of Italy on the Adriatic Coast up and across country towards Como and the border of Switzerland. Like England, the roads were manic, with cars flashing past and lorries thundering by, rocking the Cinquecento in their slipstream. Even with two middle-aged, overweight, chunky people and as much crammed in that tiny vehicle as humanly possible, it still didn't weigh enough to resist the turbulence of those huge trucks.

To put it into perspective, some modern-day motorcycles have 1500 cc under their seats and in my younger day's, way back in the early 1960s, I drove a 650 cc Panther. So it was asking a great deal of the two cylinder, 500 cc, 30-year-old tin can on wheels to perform this mission. But give credit where credit is due, the little old Fiat 500 chugged relentlessly on at the incredible speed of 50 miles an hour. OK, it did struggle with the hills where we dropped down to 30 miles an hour, but the little beast kept going. The fuel tank held about 3 gallons and lasted nearly three hours, which was the signal to refill, change drivers and push on, giving the Fiat little or no rest.

Apart from the cramped conditions, there is another less endearing feature of the Cinquecento: the suspension; or should I say the lack of it. Every bump, every hole, every ridge in the road sent shock waves through your system. But let's be brutally honest, these cars were designed for short-hop, cheap runabouts and not the crossing of the five countries.

On our journey I discovered that Mario is a worrier. I know it's true to say that no one is completely free from worry, but my philosophy has always been to worry when it happens, not if it might happen. Normally a heavy smoker, this journey made him up the ante from heavy to chain.

It's always prudent to have a contingency plan, so because Switzerland and Germany don't sell leaded fuel, Mario's strategy was to fill up the tank and a large plastic container and hope it got us to France. The fuel-pump attendant did Mario's ulcers the power of good when he told him that the police in Switzerland are red hot and would come down heavily on anyone carrying petrol in anything other than their fuel tank, especially through the tunnels.

As we negotiated the mountains of Switzerland, Mario commented that in a modern car we wouldn't even notice the steep inclines, but with this one you could hear the engine slip into groan mode; just something else for him to worry about.

It was in Germany that we discovered two problems with the ageing vehicle. An oil leak that required an infusion of one and a half pints at every refill of fuel and the other problem was with the electrics: only one headlight was working. But worse than that, the panel light was also faulty, which meant that at night we couldn't see if we were speeding or not – more opportunity for Mario to worry.

Mario asked, 'Do you think we'll get stopped by the police for only having one headlight, Bob?'

Always the calm one in stressful situations, I attempted to reassure him. 'Don't worry, Mario. If we get pulled, just tell the truth; just say that we were crossing the Alps, when we ran into this elephant.' He had to admit that I was a tower of strength.

It was late when we crossed the German border into France and smoothly coasted into Strasbourg. The fuel had lasted, but only just, putting more pressure on Mario's nerves as the red warning light flashed relentlessly. Why couldn't that particular light have blown instead?

In the hotel, I told the two young girls on reception that I wanted a double room, but not a double bed. Well, one can only do so much for a son-in-law.

But unfortunately my 'Del Boy' French was met by a polite smile and I just knew I wasn't getting though, especially as the second young Lady gave me a knowing wink! "Strewth they think we are 'An Item'!!"

Anyway, after dinner and a couple of glasses of vino it was straight to bed, thoroughly exhausted. And yes it was indeed a double bed!!

Jean had warned me about Mario's snoring and oh boy, she didn't exaggerate. In the early hours of the morning, he let out an ear-blowing snore-cum-grunt that shook him into consciousness. He got out of bed, went to the window, opened it and lit up a cigarette. The thought was good, but the breeze just blew the smoke back into the room. With the aid of some earplugs it was my turn to get my own back, sinking into a deep and snoring sleep. I knew I'd been snoring because, when I awoke, my mouth was like the Gobi Desert at high noon.

Early breakfast, the nearest garage and it was on the road again. What a difference the French roads are! Wide, straight and traffic free. It reminded me of the time Eileen and I drove down the middle of America, from South Dakota to Oklahoma. Mario began to unwind as we neared Calais, saying, 'We made the water, Bob!'

'Was there ever any doubt, Mario?'

'Yes!' came the reply.

Even though we both knew well that the English roads would be a tad busier, the motorways of France had spoilt us and we had a rude awakening as we joined in the manic furore of a billion vehicles ... going where? But we were in England and on the last leg, with just a mere 130 miles to negotiate.

Little Wratting was a welcome sight and I was glad to be home. Mario stayed for a few days and took the quicker route back to Italy, to his wife and the good life. Sally asked me how we'd got on during our epic journey and I told her, 'He's gone back to his wife, he hasn't written, he doesn't phone, it's just as if it never happened, but there will always be Strasbourg.'

The Tipster

Eileen was about to change channels from a horse racing programme, as the "sport of kings" was not the sport for her, when she heard the commentator say as the horses were being paraded, 'And here comes the Italian horse, Cinquantacinque!' Eileen hesitated as the remark had caught her attention and she immediately fell in love with it.

Eileen had never placed a bet before, so hadn't a clue how to do it. She was unable to contact me – not that I'm an expert – so she rang our daughters, one by one; but not one of them knew how to place a bet.

She was getting uptight at not being able to back the nag and the start time was getting close. Then a brainwave emerged: she would ring her brother in London, he would know. Tom explained that she would have to go to a betting shop to do the deed but, of course, it was too late to do that, so she watched the race without placing a bet.

She told me later, 'You should have seen this horse, Bob, it was gorgeous; a really beautiful animal, superb condition. I was dying to put some cash on its nose, or wherever it's supposed to go! And guess what, Bob,' she continued.

'Don't tell me,' I replied. 'It won the race.'

'No, it came third.'

'Well that's not bad,' I said consolingly.

'But,' she continued, 'there were only four horses in the race!'

Well that saved us a few bob; I refrained from telling her she could have placed a bet over the phone. Thank goodness for lack of knowledge!

MOT Time

The MOT was a month overdue. I'd forgotten all about it and the garage forgot to remind me. That's the problem when you get a reminder each year; you tend not to create safeguards, like marking the calendar or scattering notes everywhere. The only reason I did remember was a train of thought that led to the discovery. Eileen and I were returning from a shopping trip, when she reminded me that we were planning to drive up to West Hartlepool to bring her sister down for her annual two-week holiday. As they are Catholics, it meant a trip to Walsingham and, of course, other trips out.

In other words, a lot of motoring. This thought got me thinking about what sort of condition the car was in. Is it due for a service? was my next thought and as I tried to think when it was last done, my mind clicked into thoughts of that most dreaded time of the year: MOT time. At home, a search for the documents revealed that it was a month overdue.

'Can you get it in tomorrow?' was the mechanic's response to my phone call. He must have been feeling guilty, as he'd also missed that most memorable event that always creates hard cash for him.

The garage was 40 miles away. I know there are nearer places I can get it done, but this guy has done all the services and MOTs since Richard bought it for me. Also, it's only a couple of miles from Richard's place of work and it's the garage he's used for years. I set off at 7.00 a.m., planning to get there just before 8.00 a.m., but it turned out to be a journey from hell. Just a few miles from home I ran into stationary traffic – and I do mean stationary! Over the wireless came the traffic news and guess what? Yes, it told me that because of an accident there were long tailbacks of traffic on the road I was on. It was a possibility that had already occurred to me.

A few minutes earlier and I could have taken a detour, but as it was I was well and truly stuck and the news came too late to help both me and thousands of other motorists; well, it seemed like thousands. It took me an hour and twenty minutes to inch through and circumnavigate through the diversions set up to take us around the incident. Down the narrow and winding lanes, with an abundance of oncoming traffic, also being diverted from the other direction, I bobbed and wove my way through. Not the easiest place to navigate and the locals, not used to traffic, must have been gobsmacked at the interruption of their normally tranquil existence.

I finally made it and having been given a courtesy car, I cracked on with my return journey. The decision to try another route was a bad one. The A428 is a link road between the M11 and the A1. It's normally busy, but it's usually quite free-flowing. Not this time!

While the outward journey was cruel, the return one was wicked and I don't mean the modern meaning of the term. Once again, I sat, stationary, in a solid jam of traffic and once again, the wireless told me, oh too late, that an overturned lorry on the A14 had caused chaos and the problem had snowballed to the alternative routes, in particular the A428. I called Eileen on the mobile and related my sorry tale of woe. All she could say was, 'Don't forget we're going out with friends, so don't be late.'

As if I was in control! I was within ten minutes of the allotted time of our appointment with our friends as I drove into Kedington, when the mobile phone rang. I pulled over and a voice said, 'Where the hell are you? We have to be out; like now!'

'The A428,' I replied. I can't quite remember her exact words, but I interrupted her saying, 'Hang on, girl, hang on. We're moving!' I put the phone on the passenger seat, shouting as I drove off, 'We're moving! We're moving, hang on a sec, this isn't an automatic and I have to change gear.' I kept waffling on until I pulled on our drive.

I went into the house saying, 'Bloody hell, we've stopped again!' She was stood with her back to me as I opened the door and she turned to see who it was. Need I say more? In trouble again!

Bob Oliver

The Headliner

Traffic! If you haven't noticed, there's a lot of it about! I can't wait 'til I'm too old to drive and I can tell the great-grandchildren how "when I was a boy" … cars were few and far between. Horses and carts were still doing the rounds in our day, delivering coal, milk, etc. to houses. Indeed, some small businesses couldn't afford the luxury of a horse and had to push a handcart through the streets selling their wares. They'd like that one.

We kids used to hang around the Angel Pub, wait for the hawkers to stop in for their lunchtime pie and a pint and see what we could nick. Quite often, they would emerge from the alehouse, slightly worse for drink, and lurch off down the road pushing their barrow and swinging from side to side. Hence the saying "pissed as an 'an'cart!". But with little or no traffic on the roads, the only danger was to themselves.

Nowadays, it's an entirely different story, with everyone with their cars, lorries and motorbikes roaring around like people possessed. We live in a nice quiet little Suffolk village, where the traffic problems are nothing compared to London, Birmingham and other big cities. But that's not to say we're problem free. Oh no! We, too, have our fair share of traffic problems, with crazy drivers in too much of a hurry and without thought of the elderly and the kids on foot down narrow roads without footpaths.

About a mile away from our house is a large factory situated on a crossroads. One of my grandsons had a 15-mile bus trip to school and the bus picked up and dropped off at the crossroads.

Sometimes, I used meet the bus on its return journey and was truly shocked at the daily chaos at the crossroads. The time of the arrival of the kids coming home from school coincides with the factory turning out. I had for a long time thought that there was a great need for a roundabout at the crossroads, but it was really bought home to me as I sat waiting for the school bus, watching this dangerous cocktail of traffic as cars come pouring out onto the main road, where vehicles approached the crossroads at high speed. Add to this articulated lorries and school buses approaching, turning and stopping, and it's a blueprint for disaster, with only time to determine when a serious accident would occur.

It was the potential danger to the kids that stirred me into action.

I wrote a letter to my local MP and sent copies to all the appropriate authorities, including the local paper, who reacted first. Ace reporter "Scoop Hart" was knocking on my door for an interview shortly after, followed by the newspaper photographer, who took shots of me at the offending crossroads. I did, of course, object that they were being taken without the aid of a make-up artist and the wind made it very difficult to perform, causing havoc with my hair.

I honestly thought that my complaint would be relegated to a small corner of the sports page. But to my great shock and surprise, my picture was plastered all over the front page, with a full report and huge headlines reading: Action Needed at Danger Junction! I surely must have hit a slow news week. I also received a reply from the House of Commons – The Rt. Hon. Richard Spring nonetheless – thanking me and saying he would investigate. I waited, a little apprehensively, for the arrival of the autograph hunters and in fear of the paparazzi at my front door.

Instead, less than a week after I'd achieved the status of "the Headliner", the phone started ringing and I received a string of abusive calls. The first was from my eldest daughter. 'Thank you very bloody much, Dad!'

'What's up? What's up?' I retorted.

'Have you been down to the crossroads? Everyone is late for work. The traffic's tailed back for miles! There are workmen, diggers, compressors and cones by the thousands. They're ripping up the road, causing havoc, and it's all down to you!'

I tried to tell everyone that it couldn't have been me and it must have already been on the cards. No local council would act that quickly. But they weren't having any of it and no one could see the funny side – miserable gits!

In the meantime, I'd received another letter from the House of Commons, saying that the local authorities were to carry out work at the junction. Unfortunately, the local authorities had opted for the cheap option rather than a roundabout and all the inconvenience of weeks of roadworks resulted in a couple of islands and some signs that restricted your view of the oncoming traffic.

I wrote again to Richard Spring and said that my first thoughts about the changes were that it had been a waste of money. But not wanting to jump to hasty conclusions, I'd not only spoken to various people seeking their opinions, but I'd also observed the traffic at busy times at the junction. My second opinion was little, if anything, had been gained. Traffic still approached the junction at speed and now there was the facility for traffic turning right to enter a central reservation, it enabled the through traffic to blast through at speed, giving traffic entering the main road an even worse nightmare.

He swiftly replied and offered to meet me at the junction to take a look for himself. I have to admit: I didn't expect that response and was both pleased and surprised at his commitment.

True to his word, he came to my house and after a cup of tea and a chat we had photo shoot at the junction. I did say that now the money had been spent, I doubt that further funds would be available to spend on a roundabout that would have been the best option in the first place. We all know that there are more important things in the world than a roundabout, but it would become extremely important to friends and family of anyone killed or seriously injured at this dangerous crossing.

I received another letter from Richard Spring saying that he agreed with me and that he had written to the authorities, pointing out our concerns, but that he understood that the county council are under severe financial constraints.

I'm tempted to write back and say, can you not wonder at the county council having financial problems when they make such crass decisions like wasting 30,000 pounds on changes without improvement!

Bob Oliver

Scooters, Sparking Moments!

After the army in the late 1950s times were getting marginally better, rationing was no longer a consideration, jobs were aplenty and we were beginning to acquire things previously unheard of or just that bit out of reach of the majority; and, of course, that included motorised transport. My first beast was a Lambretta.

Eileen and I would burn rubber on and around the roads in our local area, putting the fear of Christ in any old dear unfortunate enough to be in the vicinity; this two-stroke engine was our very own throbbing monster. One sunny day we were returning from a great day in Southend, when our "'put-put" went "fut-fut" and we ground to a halt. I kicked it over and it burst into life, but every time we pulled away it conked out; but only when Eileen sat on the passenger seat, so I put her on a bus and I chugged along behind. She wasn't best pleased at this, as she was wearing all her scooter clobber, which didn't fit in with bus travel at that time.

The next day I consulted Dutchy, who was an expert on engines, having famously achieved a ton on the London North Circular Road on his Ariel Square Four; a feat my 150cc blue streak would never make. This consultation took place outside his house in the street in broad daylight so, as Dutchy deftly removed the side panels, he furtively glanced over his shoulder to make sure no one saw him touching this unworthy scooter. In the motorbike world it wouldn't do to touch a leprous scooter, unless of course you were kicking it.

Memoirs of a Working Man

His contempt was evident as he pointed to a wire and said, 'Listen, James Dean. This is a spark-plug lead and this is a spark plug and if they aren't connected, the petrol can't ignite.'

The lead had become disconnected and was merely resting on the plug; still sufficient to run with just me on it, but as Eileen got on the weight tilted the engine and caused the separation.

Dutchy later explained to Eileen that it was far too complex a problem for her to understand, but owing to his vast knowledge of the internal-combustion engine, he'd wrestled with the intricate problem and through sheer tenacity had figured it out and fixed it.

I can't believe she swallowed it, but she believed everything he said and I couldn't tell her the truth, as she wasn't best pleased with me after she'd been forced to ride home on a bus on a hot summer's day, fully kitted out for biking, with leather gauntlet gloves, helmet and carrying a stick of rock. My decision to change from mod to rocker and swap my Lambretta for a BSA 500 cc was nothing to do with image, because everyone knows that a duffel coat is far trendier than a greasy, clapped-out old leather jacket. No, my reason was a total lack of skill: I kept falling off every time it rained; and sometimes when it didn't. I was unsaddled more times than a bull rider in a rodeo and so it was that I made my first move forwards and took one step further towards my aspirations of owning a Jag; but that was a long way away.

Bob Oliver

Women Drivers

Women – can we do without them? Answer: probably not, but they're soft, cuddly, lovely little creatures with the ability to put you on top of the world, but my word, don't they just infuriate you at times. Especially their dubious driving skills. Anyway, my friend's Alfa Romeo broke down once and he asked me to tow him to a specialised garage about 14 miles away. When I saw the flimsy rope he proposed using I suggested that we use mine, as it was a great deal stronger, a proper tow rope. But being the Scottish bull-headed bugger he was, he insisted that we use his and so off we went.

All was well until we reached the Four Went Ways roundabout. I waited for my chance to move, which came when a very large articulated lorry approached from the direction of Cambridge on the 604. As soon as it stopped the flow of traffic pouring onto the roundabout I pulled onto it, taking the car I was towing with me, before it disappeared towards Colchester.

Just then a woman driver, who was obviously in a rush, burst onto the scene. From a standing start, she must have reached 40 mph in three seconds flat. She must have seen Jim pulling out and thought, right, it's my right of way, so out of the way – I'm coming through. She flashed between us breaking the tow rope that she obviously hadn't noticed.

I swivelled my head round and tried to gauge whether I should stop or whether Jim had enough momentum to get over the roundabout; all this crossed my mind as other motorists watched, stunned. I tucked my car on the verge and watched Jim slowly roll towards me. White-faced and trembling, he climbed out. 'Are you OK?' I asked and Jim nodded and said, 'Yes, but I need to go home and change my underpants.'

'Just think, you wouldn't have to change them if we'd used my stronger tow rope,' I said. 'We'd have been halfway to London in reverse by now.'

Meanwhile, the lady driver had pulled over, jumped out of her car, looked back at us, saw that we were in one piece, patted her hair, straightened her skirt, leapt back in her car and vanished into the distance.

Back-seat Drivers

Don't you just love back-seat drivers? I'm sure they cause more accidents than any other distraction encountered behind the wheel. Non-drivers are the best passengers, but as soon as they get the nod from the examiner, they assume far too much.

Youngsters who've just passed their test presume that because they have it in writing they're "experts" and so proceed to burn rubber and blast their horns at the steadier or older driver who, in their opinion, are holding them up. Then there are the drivers who've studied all aspects of being a good driver; they know the Highway Code backwards and have inwardly digested the "Good Driver Guide". To them, there are no grey areas.

My wife Eileen is one of the latter. A 30 mile an hour speed limit means 30 miles per hour, not 31. She continually tells me to slow down if I creep 5 miles an hour above the allotted speed limit. Have you ever tried to drive a Jag at 30 miles an hour? You would think one is parked up.

I try telling her it's just a guide and one has to use one's own initiative and drive according to the road conditions, which is something the police don't seem to understand, either. I wish someone would explain it to them.

Sometimes, her attention is drawn to other drivers. 'Look! Just look; he's driving along and talking on his mobile phone.' She considers that using a mobile while driving is against the law. I told her it's only against the law if you're caught! That was a joke – she didn't laugh. She loses her sense of humour when she sits in a car.

Then there are the occasions when I'm approaching traffic lights. You know the situation; you're 5 yards from the lights and they change, but naturally you carry on through. Her dulcet tones come from the seat beside you, 'You went through a red light!'

'The light was orange, sweetheart.'

'Rules! They just don't apply to you, do they?'

I tried to explain about the rules applying to traffic signals. Red and orange means go; green means go; orange means go; flashing orange means go; red means go with caution! I'm still not sure if she fully understands.

Back-seat drivers, eh! What can you do with 'em?

Duty-free

A few years ago Richard used to own a Saab. It was a big black beauty, turbo assisted with awesome power and was really rather comfortable. It had everything except an automatic gearbox and I loved to drive it and being a passenger wasn't so bad, either. To my great disappointment, he chopped the saloon for a more sporty-type; it was a soft-top convertible and in my opinion, not a patch on his first Saab – I like big cars with space and comfort.

Every time he picked me up for work I would find something to moan about and I was quite chuffed when he told me that ever since he'd come back from his holiday in France, the convertible hood wouldn't work. Never one to miss the opportunity to say "I told you so!", I said, 'I told you to stick with saloon type.'

Richard then asked me to get it checked out at the Saab dealers. The salesperson looked down his superior nose with obvious distaste as I entered his posh showroom. My dirty old work jeans, Wallace & Gromit T-shirt and grubby trainers – not Gucci – did little to impress him; not one little bit.

I chucked the keys on the counter and told him to get the heap repaired. Eileen has edited out my actual words, but my colourful description was flowered with profanities, though I did say it with a smile on my face to soften the blow. By the look on his face, he had never, ever encountered a cross word about any of his beloved Saabs and I left him with mouth agape.

When I went to pick it up the next day, the salesperson had regained his composure and was looking too smug for my liking.

'Ah yes, the convertible, sir.' The words came with contemptuous arrogance as he continued to relish in every word. 'Our first-class mechanics spent four hours testing the electronics and completing various other checks and were completely baffled, as there appeared to be nothing wrong. It was Mr Roberts our valet who found the problem. He discovered this jammed in the mechanism!' He pulled out from behind the counter a bottle of red wine. 'Duty-free, I assume, sir?'

An Exhausting Tale

David had a building business and as such he owns a few vans. Whenever anything goes wrong with them he gets a mechanic to repair the fault. Anyway, one of his vans had a faulty exhaust and he asked if he could leave it on my drive, so that the mechanic could come and fit a new one.

He rang this mechanic, who is a one-man band, and gave him directions to our house. I heard him tell the guy exactly where we lived and to look out for the lay-by with a bungalow in the middle. 'The house is white and the van is a red Renault and needs a new exhaust,' he explained.

The next day, I came home and the van had gone and so I assumed all had gone to plan. I didn't think any more about it until a few weeks later, when David told me that the mechanic was coming to fix the clutch on another of his vans that he'd parked outside our house.

When he arrived I thought I would go and make his acquaintance and as we chatted he asked me if David had told us about the exhaust incident on the other van. I said no, made him a cup of tea and sat and listened to his tale of woe.

Apparently, as he'd approached our village following David's instructions, he'd spotted a white house. It was on the wrong side of the road, but it was white and in a lay-by and outside was a red Renault van. Thinking that he'd found the right place, he stripped the exhaust from the van, chucked it in the back of his van and went back into town to get a replacement.

Meanwhile, the correct van owner came out of his house and started his van. You can well imagine the noise that came from the exhaustless vehicle. The irate owner immediately phoned the police, to report the theft of his exhaust in broad daylight.

A thorough investigation took place and all the usual suspects were rounded up. Anyone with a record for a fetish of second-hand, faulty and rusting pipes were taken into custody and grilled mercilessly. Even the local tyre and exhaust companies were interrogated, in case anyone had been trying to pedal a hot exhaust.

Anyway, Mick the mechanic had returned with a nice new exhaust and he proceeded to fit it to the van. The guy in the house saw Mick from his window and thought he was stealing something else from his van and immediately called the police again. Not content with waiting for the law to arrive, he decided to have a go himself. Bursting from the house, he proceeded to bombard poor Mick with a barrage of verbal abuse. Lying on his back, he peered out from under the van. Thinking it was me who was attacking him he called out, 'It's OK, guv'nor; I'm doing it for David.'

The van owner wasn't impressed and apparently couldn't give a toss if was doing it for the Pope. Naturally, his reply was splattered with an abundance of expletives. The police arrived and promptly arrested the guy giving out the verbal; a Brian Rix farce comes to mind. After some extremely confusing moments, Mick managed to convince all concerned that a genuine mistake had been made and the only loser was him, as it had cost him a great deal of time and the price of a new exhaust. The owner completely ignored Mick's pleas for the costs incurred and to add insult to injury, he insisted Mick clear his drive of the mess he'd made.

When I later asked David why he hadn't told me the story, he gave me one of his dead-pan looks and replied, 'I thought Mick wanted me to keep it a secret.'

Well, wouldn't you?

Punting in Cambridge on the Cam

Eileen's sister Lemmie and her husband Alfie came down from West Hartlepool for a few days. Cambridge was always the first place we took our visitors. The city is great, full of interesting characters, wonderful sights, buildings and excellent buskers; certainly a class above the beggar who blows on a penny whistle with little or no skill, but at least he tries to do something rather than just sitting there looking sad and asking for change.

No, these buskers were something else – from classical groups to the South American flute band and the Jamaican kettledrums. All great stuff. Quite often we saw a young American lad who played a guitar and sang songs from the sixties and seventies. He was only in his twenties, so the music he played was long before his time, but whenever I've asked him to sing a particular song, he's never ceased to amaze me by singing my request off the top of his head, without the music or the words to refer to. Then there's the river and the punts – had some great fun on these; indeed, two particular incidents come to mind.

Memoirs of a Working Man

We managed to talk Alfie, Eileen's sister's husband, into leaving the pub and got him in the punt with us. I was on the pole and he was on the paddle. As I propelled us downriver, Alfie was reluctant paddle, as this extended the distance between him and his next pint of beer waiting to be pulled in the pub he'd just so reluctantly vacated. Instead, he just dangled the paddle in the water and looked uneasy. After we'd had a nice long punt enjoying the sun and the views, with me doing all the work, I steered the punt around and headed back, when a metamorphosis occurred. Alfie took up the paddle and began to wield it into the water like a man possessed. As we rounded a bend in the river and the sight of the pub came into view, Alfie's strength seemed to do the impossible and the paddle propelled the punt at an unbelievable speed. This boy should be in the Olympics, I remember thinking.

As we closed in on the finish, devilment came over me. I had the pole and the pole determines the direction. So I swung the punt round, pointing it away from his goal. His face was a picture and his body language screamed volumes. His shoulders slumped, his lips disappeared into two white lines, his teeth ground in a grimace and his eyes burnt holes in my head. The girls laughed till they were fit to burst.

The second incident involved my sister Lily who had a bad experience in a swimming pool when she was just a kid and the experience has haunted her ever since in that she has an enormous fear of water. How we managed to talk her into a punt down the River Cam still has me puzzled; I can only think she must have had a vision of one of those huge gondolas in Venice when she'd agreed to partake.

As we approached the riverbank, I watched her face as she surveyed the scene of chaos and confusion with people milling around, embarking and disembarking from these skinny little boats as the man held the punt in place with a hook on the end of a pole. She clutched onto Des, her husband, like a leech, wide-eyed and fearful. We had three grandchildren with us and she obviously didn't want to show her fear to the children, so she put on a brave face and unsteadily mounted the punt.

We set off downriver and once again, we were lucky with the weather. It was a glorious summer's day and as we floated majestically along the Cam, propelled by yours truly, of course, another punt approached us from the opposite direction. Now this in itself wasn't unusual, because there were dozens of punts on the river. But this punt was approaching us in a zigzag manor. The pole person obviously wasn't in control and my sister began to panic. 'Bob! Look out, Bob. Look out! Look out!'

As they closed in on us, they began their pass within inches of us. On their punt were two very beautiful girls. 'Don't worry, Lily; it's obvious these lovely ladies need help.' I then jumped from our punt onto theirs and walked its length, with Lily frozen ridged and the grandchildren shouting, 'Get back over here, Grandad!'

As the two punts passed I leaped back into ours, to face a tirade of abuse from my camp and giggles from the other punt.

Peace was once again restored and we proceeded with tranquil calm along the picturesque River Cam and the words of Rupert Brooke came to mind from his poem *Old Vicarage, Grantchester*:

Say, is there Beauty yet to find?

And Certainty? and Quiet kind?

Deep meadows yet, for to forget

The lies, and truths, and pain? .... oh! yet

Stands the Church clock at ten to three?

And is there honey still for tea?

Senior Moments:

Getting Old; Better Than the Alternative

Having a senior moment has a particularly annoying effect on Eileen. Not sure if it's because we're in the senior-moment age group or whether it was because every time I opened my mouth there was a need for me to bring senior moments into the conversation, but she does ask for it.

Some time ago we were going to London and I asked her to phone my brother to let him know we were on our way. I glanced over, because she appeared to be having trouble with the mobile phone, and told her, 'Listen, dear, you might get BBC 2, but you'll never be able to get my brother on that thing you've got there!'

Yes, she was trying to make a phone call with the TV remote control! I'm glad mobiles have changed dramatically, so they no longer resemble the remote. Well, that was her excuse that they looked similar, but as far as I was concerned it was a senior moment.

But she's quick, repling, 'I wish I'd bought the television.'

'Why's that, dear?' I enquired all innocent-like.

'Because the mobile's on top of it!'

Eileen continually reminds me of many a senior moment, especially the time we went on holiday, leaving our suitcases on the drive. Well, I meant to put them in the boot, but got distracted when she asked me to go back in the house to make sure I hadn't forgotten anything. Mustn't grumble.

My problem is that inside, I still think I'm eighteen. It's when I look in the mirror and see this strange old man looking back at me that I begin to think that old Father Time has kept ticking away, without getting my permission. There are, of course, other pointers that destroy my delusions of youth. The need to stop during grass cutting, the grandchildren running rings round me while playing football in the garden – and that's the 7-year-old granddaughters – and then there are the twinges in the old back. I can find good excuses for most things, like, 'There's no rush, I can finish the grass later,' and 'You have to let the kids beat you at football; after all, you don't want to dishearten them,' and 'Backache. Oh, that's nothing. I always get backache when Eileen's pregnant!' Well, maybe not Eileen now, as she's been "done"; it must be one of the daughters – oh Gawd, I hope not; ten grandchildren is more than enough! We're now in the year 2009 and I suppose it won't be long before we get great-grandchildren.

I always put my other aches and pains down to either broken bones in my younger days or strains put on my body through football, squash and the like, but never, never down to the fact that I'm getting old.

Bob Oliver

Old Age is Upon Me!

I'm now convinced that old age is upon me. For some time now I've considered it quite normal and I often suspected I wasn't alone when I wandered round the house looking for my glasses that, unbeknown to me, are perched on my head. Then what about walking into a room, only to stop at the threshold and think, What the hell am I doing here and what am I looking for?

These things, I would say to myself, are quite common and it's nothing to be concerned about. But these past few weeks things have moved up a plane and this has me extremely concerned. The other day I was cooking breakfast. I'd set myself up, placing a bowl, some paper kitchen towel and half a dozen eggs on the work surface. Then I'd cracked open the first egg and tipped it into the bowl, placing the shell on the paper towel. Repeating the operation with methodical precision, I'd proceeded to cook breakfast. Eileen's convinced I have a touch of Asperger's syndrome, as I must have everything in its place and everything has to be neat and tidy. So I was shocked rigid when, coming to the fourth egg, I cracked it open, tipped its contents onto the paper towel among the egg shells and dropped the empty shell into the bowl of eggs.

Worrying; very worrying. That was incident number two – the first went as follows: we have one of those kettles that receives its electricity from a base, so that once boiled you remove it from its base and run round the kitchen with it, if that be your want. Anyway, I was making hot drinks for Eileen and some visitors and naturally, they all wanted a different drink: herbal tea, ordinary tea, hot chocolate, coffee, etc.

I'd completed the mission and everyone had their drinks and this just left mine. I popped a peppermint tea bag in my cup and depressed the kettle switch. After tidying everything up, cleaning the work surface, etc., I turned to the kettle to make my tea, only to notice it wasn't boiling. I studied the situation and clicked the switch several times, but the little light wouldn't come on. Has the power gone off? I thought to myself. But the electric clocks were still working, so once again I studied the kettle, thinking it must be the kettle that had blown.

Then it happened; the penny dropped and my faced glowed red with embarrassment! I hadn't placed the kettle back on its base. It stood just in front of it on the work surface and the electricity refused to cross the bridge! Oh dear; worrying; very worrying.

I quite like the following quote: Red Buttons once said, 'Old is when your wife says, "Let's go upstairs and make love," and you answer, "Honey, I can't do both!"'

Senility?

This is a true story and for once it wasn't me having the senior moment. It's about an old lady who lives down the road from us. She's in her eighties and the poor old girl'd had to have a leg amputated. She recovered from the operation remarkably well and I often saw her husband pushing her around the village in her wheelchair. A while back I stopped to have a chat and was amazed to see that she had a black eye; in fact, half of her face was black and blue.

'What the hell have you been up to, Maud?' I said.

She looked rather sheepish and her husband said, 'Go on then, tell him.'

'Well,' she replied, 'I was getting out of bed the other morning and forgot I didn't have a leg to stand on and crashed into the bed side cabinet!'

As Bette Davis said, 'Old age is not for sissies!'

In a Flap!

I came home from work to find a message on the answerphone from the better half. After work, I have a shower and zoom off to our daughter's for Sunday lunch. The answerphone message was telling me to hurry up, as dinner was ready and everyone was starving; waiting for me.

She put me in a flap – Eileen has that affect on me – so I quickly stripped and jumped in the shower, but for some strange reason my head stayed dry. I suppose it had something to do with me still wearing my hat.

Matalan Mayhem

In the year 2001 a well-meaning friend told Eileen that a clothes retail outlet called Matalan had opened a branch in Bury St Edmunds.

The chess AGM was a couple of months away and Eileen decided I was in need of smartening up. Blimey; she had more chance of seeing pigs fly. She told me I would have to wear socks, have a shave and go shopping with her to buy some clothes. Shaving wasn't a problem, as I do this at least once a week; but wear socks? Now that's where I put my foot down. I hate socks and I only wear them if forced. OK, so I was forced and what's more, I was instructed not to wear my old trainers.

I'd never before heard of Matalan. They call it a clothes shop, but Burtons it ain't. It's a bloody madhouse. I stood there completely bemused, watching women milling around aimlessly, holding garments against their hapless husbands, many of whom had the glazed, bored look of a female student attending a lecture about male supremacy. Eileen, completely at home in this – what I consider – alien environment, elbowed her way through the crowd, shoved some trousers into my hands, pointed towards the changing rooms and told me to try them on.

Naturally, there was a queue, but when it was my turn I was confronted by a large muscle-bound Amazon, who was sporting some sexually explicit tattoos, with body-piercing in places that must have hurt and been extremely uncomfortable; the young lady was also displaying the beginnings of a David Niven moustache. She looked at me and without a change in her expression, she just shook her head. I nervously glanced about to make sure her boss-eyed glare was, indeed, focused on me.

'You're in the wrong queue; this is for ladies!' she growled in a husky voice. Perhaps "she" was a "he"! After all, it's hard to tell these days.

As I shuffled away I noticed Eileen looking at me. She, too, was shaking her head, so I called out to her, 'What's up, then? That was a far more interesting queue.'

Finally, after another wait, I managed to find a cubical and disrobed. But what a shock. When I turned to look in the full-length mirror, starring back at me was this old man. Blimey!

it's me, I thought. 'Nah! can't be; I'm not that old. Am I?' I was talking to myself. Oh dear; that as well!

My self-esteem was dealt another blow when I was unable to zip up the fly; I had to go up two sizes. But what I really hated was Eileen insisting that I emerge from the changing room wearing the said garments, so she – and umpteen other nosy folk – could look me over, pass judgement and give the nod of approval or otherwise.

The worst thing to happen to me was when Matalan decided that a store within easy reach of Eileen was a good idea. Good for them – bad for me. No, that's not quite true. The worse thing was when they announced a half-price sale.

To say I hate shopping is a gross understatement, but "the order", by Noriega, came without compromise or any room for negotiation. Discussion was a fruitless exercise. She stated, 'They're having a half-price sale and *you* need new clothes.'

Not true; it's just not true. I already have two pair of jeans, two pairs of trainers, plenty of T-shirts, I don't wear socks and if she washes out my underpants every other day I have sufficient to meet my needs. She also wants me to have a suit, but I draw the line at these.

The only suit I've ever owned was the one I got married in – and that was in 1960. Not sure how old the suit was, because it was a gift from the army when I got demobbed in 1958 and Lord knows how long they kept the demob suits in those days; I suspect pre the Second World War. It was so smart I've never been able to match it.

On the way to the said sale, she said, 'If you won't have a suit, at least buy a nice jacket.'

'I already have a jacket, darling; you know, my Donegal jacket.' I was attempting to placate her.

'That Donegal jacket,' she replied caustically, 'is 30 years old!'

'But it's as good as new!' I protested.

'That's because you've never worn it.'

She did have a little more to say on the subject, but I'd switched off and sunk deeper into my already depressed state.

My depression turned into despair as the madness to greet us as we approached the store was nothing short of horrifying. On the other hand, Eileen's eyes sparkled with delight. What's wrong with women, are they sick or what?

The car park was chock-a-block, so there were cars parked along the adjacent roads, on the grass verges and in places where you would've never thought possible. After circling the car park, winding in and out of cars waiting for others to pull out, I decided that the best option was to park away from the store and walk into the mayhem in Matalan.

Trolleys were in short supply – or should I say as rare as hens' teeth. People were following shoppers with clothes-laden trolleys to their cars and pouncing on them as soon as they were emptied. I was posted at the exit door with instructions to acquire a trolley, while Eileen, mouth watering and with glazed eyes, pushed her way into the entrance. The last words

I heard her muttering was "Visa card!" Does that mean what I think it means?

With mouth agape, I surveyed the confusion and my eagle eye spotted an abandoned trolley. With catlike reactions and the speed of a compressed, curled spring being unleashed, I rushed forwards, pushed an elderly woman aside, tripped up a 10-year-old kid and grabbed the empty trolley. I looked around and dared anyone to attempt to lay claim to it. Little did it matter to me that it only had three wheels. Eileen, on the other hand, moaned all round the shop as she veered into people, collided into displays and cracked the shins of shop assistants. She wasn't interested in the perils I'd had to face to acquire this most treasured item; oh no, it was whinge, whinge, whinge!

'Try this jacket on; it comes with matching trousers,' she told me.

Now I know I'm no expert when it comes to clothes, but to me a matching jacket and trousers means but one thing and this little rabbit wasn't about to be snared. Another jacket was pushed into my hands. 'It makes me look like an old man,' I protested.

Her look was worth a thousand words! I know I'm no spring chicken, but there's no need to advertise the fact, is there? A compromise was in order, so I kitted myself out with a T-shirt and two pairs of underpants. Eileen selected herself an outfit, some bras, knickers, two pair of shoes and a handbag. Blimey! how many more handbags does she want?

The nightmare continued with the queue to pay and evacuate the premises – it was unbelievable. No doubt the half-price sale will be followed by an end of half price sale that'll run 'til the January sales that will start sometime in November. Why can't women be more like men?

The Brighton Belle

Mrs Mac is eighty-two, stands at 5 feet nothing in her 2 inch heels and is a lovely round and cuddly lady. Her son-in-law is my brother and he tells me that she's no angel. I don't believe him; she's lovely and I won't have a word said against her.

I know she called him at two in the morning to get her cat out of the neighbour's tree – big deal. OK, so the neighbour called the police because he thought Bill was a burglar and he therefore had to spend a couple of hours in the police station while they cleared him, but that could happen to anyone. Mrs Mac? Oh, she'd gone to bed.

Then one time she was on holiday in New Zealand and she fancied a chat, so she reversed the charges; it's only money, Bill! There were loads more incidents, but they were petty and easily explained, though one of her capers was really funny and even Bill smiles when he relates the tale.

Her pensioners' club had organised a trip to Brighton and when they arrived there Mrs Mac decided to take the train to Hove, which is a couple of miles away and holds many memories of bygone holidays to our heroine. She thought she'd go on her own and after a nice visit and some lunch, she would then walk the 2 miles back to Brighton – a walk she did many times with Mr Mac when he was alive years ago.

Alas, she got a little confused and started to walk in the opposite direction. After a while she must have looked lost and bewildered, because a kind policeman spotted her and went to her assistance. He assumed she was staying in one of the local hotels and said he'd take her there if she'd tell him its name. She was by now a bit nervous and couldn't tell him where she was staying and had forgotten that she was only on a day trip, so the officer took her to the station to sort things out.

After countless cups of tea and lots of questioning, the only information was that her daughter lived in Cheshunt and was named Doreen Oliver. They put their best man on the job and he went through the directory one by one reading out the addresses and finally the penny dropped with Mrs Mac and she confirmed her daughter's address. Then it was just a question of getting them on the phone.

'We've found your wandering ma-in-law and were wondering which hotel she's staying at, so that we can safely deliver her. We've rung round all the local hotels and they've no record of her.'

As Mrs Mac wasn't staying in a hotel and neither Bill nor Doreen had any information on the organisers of the coach trip, they were therefore unable to give the police any information. The police, in turn, politely suggested that they pop down to Brighton and pick Mrs Mac up. After all, it's only it's only about 100 miles each way!

It didn't matter to Doreen that she had to cancel a planned day out, because her mum was more important; but Bill was due to play a highly prestigious golf match and asked the constable if they could put her up for the night or, alternatively, if they could put her on a train.

The officer didn't have a chance to reply, because Doreen snatched the phone from Bill and said, 'We'll be down as soon as possible.'

As you would expect, Bill moaned all the way and it didn't help matters when, upon their arrival at the cop shop, Mrs Mac said, 'You took your time getting here, didn't you?'

Doreen was concerned that the coach trip organisers would be worried when her mum went AWOL, but the police assured her that the information would go on their computer and in these cases the police are always contacted. No matter what station in the area they go to, the details would be on file.

Mrs Mac slept all the way home and when they arrived back, she remarked that she hadn't had much of a trip and that her day had been spoilt. All that my unfeeling brother of mine had to say was, 'It didn't do too much for my bleeding day, either, Mum.' Me, me, me!

An old lady who lives near Mrs Mac, who was also on the trip, arrived back some time later and was amazed to find Mrs Mac already at home. Apparently, the organisers had reported her loss to the police station and a search of the area was instigated. But, surprise, surprise, no Mrs Mac. The coach trip was by now running late and the organisers had fifty other oldies to think about, so couldn't hold back any longer, leaving the problem with the local police. So much for computer communications; there had to have been a breakdown somewhere. For Bill this was the last straw and he never did forgive his mother-in-law.

Eileen's Night Out

Wonders will never cease. I took Eileen to the theatre. Hairdo, posh frock, new shoes – and that was just the men. As we stood in the queue, I whispered to Eileen, 'I wish I'd bought the piano.'

'Why's that?' she replied.

'The theatre tickets are on it!' I explained.

Bald is Beautiful

It's a fallacy that you lose your hair when you grow old. I shed my locks before I was thirty and I've had over forty years of no combing, no washing and no barbers. The time saved is immeasurable and it's always been a wonderful fascination for not only the grandchildren, but also my own kids.

I can remember going to the school to pick up one of my daughters. She'd had several other kids with her and when I arrived, she said, 'Dad, Dad, take your hat off!'

This I did and all the other kids gasped in amazement and my little angel turned to them and said, 'There, I told you my dad didn't have any hair!'

When I was young I found that other people were more concerned than me regarding my lack of thatch. My reply was always, 'I've no intention of wasting my hormones on hair; I've got better things to do with them!'

The Funeral. "No Flowers, Please!"

The funeral of my niece's husband was in London and while it was a sad occasion, it was great to get together with friends and family.

Because it was a Friday, the traffic was heavier than normal. Making it worse was what always seems to happen at funerals; it was sheeting down. The phrase "hell on wheels" comes to mind. The crematorium is like a production line: wheel them in, say a few words and then next, please. And our funeral caused the crematorium staff some anxiety, as the cortège was late. Apparently, the hearse had a puncture en route and the already horrendous traffic was placed in turmoil.

Tony, my niece's husband, always a guy that loved a laugh and a joke, would have really enjoyed the fact he was the instrument of such chaos and most of all, causing the funeral directors a deal of agitation. The mourners waited and the men in black paced, trying to look calm and unruffled, with one eye on the entrance and the other on their watches.

At a given signal, the chapel doors were opened and we were herded in. Our bums had hardly touched seats, when we were told to stand as the cortège made their entrance. I couldn't help noticing that the pace was a tad quicker than usual: the coffin was deposited on the altar, the vicar appeared, said a few words – 'The Lord giveth and the Lord taketh away; ashes to ashes and dust to dust.' – he threw a switch and then Frank Sinatra began to sing I Did it My Way. Before he got to, 'I must face the final curtain,' the side doors opened and the ushers appeared and suggested we move out of the chapel to view the flowers, of which we had to look at other peoples, as Tony had strictly requested "No Flowers; all donations to the Heart Foundation".

Goodbye, Lem

When Eileen's sister Lem died, we had to trek north to Hartlepool for the funeral. It was the fourth funeral in six months. I suppose it goes with the territory of being the youngest of large families and both Eileen and I fall into this category.

Naturally, Eileen was very upset. They were very close and her death was sudden, but the funeral was just as Lem planned it, even down to the hymns and her favourite priest Father Tom, who said the mass for her. We'd booked into a B & B and once we'd unpacked and settled in I rang Eileen's eldest niece, who was organising the funeral. Her husband Big Billy insisted that we went round for a cup of tea. Billy is 6 foot 4, built like a brick shithouse and has a face that's well lived in. I can only describe his face by saying he resembles a cross between Jack Palance, Ernest Borgnine and Victor Mclachlan. He's a giant of a man and is as hard as nails, but you couldn't wish for a nicer guy and to see him with babies is a revelation.

Over the years they've visited us on many an occasion and whenever I think of Billy I remember us walking into the local snooker hall, with me leading the way and Billy following. At one of the tables was a friend of mine and he was just getting down to make his shot, when out of the corner of his eye he spotted me. He lifted his head, saying, 'Hello, Bob.' Then he stopped, with mouth agape, as out of the gloom of the snooker hall appeared Billy, like a kraken surfacing from the sea. Jim spoke not a word, just tilting his head slightly and rolling his eyes to me in a questioning manner.

With a gesture over my shoulder, using my head and my thumb, I said, 'This is my minder, Jim.'

Now my mate Jim is a bit of a rough diamond himself and he isn't easily fazed, so his comment was even funnier than normal as he replied, mouth still agape and wide eyed, 'Can 'e be my minder as well, Bob?'

To give you an even better idea of Billy's persona, when I walked down our local high street with him I watched people's faces as they quickly crossed the road to avoid face-to-face contact. If only they knew that behind that huge frame and craggy features is a pleasant, amiable guy.

But back to Hartlepool. We said our hellos in the kitchen and as we milled around I noticed, through the open door into the living room, that Billy had acquired a huge aquarium with an abundance of exotic fish. The sight lured me into living room and as I admired its beauty, the corner of my eye was attracted to another sight that was totally unexpected. It was an open coffin and there lay Lemmie. It didn't look like her, but it was.

It's the normal thing in the North and in many other places to have the body laid out for people to say their goodbyes, but it isn't common practise in the South of England and the first time we ever got to see the coffin down south was when it arrived at the church or chapel.

As I looked, Eileen entered the room, also attracted by the aquarium, but unlike me she immediately saw the coffin, burst into tears and ran back into the kitchen crying. Emma, unaware, said, 'What's the matter, Mum; did those fish upset you?'

You're 'avin' a Laugh

Well-man Clinic

Every now and then Eileen gets a bee in her bonnet about a check-up and as I'd been feeling a bit low she told me that she'd booked me in at the well-man clinic for an examination. This is where they measure you, weigh you and check you out for cholesterol, prostrate, diabetes, blood count, blood pressure, etc. It doesn't bother me and it keeps Eileen happy, but what did bother me was the fact that I was told I was 2 – 2, mind you – stone overweight. Can you believe that; skinny me, 2 stone overweight!

I told the nurse, 'You're 'avin' a laugh!' I went on to inform her that if I lost 2 stone I would be 10 stone and that I was 10 stone when I came out of the army fifty-one years ago. I didn't have an ounce of fat on me and I was as fit as a flea. And if she thought that at the age of 71 I should be the same weight as I was when I was 20 years old, she's definitely 'avin' a laugh.

When I told Eileen, she laughed. I told her it wasn't a laughing matter and asked her when her appointment was.

'Oh!' she said quite coyly, 'I haven't got an appointment; that was for you, you fat git!'

Over the next few days my condition steadily worsened, so Eileen booked me in to see a doctor, who didn't perform an examination but just listened to what I had to say. She told me she had the results of my blood test and said they were fine. Prostrate spot on; sugar fine; cholesterol great. The doctor in her infinite wisdom didn't read on and she sent me away with advice to take two paracetamol three times a day with food. If she'd read on, she would have seen that my white blood cells were high. This, I now know, tells the doctor that my body was fighting an infection.

The next couple of weeks were purgatory as my condition slipped further into the mire. Eileen decided enough was enough and so she booked me in to see the doctor again. Fortunately for me it was a different one, who did examine me and who also read the report on my blood test thoroughly. She immediately put me on a course of antibiotics and took another blood sample.

I finally felt I was on the mend; further blood tests showed that the antibiotics were doing their job and my white blood cells were back to normal. Though she had discovered that I was anaemic and so had prescribed a course of iron tablets. But the doctor still wasn't satisfied, because she didn't know why I was anaemic, and so she arranged for me to go to hospital for further tests. She told me that she would arrange two appointments for me, one where they insert a camera up my backside that is known as a barium enema and the other was for an endoscopy, involving a camera being shoved down my throat. I said to the doctor, 'Please, doc, if they use the same camera can I have the endoscopy first?'

Not so much of a hint of a smile came from her, just, 'It all depends when they can fit you in, Mr Oliver!'

In the meantime I was feeling a little better and was getting fed up with weeks of being shut up in the house, so I decided to go for a walk round the village. Big mistake, after weeks of inactivity I overdid it and tore a muscle in my leg. Oh woe is me! So it was back to being incarcerated in the house again. The pain was unbearable; we tried rubbing in gel and heat treatment, but all to no avail. After a couple of sleepless nights, Eileen got me an appointment with the weekend emergency doctor, who told me I'd torn a muscle – always nice to have second opinion. The doctor prescribed anti-inflammatory tablets and painkillers. I'd already tried painkillers, but because I'd been taking them throughout my illness they'd lost their effectiveness.

After another twenty-four hours of continual pain, Eileen suggested that instead of heat that had proven useless, perhaps we could try a cold compress. I was in such a state that I would even have agreed to an amputation, so Eileen took hold of a packet of frozen peas and strapped them to my leg. The effect was nothing short of miraculous. After just ten minutes the pain subsided and as long as I sat still I was pain free. The relief was wonderful. OK, I could still hardly walk and hobbling along was painful, but to be pain free while sitting still was truly magnificent. Pain relief courtesy of Captain Birdseye! what more can I say.

My first appointment at the hospital for the anaemia problem was looming fast, but before this could take place I had to attend a pre-consultation interview. For the innocents among you who are unaware of what a barium enema is I will explain.

Barium and air is pumped into your bowels and X-rays are taken from all angles.

The consultation interview was, I thought, just a question-and-answer session to ascertain if I was fit enough to have it done and for the most part it was. Until that is the lovely young nurse said, 'Right, Robert, I have just a couple of checks to do; go behind the screen, take off your trousers and lay on the bed on your left side.'

Why one has to go behind a screen is beyond me. As she was inserting a "hose pipe" up my backside I said, with eyes watering, 'Tell me, nurse; what do you say when people ask you what you do for a living?'

She had to pause from what she was doing while she had a good laugh and then said, 'First, I say I'm a nurse; if they pursue it and I start to explain, they decide they don't really want to know, after all.'

After she'd finished her inspection of the inside of my rear end, she removed her equipment and said, 'Stay there, I've just got to wipe the ointment off.'

'There!' I said. 'That's what you can tell them. You wipe old men's bums!'

All was well with the consultation interview, so she booked me in for the real thing. Now, for the real thing one has to have a day of preparation the day before the actual event. Looking back, I can honestly say that the prep day was worse. You have a strict diet to follow, but that was the easy part. The tough part was the evil mixture you had to drink at 8.00 a.m. and 5.00 p.m. This can only be described as a Jekyll and Hyde blend.

You mix the powder with a little water and the mixture then gets hot; unnerving or what? Then you have to leave for five minutes, before adding water to make it up to a half a pint, and drink it down.

Within the hour you're making a rapid approach to the "littlest" room. Fortunately for me we have a downstairs loo. Even so, I only just made it in time. I did survive the prep day and the next day it was back to the West Suffolk Hospital for the barium enema.

We booked in and a rather butch, stocky, muscular-looking lady called my name and beckoned me to follow. Still struggling to walk because of my strained leg muscle, I hobbled along behind thinking, will it be she who'll do the deed? She led Eileen and me to another waiting room with a row of changing rooms along one side.

Attila gave me a garment that had an opening at the rear; she explained that it's where the opening had to be, naturally. She also gave me a dressing gown – a saucy little number that just covered my bum; just as well with the design of the inner garment. It was a little too feminine for my own personal taste and the floral pattern was badly faded. Oh yes, and there was the shopping basket. No, no, this was for my clothes that I had to take with me.

After changing I emerged from the dressing room into a crowded waiting room, swinging my shopping basket nonchalantly. Placing my hand Noel Coward like in the dressing gown I began to sing *A Room with a View and You*.

Unfortunately, only Eileen laughed, while the other patients obviously thought I was an escapee from the nearby asylum and put their heads down and refused to make eye contact. Finally, it was my turn to be done and Attila escorted me into a room where three – yes, three – young, rather good-looking girls waited to look after me. I'm sure I saw one rubbing her hands together in anticipation. How come it's always young girls that do these jobs?

The barium enema examination wasn't that bad once you got over the embarrassment of young girls putting Gawd only knows what up your bum. But I couldn't help smiling when I was told to give a little cough to assist the camera's evacuation!

On a lighter note, this illness helped me to lose a stone and Eileen was dead jealous of my flat stomach, so she got busy cooking me fruit pies and rice pud to fatten me up again; wish I'd had the appetite to eat it, but hopefully that would come soon.

I told Eileen, 'I'm going to earn a fortune; I've discovered how to lose weight. Just stop eating!'

After the barium enema came the endoscopy. I was told I couldn't eat or drink for four hours before the appointment time at 8.30 a.m. This meant if I wanted to have something to eat and drink close to the deadline, I would have to be up at 3.00 a.m. Now I know I'm an early riser, but not that bloody early and besides, who wants to eat at that time of night?

We had our evening meal at 5.00 p.m., knowing full well that I could easily last without food until mid morning the next day. Drink was the real problem. I don't like to drink anything after 7.00 p.m.; otherwise, I would be up and down all night visiting the loo. But to get up in the morning and not have my usual drink of tea is really alien.

We arrived at the hospital just after 8.00 a.m., whereupon a nurse immediately took me aside for a question-and-answer session and then escorted me back to the waiting room. She told me the endoscopy only took five minutes, that I was second on the list and that the doctor started at 9.00 a.m.

It was twenty to nine, so I thought this is great, I'll be out of there by half past nine. Anyway, half past nine came and went. Ten o'clock came and went. Half past ten came and went. Then the news filtered through that the doctor was stuck in a traffic jam on the A14, but he'd phoned in and he was on the move. The waiting room, meanwhile, was full of starved and thirsty patients waiting for a most unpleasant experience to be performed on them. Not my happiest of times.

Finally, the doctor arrived and the first patient was taken in for fifteen minutes. At 11.45 a.m. it was my turn.

I told the doctor, 'Listen, doctor; I know you're all behind, but I don't want you rushing things and all those patients out there in the waiting room have all the time in the world.'

But I should have saved my breath, as he was completely devoid of any sense of humour. He just grunted, 'I never rush.' I thought to myself, yes, I know that from the time you arrived at work.

The actual deed wasn't so bad. A little unpleasant to begin with, but once they got it down it was fine. Someone likened it to swallowing a boiled sweet. Then it was back to the waiting room within ten minutes, desperate for a cup of tea. But I was advised to wait for an hour longer, so that the anaesthetic they'd sprayed onto my throat wore off. Boy did that tea taste good when the allotted time came round. Fortunately, I didn't get the sore throat that they said I might.

After a couple of weeks I got the results, but the mystery still remained and I'm none the wiser about what caused my problem. At least the torn muscle in my leg had healed nicely. The good news is that the tests all came out fine and they found nothing untoward either up my backside or down my throat, so it's nice to know that there's something normal about me, but it's very frustrating not knowing what caused it. I'm still taking blood tests on a regular basis, checking on my anaemia and investigating why I'm anaemic, but I suspect I'll never know the full story. You have to be tough to go through old age and there certainly isn't any room for sissies.

Apart from that first doctor I saw, who put me through an unnecessary fortnight of pain and misery, I have nothing but praise for our National Health Service. I suppose we're very lucky to live in an area where we have three excellent hospitals and the second doctor I saw was so on the ball that the incompetent one paled into insignificance.

Apart from one or two minor illnesses – and I'm not talking about sporting injuries and the like – I've sailed through life unhindered by any problems and, in fact, I have had little time for people suffering in one way or another. But not any more. I'll never take good health for granted ever again and I'll be more sympathetic towards others.

The Trouble with Eileen

Eileen was a volunteer at our local hospital, where they were testing various effects on the link between blood pressure medication and diabetes. She's on medication for a blood pressure problem herself, but apart from that she's as healthy as a horse and so was a perfect candidate for this experiment.

I took her to the hospital on Wednesday for her four-hour session of blood tests, etc., while I went for a walk. Then it was back to the car to listen to the radio, study some chess variations and have a kip while they did the business on her.

Now at this point I need to explain that Eileen, from time to time, normally every three or four weeks, has an attack of palpitations. These normally last for five or six minutes and then her heart rate and pulse return to normal; or as normal as one can get with Eileen.

Back in the hospital Eileen, having starved since 10.00 p.m. the night before, was given an obnoxious drink that she tells me is truly vile. The nurse then proceeded to do different tests and at various intervals she drew small quantities of blood. Then she was left to read her book for about half an hour before the procedure started over again. Now it's a mystery why these palpitations occur, but this time it happened in the ideal place. Eileen, who is very used to these happenings, calmly called the nurse and said, 'I'm just having an attack of palpitations, nurse, it'll soon pass.'

Before she knew where she was, she was flat out on a bed surrounded by a team of medical staff and she was sure the cleaner was also in there somewhere. Quickly, the screens encircled her and a handsome doctor at her side began frantically undoing the buttons on her blouse, while an ECG machine was dragged into the bedside area and all manor of wires were attached to her personage. At this point in time all Eileen was thinking was, typical – I haven't got my best underwear on.

By the time they got the machinery in place, as she predicted, the palpitations had passed and the look of disappointment on their faces was tangible, as they wanted to record this event for their files. Anyway, the drama was over and the pulse, blood pressure and heart rate were completely back to normal, having risen to over 200.

Eileen being Eileen was embarrassed by this event and she kept apologising for the inconvenience. Mr Handsome Doctor waved her apology away and thanked her for her cooperation, but she replied, 'No, doctor, thank you. How many women of my age can boast that they've had their blouse ripped open by a handsome young man? And next time, for your convenience, I'll replace the buttons with Velcro!'

Let's Get Serious

I'd had a frozen shoulder and was going to see the doctor, when Eileen said, 'While you're there, get him to have a look at your waterworks.'

I think most men have this sort of problem, but aren't keen to discuss it. Let me explain: you want to go to the toilet, but all you do is stand there, wanting and waiting; waiting and wanting. Then, if you're lucky, you manage a little sprinkle. Thinking that's it, you prepare to leave, when suddenly your brain tells you – wait. It's not over. There's more. You stand there alone in the loo, dejected and very miserable, thinking that you're getting old and your body is cracking up.

You don't go to the doctors because you've read all about the prostrate gland and its precise and detailed location. It's alright for women, as they're used to being investigated in all those extremely private places, but we men don't like that sort of thing, Anyway, I went to the doctors and after he'd examined and treated my frozen shoulder, I plucked up enough courage to mention my waterworks.

'OK,' he said, 'go behind the screen, take off your trousers, get up on the bed and face the wall with your knees drawn up to your chin.'

'Oh dear me.' I let out a moan of impending doom.

Climbing up on the bed I lay on the cold, clammy sheet and with my teeth firmly clamped on my right knee, I listened as he put on the rubber gloves. Was he giggling? I could swear he was giggling! So this was how he got his kicks.

'Relax, Mr Oliver.' Was he taking the mickey or what? 'Are you ready, Mr Oliver?'

The question generated goosebumps on my goosebumps, but I closed my eyes and gritted my teeth.

'Relax!' He was definitely taking the old mickey.

My God! was that his finger or a 10 ton truck entering my rear end?

'Er, doc,' I groaned, 'that's not the Blackwall Tunnel!'

After I got dressed he explained there was a year's waiting list for a prostrate operation. 'What do you think then, Mr Oliver, shall I book you in?'

Bob Oliver

'What I think, doctor, is that after all we have been through, don't you think you should stop calling me Mr and start calling me Bob?'

It took nearly a year for me to get to see a specialist, but I wasn't in a hurry, even though going to the toilet was always an adventure.

My first visit to the specialist was a repeat performance of the doctor and I wished I could have cut out the middle man. The specialist told me that it wasn't that big. I told him, 'Listen, doc, can we keep this between me and you, as my wife is convinced that I'm hung like a donkey!'

'No, no, Mr Oliver. Your prostrate isn't enlarged; your problem is with the neck of the bladder.'

He told me that he would arrange for me to have further tests, but of course it would take a few months before he could fit me in.

'Oh dear, what a pity,' I told him and went out feeling quite relieved, thinking that a few months was a long way off. But it soon came round and I was back again.

Before my tests I had to drink my fill of fluids and when I was bursting, a gorgeous young nurse gave me a scan. This is a rather nice little test, apart from one's bladder being at bursting point. You lay on a bed and the nurse covers your belly with K Y jelly; talk about jelly on your belly: Oooo baby. She then proceeds to pass a gadget across your personage, to check of all your internal organs: liver, kidneys, bladder the lot.

I had a good laugh when I was waiting to go in, for there were four people in front of me when I arrived; an old man and three young ladies. The door to the scan room burst open and out ran a rather large woman and with great haste she made for the toilet. We all looked at each other knowingly.

The old boy was next to go in for his scan and I honestly didn't think he was going to make it, let alone the examination and the repeat trip back out to the loo. He stopped three times on the way to the door and each time I scanned the floor for a puddle. About twenty minutes passed and then we were treated to a repeat performance of the large lady, except that the old boy was quicker. I would have never thought him capable of such speeds; it just shows you how adept the human body is.

The next two young ladies came and went without too much fuss, but the funniest was yet to come with the last of the young ladies. By this time I knew the pattern and was counting the minutes for my turn. I wasn't, yet, that desperate, but I was a little concerned when she exceeded my idea of how long she should have been in there.

I watched a woman come into the area and go to the loo. I read the situation as the door to the scan room opened and out came the girl, who calmly made her way to the toilet, with an air of, "I'm in control"! Her face was a picture as the realisation crept across her features – her eyes widening, her nostrils flaring and her mouth dropping open in disbelief – when she discovered the Ladies was engaged! She was suffering.

Like the gent that I am, I came to her rescue. Striding manfully over, I told her that there wasn't anyone in the Gents and that I would stand on guard for her. She didn't need any persuading and in she went.

Anyway, I got distracted by a bloke in a wheelchair and was assisting him into the disabled toilet, when this red-faced old man appeared from nowhere with his flies undone and gushed forth into the Gents.

It wasn't my fault and I tried to explain to the girl when she reappeared, but she couldn't have cared less if a regiment had been in there. She was now back in control, with an empty bladder. I can understand why they don't have locks, just an engaged sign, but it is inconvenient.

The next step for me, after the very pleasant experience of the scan, wasn't so pleasant.

'Go behind the screen, get undressed and climb up on the bed,' the young nurse instructed me. I could think of times when this sort of invitation might well have been desirable, but I could only think. Oh no, here we go again. Knowing full well that the doctor was going to do cold, clinical, nasty things to me, I wasn't at all H.A.P.P.Y. The next twenty minutes of my life was among the worst moments I've ever experienced and I wondered why they even afforded me the privacy of a screen to get undressed behind.

Without anaesthetic, they sent in a camera crew into my bladder via the small hole that I pee through and after taking a few shots of the less pretty scenery they pumped me full of water. I guess, though, that it was slightly more unpleasant when they beat a retreat from the battle scene than the initial advance, with only a little KY jelly for help.

With my bladder bulging to capacity, I was told to pee into a machine, so they could measure the flow. I stood pointing "Percy", expecting a Noah-like flood, but to no avail. It was a strange feeling, as I was absolutely chock-a-block, but nothing would come.

I was reassured by the specialist, who told me that as the muscles began to relax I would be able to pass water. What he didn't tell me was the pain that I was about to experience would give me a headache. Well, wouldn't your head ache if you headbutted the ceiling?

He told me that I needed a small operation on the neck of the bladder. Hang on a minute! I thought. Didn't he tell me that after that last examination? And has all this been really necessary? But you never ask these people these questions, you just smile or, in my case, grimace and nod your head like an idiot. He also told me it might be as long as a year before it was my turn.

'Listen, guv'nor; I'm in no hurry,' I told him.

The year went by in the wink of an eye and then I was once again back at the hospital, but this time was for real: pyjamas, toothbrush the lot.

I pushed Eileen and my daughter out of the door of the hospital, because they were completely devoid of sympathy and were only content in my ridicule. They had a great deal of knowledge of gynaecology and thought it quite entertaining that it was my turn. I, on the other hand, was not amused.

My first task in hospital was to produce a sample of urine. The nurse went into great detail on how I should perform this little task and then she gave me a box and a bottle and said, 'I want you to start by doing some in the bottle and then put your mid-flow urine in the box and the rest in the bottle.'

I took the box and the bottle into the toilet and fulfilled the function. On the wall of the toilet was a notice saying "Place a bag over your sample". Well, it's a stupid idea to have an open box for a urine sample. In my attempt to place the box in the bag, it slipped and the box upended itself and landed face down on the floor. After I'd cleaned up I tipped some from the bottle into the box and said, 'Sod it!' Nothing was said and they seemed quite happy with what they got.

There were times during my stay that I wished that I'd chickened out, but as the specialist told me, it would only be a matter of time before it caught up on me, so I thought I'd better brave it through. The anaesthetist missed the vein in my left hand and had to try the right hand, but I didn't have time to worry where next he might try if he'd missed that one, because the next thing I remember is a fog in the recovery room and to my great disappointment, there were no out-of-body experiences; just oblivion.

As soon as I could I was up and walking about. I found that sitting for a short while created a build up of fluid and when I rose to my feet to stretch my legs, something happened. After about forty seconds, I suffered excruciating pain as the fluid drained away and unfortunately, the catheter was unable to cope with the fluid, which would leak from the join. I was caught short the first time, but thereafter I would wrap tissue around the join and make a dash for the toilet, pushing the contraption holding my drip and carrying my unsavoury bag.

Arriving at the toilet, I just about had time, although it was touch and go, to discard my dressing gown. Frantically dropping my pyjamas, I would attempt to direct the flood down the loo, while banging my head on the wall and suggesting that all and sundry were of doubtful parentage. I had strange looks from a lady in the ward opposite the loo, but I think it was because of the frequency of my visits and not that she'd heard any of my ranting. What I do remember is that the pain was indescribable.

The specialist, beautiful young assistant, listened with such patience and understanding while I poured out my concerns over the effects that the operation might have to my special equipment. She being so young must have thought it obscene that an old man like me would be so concerned about that sort of thing and my three daughters say, 'Surely, Dad, you're not still doing that.' To my great relief, the young assistant explained that my playground would be unaffected.

The hospital and staff in Bury St Edmunds were great, from the specialist right up to the top; not to mention the cleaners and the tea ladies. Although I thought I detected a slight smile on the face of that lovely night nurse as she pulled out my catheter – a pain worthwhile after what I'd been through; just to get rid of that bag was really great. Having said that, I know that my problem was oh so minor compared to many that I encountered during my stay. You don't have to look very far to realise how lucky you are.

My granddaughters were too young, but the three grandsons all had funny things to say. Sam said, 'Have your eyes stopped watering yet, Grandad?' Apparently, he'd heard Sally saying to her husband David, 'I bet that made his eyes water!'

And Jack said, 'Were you dead, Grandad?'

While Joe said, 'Have you got hair now, Grandad?'

Bob Oliver

Grandma's Little Problems

November 2008 saw a week not to remember! Oh what a week it was; it really was such a week, etc., etc. Grandma had to have two operations: one on her booby and one on a birthmark on her head. The booby one was because of blockages and infections and the birthmark one was because it had turned nasty and was on the verge of turning into something worse. With our experience of the NHS, I can honestly say I won't hear a bad word said about them.

I know we were fortunate enough to live near Cambridge and have Addenbrooks Hospital, but in addition, the Bury St Edmunds Hospital is also excellent and Newmarket sees to our X-rays and the efficiency there is also brilliant. And all are within easy reach.

After preliminary examinations, scans, X-rays, blood tests and so on, the surgeons decided sooner rather than later was the order of the day, as both procedures were potentially problematic. The one drawback was that Eileen was being treated by different surgeons at different hospitals for the two ailments. The result being that Eileen received notification from Addenbrooks Hospital for the booby op and a few days later got the notification from Bury St Edmunds for the removal of the birthmark. This caused a little consternation on our part, as both operations were scheduled within two days of each other. The booby one on a Tuesday and the removal of the birthmark on the Thursday.

We considered postponing the Thursday op, but Eileen was concerned that if she did, it would put her to the back of the queue, so we decided to go for broke. We later found out after that under the circumstances, she would have been rescheduled sooner rather than later, as soon as a reasonable recovery time had elapsed from the booby op, but unaware of this she went ahead and had both ops done in the same week. Grandma did suffer, but was glad to get both over and done with.

I had to get Eileen to Addenbrooks Hospital on the Tuesday at 7.30 a.m. Going into Cambridge at that time of day is a nightmare, but we'd done it so many times before that I was prepared and knew I had to be patient and shunt along with the tailbacks of traffic. At the hospital they are so well organised: first, you book in, then she was checked over by a nurse for blood pressure, etc., and after the anaesthetist has a chat, followed by the surgeon.

The surgeon made a thorough examination of her boob and after discussing the operation said, 'Have you any questions, Eileen? I may call you Eileen, I take it?'

Eileen replied, 'Well, doctor, I think after what we've been through darling is more appropriate!'

From the main waiting room you're then moved into the inner waiting room and there she was decked out in the most becoming nightdress that one could ever imagine in your wildest dreams. Into the operating theatre she strolled and Eileen told me afterwards that she was doing what she does best: non-stop talk one moment and the next she was regaining consciousness with a nurse holding her hand.

An hour later we were winging our way home. Years ago it would have meant at least a week in hospital. Eileen hadn't recovered fully when on the Thursday, just two days later, we were on our way to The West Suffolk Hospital in Bury St Edmunds to have the birthmark cut out. This time it was a local anaesthetic, in which they stuck a needle in her head, numbing the area. Although she said there wasn't any pain, she could feel the scraping sensation as the surgeon cut and scraped away at the effected area. Apparently, there was a lot of blood loss, but again the staff were wonderful.

With the boob op they removed the blocked bits, but found rather a lot of infected areas and we were told that it might need a second op if the very strong antibiotics didn't clear it up. The birthmark could also mean a second go at it, as they couldn't be sure they'd got it all until it healed.

Another Op

Hospitals are a fact of life the older you get. I've had a few and Eileen has had her fair share, too. The latest for Eileen was the "two in a week" and yes, there is another one looming for her as I write this In May 2009. But before "she gets hers", I had my own to negotiate.

I was working in the garden thinking I was still in my prime and forgetting I was 71 years old, when "pop", I felt a sharp pain in the groin area. It happened a couple of weeks before we were due to go on holiday to Montenegro, but not wishing to miss out on our holiday I decided to seek the advice of our GP.

I didn't want to worry Eileen, so I told her it was to get my hearing tested. She'd been nagging me to get a check-up for some time, so she thought I'd finally come to my senses and swiftly booked me in.

I told the doctor I had three problems, to which he replied, 'You have ten minutes; that's the allotted time per patient!'

'Okay,' I said, 'I'll talk quickly! Can you have a look to see if I need my ears syringing? I think I've popped a Hernia, can you check it out. And my third problem is that we're off on holiday and can I still go if I have a hernia?' I then added, 'Well don't just sit there; time's a ticking; get on with it.'

Well, if truth be told, I was only thinking that and dare not say it, as Doctor "Q" is quite formidable and is not a lady to be messed with! She took a "butchers hook" in my lugholes and then had a grope in my groin area! Not an unpleasant experience, but I resisted the urge to smile!

She referred me to a hospital and told me the holiday would be okay as long as it wasn't rock-climbing, skiing, hang-gliding or any other such physical activity. At the age of 71, all those things are far removed from my idea of fun, so we needn't have worried.

The holiday came and went and soon after I was booked in for the op. It was for, I thought, an internal laparoscopic hernia repair, meaning keyhole surgery. This is where they send a camera in and the surgeon carries out the repair, by inserting the necessary instruments, leaving just a couple of small scars.

I gave little thought to the surgeon's suggestion that I should have a general anaesthetic instead of the local that I'd requested when interviewed, but still said I'd prefer a local.

I was wheeled in and there was a hive of activity as everyone went about his or her business. A young nurse busied herself shaving the "relevant area"; again, not an unpleasant experience, but I still resisted the urge to smile, especially as she blew the hairs from, shall we say, the Old John Thomas! However, I did say, 'Excuse me, nurse, have you any Old Spice?'

After the area had been anaesthetised, the surgeon and his compadres went to work. A young nurse asked me if I was okay and I got chatting to her. After a few minutes I heard the surgeon snap, 'Please stop talking to the patient!' It was my fault, as I was doing all the chat, but she got the telling off. My chattering was obviously affecting the job he was doing! Maybe my hand gestures didn't help and were causing movement where he could well have done without! Eileen says she thinks there's more than a little Italian in me as I find talking without hands quite difficult.

It was then that I realised why the surgeon had suggested a general anaesthetic instead of the local that I thought I was having. For some reason they were doing the op the old fashion way – I was under the knife! – and my chattering was interfering with his scalpel skills. I quickly shut up and declined to utter another word until I'd been stitched up, before I was stitched up good and proper.

My after-op instructions, or should I say "procedure" instructions, were: extreme care for forty-eight hours; keep the dressing dry. After forty-eight hours I was to remove the dressing and shower daily. I told the nurse that I normally shower every six months if I needed it or not! Well what was good enough for Queen Elizabeth was good enough for me! I don't think she got the connection, as she insisted that a daily wash "down there" was essential to keep the area clean and sterile.

There was to be no heavy lifting, contact sports or sexual activity for two weeks! Blimey that's an awful long time between drinks! When I told my daughter she said, 'Surely you're not still doing that at your age, Dad?'

I replied, 'Well, it helps pass the time and I didn't realise there was a time limit on such activities!'

Reminiscing

When I joined the army in 1955 I missed my mum more than anyone else. Apart from army food being a far cry from the Egon Ronay cuisine I'd expected, I realised how I'd taken a million and one things at home for granted, in common with all other teenage boys. Thinking back, I was barely out of nappies!

No matter how many times my sergeant insisted that 'I'm your muvvah nah, son', it never quite rang true. He didn't make my bed, do my ironing, polish my boots or any of the things my mum did. He didn't even do my sewing for me; he did yell a lot, though, and most of it was directed towards my personage. Apparently, I wasn't a soldier, I was a donkey.

I told him that the recruitment officer didn't agree and, indeed, insisted that I was a natural born soldier, but my sergeant didn't share his optimism and I watched the blood vessels on his neck rise ever outwards until I thought they would explode; unfortunately, they didn't.

Our rescuer turned up in the form of a boy soldier, who'd been in the army since he was 15 years old and taught us all the tricks. We learned how to shrink our berets with hot and cold water, so that we didn't look as if giant birds had crapped on our heads, and how to put razor-sharp creases in our uniforms with wet brown paper and a really hot iron; this included boxing the sleeves and squaring the back of the uniform jacket.

Blankoed webbing and polishing brasses were also learned, with none of the modern stay-bright buttons and buckles, and labour-saving polishers and cleaners had yet to be invented. We could iron out the pimples in our boots by heating a spoon over a candle and rubbing it hard on the coarse leather, until it was as smooth as a baby's bum. Then, with an abundance of spit and polish, we transformed the dull leather into a black mirror that you could have a shave in; all clever stuff. We had one pair of boots that were never to touch the floor; these were used for inspection only. He also taught us how to lay out our beds for morning inspection, for we had an hour to complete this task.

The sergeant gently introduced us to the day at 5.00 a.m., though his approach was a bit different from my mother's gentle arousal with a cup of tea in her hand. He had a voice like the crack of doom and would strut the length of our barrack room banging his pacing stick on the metal frames of the beds, screeching at full volume that we should remove our hands from our private parts and place them on our socks; this did nothing to endear him to us, but it was bloody effective.

Our kit had to be laid out on our beds with microscopic accuracy in its arrangement and had to be cleaned way beyond the realms of hygiene. Blankets were to be folded, boxed and squared at the bedhead, with the rest following uniformly down to the foot, where the gleaming bots stood proud. Not only did the kit have to be laid out in perfect precision, but yourself and the billet also had to be in tune with army regulations; one speck of dust would bring down the wrath of the sergeant major. The sergeant was a gent compared with the SM, but he was awesomely terrifying to us 17 year olds.

The word "Reveille" sounds quite nice, doesn't it? Well, how can something that sounds so nice be so bloody awful? After reveille at 0500 hours came the billet inspection at 0600 hours. The sergeant would enter the billet with shouts of, 'Stand by yer beds', and a wave of fear would surge through us. We had only seconds to get in place and be ready for the inspection by the SM.

Some days he would march up, down and out onto the next billet without even a glance, but at least once a week he would scrutinise everybody and everything. We knew that when this happened he would find something not to his liking and all hell would break loose. Lockers were upturned and beds and kit were ripped apart and chucked everywhere, while we stood rock still, not daring to bat an eyelid.

One morning, he stopped and stared straight into my eyes. 'Did you have a shave this morning, soldier?'

At that time I hadn't yet reached the age of shaving and didn't have a hint of bumfluff on my chin.

Instead of saying, 'Yes, sir,' I foolishly explained, 'I don't shave yet, sir.'

I thought my day had come as he launched into a stream of verbal abuse, after which the corporal was ordered to escort me to the latrines – at the double, of course – for a shave. I tried to explain that I didn't own a razor yet, but my friend the corporal, as if by magic, produced from his pocket a filthy razor and a lump of lifebuoy soap, barking, 'One razor for the use of and shaving soap for the use of.' It took a month for my face to recover.

Every day was a learning experience, but apart from the uselessly hard lessons there were also useful ones. The others taught me the importance of sewing and, more importantly, darning. Now that one I took to like a duck to water and I would defy anyone to show me where the darn finished and the sock began, such was my expertise.

After the army, Mum took over these chores, so it was only natural that after I married Eileen, when one of my socks produced a hole, I expectantly passed it to her for repair. Imagine my shock when she chucked it in the bin. I gently chided her, saying that these socks had cost me all of two shillings and eleven pence and that my mother had always darned my socks.

She pointed out that she performed duties my mother didn't, that this was 1960, women were equal nowadays and as we were both working full time, she had no intention of spending her evenings darning cheap socks. I was flabbergasted, but thought I would solve the problem at Christmas, by buying my bride of three months a workbox complete with darning equipment. Oh boy, to say she wasn't delighted as she unwrapped my thoughtful present is an understatement and the handle is still broken where she threw it at me.

For the last fifty years I've never even so much as looked sideways at a needle and cotton. Then, the other week, Eileen bought me a pair of trousers that, although perfect on the waist, were a tad long on the leg. She was out and I thought

I'd tackle the job and rekindle my old needlework skills. But the cotton seemed to have thickened and the eye of the needle had shrunk, though I stuck at the job and with the help of a magnifying glass and a bright light, I managed to thread the needle. Measuring the length, I folded the cloth and with a wet tea towel and a hot iron I pressed the trouser legs.

Using a loop stitch I began to take them up. The material was quite tough, so I used a spoon to push the needle through. Not sure how it happened, but somehow the needle passed through the material and up and under my thumbnail. The pain was excruciating and it's a good job the house was empty, because she doesn't know I swear.

After I'd run through the rooms hollering and screaming, I submerged my throbbing thumb in the freezer. Unbeaten, I returned to the task, stitched one leg and turned it over, only to discover that I'd stitched both sides together. I subsequently chucked the trousers in the bottom of the wardrobe and had a cup of tea – always a good thing in a time of crisis.

The next day I came home to find them perfectly altered and hanging in the wardrobe. Nothing was ever said by either of us, but I guess she must have noticed the sticking plaster on my thumb and the kick marks on the sewing box.

Sport

Heroics of a Working Man

At the outbreak of war in 1939, Arsenal Stadium was requisitioned as an ARP station, with a barrage balloon operating behind the clock end. The stadium continued to operate as a football ground for the armed forces, often with two or three games being played on it daily. During the Blitz, a 3,000 lb bomb fell on the north bank stand, destroying the roof and setting fire to the scrap that was being stored on the terrace. Arsenal played their wartime home games at White Hart Lane, courtesy of their local rivals Tottenham Hotspur. After the war, the Arsenal board presented Spurs with a cannon as a gesture of thanks.

 I was born in London and my dad took me on occasion to Leyton Orient. Dad was born in Bow and played for Leyton Orient when they were just an amateur team. Standing on the mud terraces of Leyton Orient along with the huge, jostling crowds of at least two or three hundred, I soon realised that "The Os" weren't the team for me; somehow, they lacked colour and attraction. Give Dad his due, he tried to increase their supporters by taking all of his sons at one time or another along to a game, but what was on offer was pretty grim. Having said all that, I still look each week to see how they fare.

Memoirs of a Working Man

When I was old enough, my brother Arthur was told by Mum he had to take me to watch the football match; not once, but every Saturday. It was a way of life. Saturday meant football. Indeed, it was unthinkable to miss the game. Mum had finally given in to my whining and agreed I could go if my big brother would take me. I could tell it didn't go down too well with him by the way he looked at me. You know, the loving look big brothers give their younger siblings.

I can't remember exactly how old I was when I started to go to football matches, but I can remember watching Arsenal playing their home games at Tottenham, so my guess would be around 7 years old. I can also remember that teams had guest players playing for them, because players were in the armed forces, so they would guest for teams close to where they were stationed.

One such player left an unforgettable impression on me; his name was Jimmy Wrigglesworth and he normally played for Arsenal on the left wing and dazzled defenders. Wrigglesworth was an apt name, because he wriggled his way through the game, making and scoring goal after goal with his wonderful skills.

Later, when Highbury reopened, Arthur used to take me to watch Arsenal and Tottenham on alternate weeks on their own grounds. It was in the days when crowd segregation was unheard of and Arsenal and Tottenham supporters stood shoulder to shoulder on the terraces and the worse thing to happen would be a verbal punch up. And if one of them swore in earshot of us kids, the other bloke would say, 'Watch your marff in front of the kids!' And always an apology came back. A bit different from today, where foul language is accepted without so much as a raised eyebrow.

We normally arrived very early and so managed to get pitch-side positions, but I remember being late once and we ended up being stuck right at the back. A couple of blokes noticed this and they just hoisted us little ones up and with shouts of 'Kids coming through!', they passed us over the heads of the supporters right to the front.

My team, the team I was to support the rest of my life, had to be *the* Arsenal; the colour, the atmosphere and the excitement all added to the allure of that fantastic ground. Tottenham paled into insignificance and poor old Leyton Orient didn't have a hope in hell, so my family was split: Leyton Orient, Tottenham and Arsenal. The arguments were choice, but they were all our local teams.

In those days we had a season for football and a season for cricket; the cricket season stared when the football finished, enabling players to play both football and cricket. Three such players that I can remember were Arsenal players that still stand as all-round, all-time greats. Denis Compton CBE played football for Arsenal and England. He was also an English cricketer who played in seventy-eight Test matches. He spent the whole of his cricket career with Middlesex and the whole of his football career at Arsenal FC.

His Brother Leslie Compton also played football for Arsenal and cricket for Middlesex. Together with his brother Dennis, Leslie won the 1947 County Championship title with Middlesex, making them the only brothers ever to have won the national title both in football and cricket.

Arthur Milton played on the wing for Arsenal and England and he also opened the innings for Gloucestershire and England. As such, he was the last of the double internationals. In his time, Arthur Milton was as big a name as Alan Ball, the World Cup hero. At Highbury, Milton was remembered as a slim, small, fleet-footed outside-right, an admirable partner for Jimmy Logie, who graced the red-and-white shirt.

When we moved to Suffolk I was truly amazed to find that the young Suffolk lads supported teams from all over and not their local teams. I suppose it all boiled down to who impressed them most as they became aware of the greatest game in the world. One of my son-in-laws supports Liverpool – don't ask me why; he was born in Suffolk. It never ceases to amaze me. I suppose it's down to a lack of parental guidance.

Nowadays, with Sky Television, they have a far wider education than our trips out on a Saturday afternoon. Their knowledge of the game is unbelievable, not to mention the skill they show playing the game. Not only do they have the advantage of seeing top-class footballers in action almost everyday of the week, but they also have far superior equipment. For starters, they have a ball that they can move at speed.

The ball we had was made of leather and I couldn't even pick it up, let alone kick it. If anyone was stupid enough to head the ball and unlucky enough to make contact with the protruding leather lace, not only did it knock you flat on your back, but it also tore lumps out of your skull. Boots were like two concrete blocks, shin pads were thick, heavy and cumbersome and the woollen socks weren't too bad until they got wet, when you'd have a problem.

My grandsons have a variety of football kits and as you may or may not know, the football teams have sponsors and on the shirts is the name of the sponsor; Liverpool's sponsor is Carlsberg lager. One of my grandsons had been given a Liverpool kit by his misguided father, but time was on my side and he grew too big to wear it. Foolishly, I thought that was the end of a passing phase, but he passed the kit onto his football-crazy cousin, so I had to endure the Liverpool shirt once again.

His cousin was my then 6-year-old granddaughter Libby, or Lippy as her 2-year-old cousin called her. Lippy, along with her twin sister and cousins, had been set a task by Grandma to write a story, using words and pictures. Football-crazy Lippy naturally decided her theme would be football. The pictures were great, especially the one of bald-headed Grandad scoring a goal. She turned the page and said, 'Look, Grandad, I've written Liverpool; I copied it from my Liverpool shirt.' In big, bold letters she'd written the word "Carlsberg"!

Are you into Football? Do you Love the Game?

I'm talking English football here, not the American type. Why they call that football is beyond me, for they don't use their feet and neither do they use a proper ball. As to why they call our national game "soccer" is also beyond me and I wince every time I hear it said. Soccer! I mean, soccer – what the hell is soccer? It's football! Foot-ball, a highly skilled game, played with the feet, running and kicking, nothing at all to do with socks.

I can live with them changing our rounders game to the word baseball because there's an association of sorts: one runs round in circles to get back to base. But where do they get the name soccer from? The other thing that annoys me about the greatest game in the universe is that foreigners are now teaching us a thing or three about the noble art. This certainly makes a fellow weep. But the thing that really hurts, and I do mean really hurts, was when my American friend told me that soccer is an old English name for football derived from association football. Cor blimey – what a shock! But I don't care; it's still all football to me.

Even when I was at the age of 65 I still couldn't resist the urge to kick a ball and my three eldest grandsons, then aged 7, 12 and 13, knew that I needed no persuasion to give them a game. It was OK when they were a few years younger, because with the help of a couple of younger granddaughters we could roast them, but now it was getting more serious. After half an hour of crunching tackles and being run ragged I was ready to drop, with aching bones and the blood coursing through the protruding veins on my hairless head.

Eileen looks at me disapprovingly and says, 'Now, Bob, you are silly; you're not a youngster any more.' She was, of course, right, but my brain insisted I could do it and that I was still only eighteen; the problem was that my body knew it couldn't, being a tad past it with eighteen being a long, long way back.

When I came out of the army I started taking my boots over Hackney Marshes, where they had hundreds of pitches. To get a game, all you had to do was hang around the changing area and before long, one of the team managers would say, 'You

Bob Oliver

looking for a game, mate?' There were always teams that were short of players and anybody would do.

They supplied a shirt, you supplied boots, socks shorts and pads and bingo! you got a game. One Saturday afternoon I was at my usual place waiting for a game when a guy from work spotted me and asked what I was doing there. He was the manager of the factory football team where I worked and he gave me a lecture on the stupidity of playing without insurance. He signed me up there and then and I played for them until we moved to Suffolk and through them I got my first Cup Final ticket.

When we first moved to Suffolk I signed on for the local village football team. The manager-cum–trainer-cum-physio-cum-Uncle Tom Cobley and all was of the old school and he only had one cure for all ailments; yes you guessed it – the dreaded magic sponge! At the slightest hint of one of his players being injured he would charge on, with or without the referee's permission, and plummet his magic sponge into his bucket of ice-topped water and plunge it down the front of the injured player's shorts. Needless to say, this treatment ensured a quick and immediate recovery. It mattered little to Arthur that the player had a busted leg, a split head or a twisted ankle – the sponge went unceremoniously down the front of your shorts.

As a naive new player I wondered and was indeed impressed by the bravery of my new team mates who, after suffering the cruellest tackle, would leap to their feet and run the injury off. I can remember thinking – God! these country boys ain't half tough.

It was my third game and we were midway through the second half. I was having a good game, scoring the first and making the second, when I received an inch-perfect pass from the left half, skipped a lungeing tackle from their right half and made like the wind down the left wing. Now I can only assume their left back was a bit brassed off, 'cos his team was on the receiving end of a hammering and his captain was giving him stick for not stopping my crosses, because he'd made no attempt to get the ball and it was obvious that there was only one thing on his mind.

Anyway, he hit me so hard that I ended up 10 yards off the pitch. His nail-exposed studded boot ripped the shin pad from my leg and left me bruised and bleeding.

As I rolled in agony on the floor, Arthur made his move and appeared with his first-aid kit and equipment – the bucket of iced water and the sponge. I thought the tackle was bad enough and I didn't know what had hit me. If only it had been televised; I would've loved to have captured the look of sheer amazement on my face as Arthur did the business.

'It's my leg!' I screamed, but he was completely oblivious to my pleas as he pushed me back on the pitch saying, 'Go get 'im, Bob!'

It was then that I realised my team mates weren't so much brave as bloody cowards. They all had a good laugh at my expense; especially our goalkeeper, who was a right joker. But never throw stones if one lives in a greenhouse, for it was the same keeper the very next week who gave me one of the greatest laughs of my life.

He took a bad knock and the pain made him momentarily forget himself as he fell in a crumpled heap on the floor. The sight of Arthur running towards him with bucket and sponge at the ready had wondrous healing powers. Jim, the then goalkeeper, wrapped himself around the goalpost and screamed, 'Arthur, I'm alright, Arthur; honest I am!' There was genuine panic in his voice and anguish on his face.

I fought hard with my conscience, but was unable to allow the moment to pass. Grabbing Jim firmly, I dragged him to the ground and shouted to Arthur, 'It's his leg, Arthur; quick, it's his leg!'

Arthur didn't have to be told to twice. Oh no, he was quicker than anyone could imagine and Jim has never forgiven me even after fifty plus years. Whenever we meet, he says, with pointing finger, 'I haven't forgotten, Oliver; oh no, I haven't forgotten!' But then again, neither have I.

FA Cup Final

In 1961 I was lucky enough to get an FA Cup Final ticket. I played football for the factory team and every year each team were allocated two tickets from the Football Association. Our manager always had one ticket and the other was given to one of the players. All our names were put in a hat and the fist name out was the lucky guy to accompany him. This particular year our centre half Johnny Burns was that lucky guy.

On the Thursday before the Cup Final, Tony Wright, the captain of our team who worked in the offices, came to see me in the workshop. He said, 'Bob, Johnny's still in hospital following that operation on his knee, so he won't be able to go

Memoirs of a Working Man

and see the Cup Final. What do you think we should do with the ticket?'

'Well,' I said, 'we'll have to put the names back in the hat again, I guess.'

Tony replied, 'We did and your name came out!'

It was a particularly difficult moment for Tony, as he was a Tottenham supporter and the Cup Final was between Tottenham and Leicester. He did offer to buy it from me, but even though I'm an Arsenal supporter I wouldn't have missed the chance to see my first Cup Final.

The Leicester team had among its ranks great players like Gordon Banks, Frank McLintock and Albert Cheesbrough, while Tottenham could boast Dave Mackay, Danny "not on your life" Blanchflower and John White. Not to mention Bobby Smith who got the winning goal and Les Allen, father of Clive, who signed for Arsenal in the 1970's but never played for them. He was signed for a million pounds in the closed season and was resold before the next season.

It would be impossible for me to relay the wonderful atmosphere that prevailed, but although I wasn't a supporter of either of the teams, there was a tremendous thrill of the occasion. Soaking up the atmosphere, I walked Wembley Way savouring every moment.

I had the opportunity to see another FA Cup Final twenty-two years later in 1983; the finalists were Brighton and Manchester United. A couple of the lads were picking me up at half past ten on Saturday morning and I had a game of squash arranged for nine o'clock, which was a hard match that went the full five games, so I felt absolutely shattered.

On the road to Wembley, the feeling of excitement was in the air. Brighton was the team I was going to shout for, because they were the underdogs. My mates, on the other hand, were ardent Man U supporters, so there was plenty of banter going on throughout our journey. What the swines neglected to tell me was that we were destined to be penned-up with the Man U supporters. My face must have been a picture when we were herded into the enclosure with 5 million red-and-white clad yobs chanting, 'Going down, going down, going down'! Indicating to the Brighton supporters that their team had been relegated; in the nicest possible way, of course.

At the other end, the Brighton supporters chanted, 'Sea gulls, sea gulls, sea gulls.' Wanting oh so much to join in, I had to button my lip. When Brighton scored, I momentarily forgot myself and quickly had to change my shout of joy into a gasp of anguish. I clasped my hands over my head, peering through my fingers to see if anyone had twigged me.

A rather unsavoury Neanderthal was looking at me! 'Oh dear!' I said nervously, 'that's really tough; they've scored a goal!' He grunted and shrugged his 6-foot bulky frame as he continued urinating on the floor! Manchester equalised, but in the dying seconds Brighton had the chance to clinch it, but the centre forward shot straight at the goalkeeper. The full-time whistle went, but the nightmare continued as the match went into extra time. My back and legs ached and I wished I hadn't played that game of squash; I was 45 years old and felt more like 90.

Fortunately, the match ended in a draw, for I feel sure a win either way would have spelt trouble. They mumbled to each other 'Back Thursday', when the return match was to take place, and seemed quite pleased to think they'd be seeing another game. I, on the other hand, had no intention of coming back next Thursday. This, my second Cup Final, was oh such a different experience from the 1961 final.

It was nearly eight o'clock by the time we arrived home and I'd just about had enough. Eileen greeted me with, 'The factory's been on the phone. Apparently, you were the last one to have the keys to the squash court. You took them with you and can they please have them back?' Dragging my tired old bones down to the factory I apologised, explaining the keys had been to Wembley to watch the Cup Final.

The security man told me to save my apologies for Brian, the secretary of the squash club and keeper of the spare keys; apparently, he'd been watching the Cup Final when he was dragged away to unlock the squash court. It was beyond my comprehension that anybody should want to play squash when the Cup Final was on, but there you are; it takes all sorts. Brian is a nice guy and he forgave me when I made him a present of the Cup Final programme. Yes, I'm definitely in favour of all-seater stadiums.

Sunday 29 April 2007

I had a great treat on Sunday 29 April 2007. No, no, I didn't go to church, it was a religion of another kind. I was up at 4.30 a.m. and off to work at 5.00 a.m. at Richard's factory until midday, as Richard had a special treat lined up for us. After lunch, we were picked up by a driver who drove us to London; North London to be precise. The Emirates Stadium to be even more precise. The New Highbury for the Gunners; wow! what a football ground that is, absolutely fantastic. It was my first time and to have a driver take us to the stadium without the hassle of public transport was the icing on the cake.

We were really early and consequently we had time to look around and do a bit of Arsenal shopping, so I now have an Arsenal dressing gown courtesy of Richard, who suggested I wear it at the chess club AGM, but I don't really think so.

Inside the stadium the atmosphere was fantastic and the turf looked for all the world as if it was the first game of the season, instead of the last bar one game. In the first half Arsenal should have had four goals, a repeat of the 2006/07 season, if it wasn't for the second half, which told a different story. I couldn't believe what I was seeing. During the first half the Gooners played fantastic football and scored once, but when they came out in the second half they look jaded and played like Bolton with long balls and without the neat passing game they'd been playing earlier and what we'd all expect from the Gooners. The longer it went on the more I feared the worst and kept saying to Richard, 'One goal is not enough.'

And sure enough, with only a short time to go, Fulham got a well-deserved equaliser. Our hearts sank, but we didn't have long to grieve, as that goal seemed to spark our team back to life as they eventually ran off as the winners, three goals to one. So we could go home very happy and very tired, but at least happy.

Memoirs of a Working Man

Football Crazy

As you might have guessed, I'm an avid Arsenal supporter and Richard bought me for me seventieth birthday a signed Arsenal shirt; signed by Arsene Wenger and the 2007/08 team. He'd had it framed and I hung it in our hall for all to see and admire, especially any Arsenal supporters.

Come August each year we have our chimney swept in readiness for the winter. I was unable to contact our regular guy, so Eileen found an alternative on the Internet. The sweep turned up as arranged and I detected a strong accent in his voice that I just couldn't place. So being of an inquisitive nature I enquired as to its origin. He told me he was Polish and had lived in England for five years, most of it in London, so his accent was of cockney-Polack, with a hint of Geordie, where he'd spent a year on contract work. Blimey! what a mixture; no wonder I couldn't place it.

As he unloaded his van he stopped in the hall to admire my framed Arsenal shirt. 'I see you're an Arsenal supporter, kiddo,' he said.

'Ah yes, I'm a Gooner alright. I didn't always live in Suffolk. I was born in London,' I replied.

'I vill tell you a funny story about Ars-in-al,' the sweep exclaimed as I listened intently to his enriched tones and pronunciation. 'Five years ago, when I'm first coming to England, I was sent to a lodging house in Holloway Road near the Ars-in-nal football ground. The landlord was very grisly and as he showed me in, he asked, with dees funny looks in his eyes, if I liked football and, of course, I told him that all Poles loved de football. He then asked if I had a favourite English football team. Well,' the Pole said to me, nodding his head knowingly, 'Me momski no breed dem idiots, me telling you, matie, and nun mistakes! I was in North London near the Arsenal ground, so I told him I'd always supported de Ars-in-nal! He unceremoniously showed be to the door and, pushing me into the street, said, "No Arsenal supporters in my house!" Wait, wait, I said. My English is not good. I meant Tott-in-ham!'

'"That's worse!" he snapped. "Only Liverpool supporters in my house!" If only he'd had a Liverpool picture in his hall!'

'Blimey!' I said. 'A bleeding Scouser in the Smoke!'

'No, no!' replied the Pole. 'I no smoke!'

I did think about explaining that "the Smoke" was slang for London, but that was when I was a kid, so I just nodded and said, 'That's good!'

Eileen's Encounter

In 1960, Eileen was working for a company who had their premises in White Hart Lane. One day, as she was leaving work, she achieved her claim to fame. As she turned a corner she was knocked to the ground by none other than Danny Blanchflower, who was making his escape from a crowd of autograph hunters. Only her stockings were damaged, but he offered to pay for them. She declined the offer, before he once again took flight from the chasing horde of young girls.

Eileen didn't even know who he was until one of the pursuing crowd asked her what he'd said to her. After she'd told her, she asked the girl, 'Who was it, then; a film star?' The young fan was suitably disgusted with Eileen at the thought that there was a person on the planet who didn't know Danny Blanchflower!

Years later, we were in Cambridge and we met some old friends we hadn't seen for years. While the girls spoke of trivia, we blokes talked of more important things. This guy, a poor, misguided fool, is a Tottenham supporter, so naturally the chat was of an aggressive nature.

When Eileen heard the words White Hart Lane, she stopped talking rubbish with her friend and added to our more intellectual conversation by mentioning that she'd once worked in White Hart Lane in the 1960s. This impressed Dave no end, as it was at a time and place in history when Tottenham had the best team that has ever worn the Cockerel.

His mouth was agape as she retold the story of how Danny Blanchflower had offered her compensation for her damaged stockings! In a crowded, hustling, bustling Cambridge high street, he fell to his knees and began kissing Eileen's feet, much to her great embarrassment. Now if it had been Denis Compton I could have understood it!

The Varsity Match

I've seen a few rugby matches, but the one that'll always stick in my mind was the first time I went to Twickenham to see the Varsity Match between Cambridge and Oxford on 12 December 1995. Richard told me that after a great deal of wrangling, he'd managed to secure me a ticket to see Cambridge play Oxford in the Varsity Match at Twickenham. I had a bit of a dilemma, as my brother and his wife had arranged to visit us on the day of the big match and what made it worse was that we'd already put them off once because Eileen'd had a hospital appointment.

Richard gave me an old-fashioned look and said, 'Bob, there can't be any contest! The Varsity Match comes but once a year! And besides, it won't cost you a penny.'

That did it and so Bill and Doreen were kicked into touch. It was to be a day of food, booze and rugby.

The day was due to start at eight forty-five, with breakfast at a posh hotel just outside of Cambridge. I obviously thought that Richard would pick me up at eight o'clock and we would have a steady drive to the hotel. But no, 'I'll pick you up at six,' he said. Yes, we were going to work first; even on his day's holiday there was no keeping him away from his beloved factory. At eight forty-three, he said, 'Grab your coat, Bob, we're off.'

Nigel, his partner, was to follow in his car and as we roared down the road we could see traffic as far as the eye would stretch.

'I know a short cut,' he said.

He didn't actually *know* a short cut, but he did know there was a short cut, somewhere! After five minutes of imitating a headless chicken, he instructed me to, 'Phone Nigel on the mobile; he'll direct us.'

'Where are we, Nigel?' I said.

The reply was tart. 'How the bleeding hell do I know?' After some banter, he screamed, 'Tell me exactly where you are and I'll talk you in.'

Richard told me to tell him we were at number sixteen. Nigel began to lose his rag and this made it worse, so we gave him a further string of ambiguous situations. Finally, I thought I'd better bring some sanity into the situation and convinced him of our true location.

'You're heading in the wrong direction. Turn round and come back through the village. Turn right, follow that road and I'll be waiting for you about a mile down.'

As we approached his position, Richard suggested we phoned him and wound him up some more. He loads the bullets and I squeeze the trigger.

'Now what?' Nigel snapped.

The village in the opposite direction was called Over, so naturally I told him we'd reached Over and what were his instructions now. I thought the poor sod was going to have a coronary.

'Stop! Stop! Stop! Just stop – I'll come and get you!'

'But Richard said if we do a right it'll bring us round to you.'

'No, no, no, just stay where you are!'

All this was punctuated with a few descriptive "doing" words I once heard at a judges' convention. Something to do with sex, illegitimacy and personal parts of the female anatomy. This colourful language had me wondering what else they'd taught him at university. He was halfway through a three-point turn, when he caught sight of us, directly behind him. He abandoned the manoeuvre and roared off down the road with us in hot pursuit.

The rest of the group we were to meet had finished their breakfast by the time we arrived, but they were quite content to wait for us; especially as hip flasks of brandy and whisky were being passed around the breakfast table. The group were already very happy and were full of banter and rugby stories. Obviously, being all ex-rugby types, there wasn't one under 6 foot.

Richard declined the flasks with the excuse that we hadn't decided who was to drink and who was to drive. In actual fact, he'd already adjudged that I would be the sober one and he intended to get well oiled. But he whispered to me, 'I don't like the idea of partaking from the same flask as this load of macho machines.'

The breakfast was first class, but for ten pounds fifty it should have been in the premier league. I'm glad I didn't have to pay and when Richard found out how much it was to cost, he decided to get his money's worth and walked out with pockets bulging with mini packs of Coco Pops, Frosties, jams, marmalade and the like. He was unable to involve me in his illegal activities, although I did collect all the uneaten toast and put it in the overcoat pocket of a 7 foot guy who'd gone to the toilet.

There were twelve of us and we all piled into this twelve-seater minibus, but the problem was that the seats weren't designed to take 17 and 18 stone monsters and to say we were cramped would be the understatement of the century. The bus had seen better days and the driver looked in worse condition.

I asked Richard why they called the driver "Shoulders" and was it because he was thickset. 'No, no!' Richard explained. 'He earned that nickname because he drives close into the left and on motorways he spends most of the time on the hard shoulder.' Oh shit! I thought.

The fog was quite thick, with visibility down to about 50 yards. Shoulders was bombing along with two wheels firmly entrenched on the outer parameter, the boozy, bulky bodies full of fun and cackling worse than any group of women. Richard was still declining to drink from their flasks, although the temptation of a slug of whisky was great, but opted instead to munch on his stolen Coco Pops and mumble, 'I wish I had a slice of toast to go with marmalade.' The 7 foot guy was still quite oblivious to the toast overloading his overcoat pockets.

Suddenly, the noise in the bus melted into terrified silence. Shoulders had jammed on the brakes and with all four wheels locked, the rear of the vehicle began to overtake the headlights. It was like a roller-coaster ride, complete with contorted faces and white knuckles. It wasn't skill at the wheel that enabled the driver to avoid the other vehicles – just pure luck and providence. But, fortunately, Shoulders lived up to his name and that's where we ended up. Alas, we were facing back towards Cambridge.

We sat helplessly watching as he attempted to turn the bus with cars appearing out of the fog and screaming to a halt all around us. At this point, Richard decided that drinking from their flask was no big deal and he emptied the half-full flask of whisky down his throat.

The traffic in London was the usual nightmare and no one seemed to mind us cutting them up; either it's the done thing in London or could it have been the eleven "mini mountains" glaring out of the windows? Little did they know how petrified we all were. At least I was well protected, being cocooned in the middle of a mass of flesh.

Bob Oliver

It was just after one o'clock when we ground to a halt. Kick-off was at two thirty, so it was a mad scramble to the pub to sink as much alcohol as possible, or in my case a glass of coke and a hot dog. Bellies full and flasks replenished, we were off to the match, where history was to be made. It was the first in the series of games at Twickenham to be played under floodlight, in front of a record crowd, in excess of 70,000. It's quite incredible to think a rugby game between two schools can create so much interest. Indeed, sixty-nine games have been played at Twickenham: Cambridge has won thirty-seven, Oxford twenty-eight, with four draws.

There's something special about being at a match like this: the atmosphere is electric, with everyone excited and full of expectations. After watching many top-class football matches, I was impressed that there wasn't any need for crowd separation and the good-natured banter between fans added to the ambience of the occasion.

Within minutes of the kick-off, Cambridge went three points up from a penalty kick and I thought this was it; we were going to bury them. But our high hopes were soon dashed as Oxford took the lead and dominated the play, even though I was giving them as much encouragement as possible, with shouts of, 'Come on, chaps, stop messing about!' in my best Cambridge accent. Although my cockney did slip through now and then with, 'Gert you cowson!'

I was screaming at the top of my voice as Oxford converted a penalty; then an announcement came over the tannoy, 'Will supporters please refrain from calling out when the players are about to take a penalty. This has always been a tradition at Twickenham!'

I replied in my usual suave manner, 'What do you think this is? A sodding snooker match?'

The crowd was in uproar and years of tradition were flushed down the drain as they hooted and howled at every penalty kick. Alas, it backfired on the Light Blues supporters, as it was the Cambridge kicks that went astray and Oxford marched on; at half-time we were sixteen to three up. We were down and out and with the way Oxford were playing, there was no way back. Of course, down in the bar at half-time, as all the lads were drowning their sorrows, there were plenty of people who could have told the players just exactly where they were going wrong.

But our fears were unfounded, for the Light Blues came out like tigers during the second half and played out of their skins, giving us all plenty to shout at. Mind you, it was touch and go 'til the very last second of the match and when Oxford hit the post with a drop kick, I thought my heart would never start again.

With the last kick, Cambridge nicked it by one point: 22–21. One couldn't help feeling sorry for Oxford. Ha, ha, not really. Come on you super Sky Blues! After a few more celebratory pints, with me the only sober one amongst them, we made our way to the place where we were to meet the driver from hell. As we waited, we started to get cold, so "Seven Foot" put his overcoat on and discovered the toast in his pocket. Richard lost no time in telling him who'd planted the stolen property and I had to use my best silver tongue to get me out of that one.

Shoulders had sat next to him at the breakfast table, so it was only natural that he should get the blame and in any case, he was late, so it serves him right. We were freezing our extremities off and were choking from the fumes being discharged from the packed-solid traffic, merely inching along while we waited. He finally picked us up three quarters of an hour late, without so much as a by your leave. It was a nightmare journey home, taking five hours to do the usual two-hour trip.

The fish and chips in Baldock went down a treat and Richard managed to empty all four flasks, much to the disgust of the other drunks; but no one can keep up with him when he's in full flow. I did get to drive his super Saab, though; something he would never have let me do when he was sober. We arrived home at eleven o'clock; it had been quite a day with the Light Blues getting a great result.

How Many Types of Fishing are There?

I tried river fishing when I was young, but couldn't see much fun in it. A bloke I worked with was a fishing fanatic and at every opportunity he would load up his car and make tracks out of London to his secret destination, where, so he told me, there was the greatest fishing in the country.

One day, he talked me into joining him on one of his treks into the unknown. I was young, gullible and oh so willing to believe all he'd told me about the pure excitement of hooking the big one. He spoke of trout, bream and the biggest pike you could only dream of; I think most of it was in his dreams!

We cracked off at two o'clock in the morning on a cold and dank November day. 'Must get there before sun-up; that's the best time to fish,' he told me. To this day I still don't know where we went. I know it was North of London and it took us about two hours to get there, but I slept most of the way.

It was then that I discovered why Frank had talked me into coming along. All the equipment had to be carried to the river. It was a mile walk from the car park and you wouldn't believe the amount of stuff these fishermen take with them. Finally, after slip-sliding through terrain that reminded me of the tank tracks where I'd done some of my army training, we found a spot where we couldn't fail to catch the biggest and the best fish in the river.

Frank set up his equipment on a muddy riverbank and under strict instructions on how to hook and play for our would-be dinner, he left me to try for that pike that had slipped his grasp last time. Apparently, the place for pike was at the weir just a few hundred yards up river.

The early morning drizzle developed into a steady downpour, but worse than the cold and the rain was the boredom. I sat on a stupid little stool, squinting by torchlight at a float oscillating on the ripples of the water, which refused to disappear and be pulled under by a hungry fish to ease my monotony. It wasn't as if I could slip back to the car for a warm up, for apart from the distance, I doubted if I'd ever be able to find it.

Daylight was late in arriving and the sky hung thick with cloud; not a star or the moon could be seen. Frank's words kept echoing in my brain, 'Must get there before sun-up.' Sun? Oh for a bit of sun! My fingers and toes were so cold I was fearful of them snapping off. The hours slowly crept by and my misery increased as the damp seeped through my clothes onto my skin and even my bones seemed damp. After a while I got fed up with staring at the float and looked about me. I suppose if it hadn't been so cold and the persistent rain had eased or, even better, stopped, I might have been able to enjoy the beauty of that peaceful, idyllic spot.

The winding river lapped against the tree-lined bank, the trees were almost bare and the ground lay heavy with autumn leaves. After several hours, Frank returned all excited. 'I had it on my hook!' he blurted.

'It was enormous. I nearly had it in my net when the line broke!' Oh blimey, not "the one that got away", I thought as my eyes glazed over. I suffered for my day of pleasure with a sore throat, a blazing head and every bone in my body ached ... and not a fish to call our own; all in all, a most ravaging day. After which I've resisted all attempts to partake in that most dubious of sports.

Many years ago I did a bit of trawler fishing with our friend in Barrow-in-Furness. He was a shipwright in the shipyard on Barrow Island and he and his mate had built a small trawler in their spare time. I was always in awe of Frank – yes, another Frank: are all fishermen called Frank? His skill was second only to my dad, who was a builder of a different kind. To build a trawler with only the help of one mate, who was a railwayman named George and who knew nothing about shipbuilding, was an unbelievable feat.

Now I quite enjoyed trawler fishing and we would chug out to sea, chuck the nets overboard, find a comfortable spot, soak up some vitamin A – I think that's the vitamin you get from the sun – and suck back a few beers, dreaming of nautical things.

Then came the hard bit – manually pulling in the nets! None of those winches that the softies use; this was real trawling.

The other type of fishing that was more to my liking and which was something I could equate to was long lining. Frank's son Steve taught me all about long lining. He had these fishing lines that were about 200 yards long, with a hook positioned at every metre; I thought I would slip a bit of metric in, to prove I'm up with the modern times. When the tide was out we would lay these lines out across the estuary and go off and do more interesting things like swimming, squash or football.

Returning after the tide has been and gone, we would pick up the lines along with the fish that had been nice enough to offer themselves up for supper. Dinah, Steven's grandma (Frank' mum) was a master with the boning knife and was an absolute pleasure to watch as she transformed those smelly, wet, slimy creatures into a culinary dish fit for a king.

Ah yes, I forgot to mention cockling – another little pastime that young Steven introduced me to. Or at least I suppose scratching the sands for cockles is a form of fishing. Not too keen on this one. Not only is it back-breaking, but the little gits spit at you when you uncover them. Neither did Dinah enjoy the chore of cleaning and preparing them to eat. She would sit for hours cursing our good harvest or thanking the Lord that we'd a bad day and the haul was poor. All things considered, I think the chip shop is the best place to catch a nice fish.

My Obsession

Chess.

My introduction to chess came in 1958, having just been demobbed from the army, after which I started work in a factory in North London, working as a pipe bender. The guy who introduced me to the wonderful game was a welder. He used to organise competitions and tournaments during tea and lunch breaks and his name was Tub Woolin – one of the all-time greats of the National Correspondence Chess Club.

The factory operated a twelve-hour rotating shift work set-up. The hours worked were 0800 hrs to 2000 hrs days and 2000 hrs to 0800 hrs for the night shift. The factory ran everything on a piecework system, where one made many items per hour for our money. I didn't like the night shift, but it paid better and there were far fewer guv'nors about. The great plus with the night shift was that we were able to crack on with the work and finish in the early hours of the morning. But there was no getting our heads down: it was out with the portable chess sets, into the welding booths and let battle commence. The guy I played mostly was a West Indian named Jimmy Bell and he thrashed me unmercifully; but I was learning all the while.

Eileen and I were courting at the time and I was living with the folks. The rotating shift work was murder. Everything was in turmoil: sleep, meals and social life, continually being turned upside down and inside out.

I can remember one day in particular. It was in 1959, a glorious hot summer's day, the sort of weather we had before they ruined it with their infernal A-bomb test; that's what we blamed for the weather changes in those days, not today's Jet Stream. My fortnight of nights was almost complete and finally, after seven hours of work and five hours of chess, my shift was over and I headed for home. The morning sun had already gathered in strength and with a cloudless sky, it was obviously going to be a hot and sticky day. Too tired to care, utterly shattered, I crept into bed and sank into a stupefied sleep.

Suddenly, a knight on a black charger roared forth and slaughtered a poor, defenceless white bishop. A white foot soldier leapt forwards, his shield held high as he lunged with his dagger. Sadly missing, he tumbled and was gobbled up by a greedy rook. All around was oppression and King John sat smugly as his troops crashed onwards. Then the remaining bishop, who had slipped in quietly, removed John's head with speed and efficiency and dumped it in the basket.

'What are you doing out of bed?' The voice shattered my dream. I was downstairs in the living room, looking down at an empty chess board. The words bellowed once again in my ears. 'What are you doing out of bed, you silly sod?' The old lady was stood at the door, not realising I'd been sleepwalking. My mind was hazy as I fought for clarity.

Mumbling some excuse, I shuffled off, my mind still confused. Dragging my half-conscious body back upstairs and into bed, I looked for a long time at the alarm clock, but my brain wouldn't accept the fact it was only five minutes after I'd closed my eyes.

I married Eileen in 1960 and we returned from honeymoon to find eighteen window envelopes containing thirty-six chess games. It was then that Eileen began to realise she had married a chess nut! She sent the following poem called Checkmate to her sister Lem:

> Up the stairs at night I creep,
>
> He, I know, is fast asleep.
>
> Every night seems the same,
>
> Chess is his nocturnal game.
>
> He rambles on and sheets are rent,
>
> Shouting "Les" for president.
>
> Does he dream of girls galore?
>
> No, not him, it's pawn to king four.
>
> To my sister Lem I write
>
> And tell her of my awful plight.
>
> Her reply is swift and straight,
>
> Tell him, dear, that it's "checkmate".

But she did learn to live with my obsession and it wasn't long before I introduced my lifelong buddy Les Dutch to the delights of postal chess. He became more involved in Natcor than I did. Not so much with the amount of games, but with the social and letter writing side of things. Then it was his turn to introduce me to that side of things, for in 1964, he'd taken over the job of boss of the mail and, of course, got me involved.

His job as Boss of the Mail was to coordinate bundles of letters being passed around the country to a small group of like-minded members who enjoyed writing and receiving funny or interesting letters. It didn't take him long to realise that there were problems with the system. The bundles of mail took forever to circulate, holidays caused delays and some members left letters in the bundles that should have been pulled doing the circuit, resulting in huge bundles costing more in postage than necessary.

Then Les, alias Dutchy, came up with a great idea. He got us all to send to him any funny or interesting letters and then, with the aid of his wife Carol, who did all the typing, he created a magazine and called it *The Oracle*, which was sent out to all members who subscribed. At the time that I'm writing this in 2009, *The Mailers Oracle* will have been produced for forty-four years by a number of different editors without missing a single month.

In the beginning, there were a few committee members who were against a second magazine for Natcor. *En Passant* is the official magazine for Natcor, strictly a purist mag, with only chess-related items, tournaments, etc. Whereas *The Mailers Oracle* is the social side of the club and enlightened members could see that it would compliment Natcor and not detract from it as some feared.

Some did their utmost to outlaw *The Oracle*, but I'm glad to say they didn't succeed. With over 300 members, my involvement in the chess club was great, in the early days being

Distribution Secretary for a number of years, followed by CT Controller, finally handing over the reins to Danny Kerr, both positions having been granted by Reg Gillman, another Nactcorian great. Too many home commitments forced me to back off and for many years I sat back and just enjoyed Natcor, the chess – albeit fewer games – and both of Natcor's magazines. I was then very proud to be elected President.

Several years ago, Les got Eileen to take over the distribution of *The Oracle* and another friend of ours Stan Warren recruited me to take over as Natcor's secretary.

My Chess Opponent

I played postal chess with Eileen's nephew, who now lives in Hartlepool in the North-East of England; you know: the deprived area of Britain. Deprived?! If you believe that you'll believe in the illuminati!

His short notes included: I'm not playing so good these days; I'm making silly mistakes; I'm getting old; I'm losing it.

I told him, 'Just stop it, Alf; you can't kid a kidder. I've heard it all before.'

He actually started out by saying, 'My word, that's an interesting opening; I'm most impressed.' But as the game progressed, he slipped in little comments like, 'You have me baffled there'; 'You're far too good for me'; 'I can't compete with you; you're way out of my league'; 'That was a really fine move; I can't see what you are up to and don't know how I'm going to stop you'. Then he came up with one I had never heard before. 'Do you think you can tie one hand behind your back, so as to

Memoirs of a Working Man

give me the slightest hint of a chance?' Then comes the sucker punch. 'Boy, am I lucky or what? Just spotted a mate in both the games!'

Thanks for the games; I think you've taught me a great deal.

Pawn to Kings Four (P-K4)

When I joined the National Correspondence Chess Club fifty years ago, life was oh so simple; it was plain old P-K4 in wonderful plain English, without any complications. For years and years I was content with the good old English descriptive notation: win a few, lose a few. Making an odd clerical error or the occasional ambiguous move that spiced up the correspondence and, of course, meeting the members who, like myself, were just as interested in the letter writing as in the chess, merely added to the enjoyment.

Then my world began to crumble and cracks appeared in what I had considered to be a fortress. I'd been paired with a bright young sprog, who told me that my beloved P-K4 type notation was outdated and that I should, *Get into the Groove*, man, and change my notation to E2-E4.

Naturally, I was confused. But not wishing to appear to be an old stick in the mud, I allowed him to explain this new revolutionary system. Determined not to resist change for the sake of just resisting, I buckled down and conformed.

After a while, I mastered it and had complete understanding, only occasionally getting confused and slipping back into the odd P-K4. Then a geezer, who will remain nameless, but has a highly paid committee post, has a name of a chess piece that stands next to the queen, has been in the club for more years than me and should know better, told me to forget all about P-K4 and E2-E4. 'You should write your moves like this "e4".' Now I ask you, what do I make of that?

Once again, being of a rather servile nature and not wishing in any way to upset this kingly figure, I knuckled down, put my brain under a tremendous amount of pressure and changed systems once again. But that wasn't the end of it and I was set yet another challenge.

A few years ago, I was paired with a Swedish South African, who introduced me to yet another way of playing correspondence chess. He was 82 years old when I played him and he told me, 'Get with it, son! Drag yourself from the Dark Ages and look forward to the new millennium. At the time, I didn't even know what a millennium was. The upshot of this other system was that each square on the chess board has a number and all one has to do is write, "number to number". Can you imagine me trying to work out what the bloody hell 5153 if 5755 – 7163 was?

It was Richard who came to my rescue and who, incidentally, has never played chess, but was able to explain to me how these numbers came about. I can't remember what he said the method was; all I do know is that it has nothing to do with chess.

So you see, I'm now stuck with international, algebraic, co-ordinate, long algebraic and the good old English descriptive! Oh my Gawd! Me bleeding 'ed 'urts – why can't life be a little simpler? Maybe not. Simple is boring, give me complications any day. It all helps to add some spice to life.

Progressive Chess

It was Les who introduced me to progressive chess. When he was editor of the *Mailers Oracle* he ran a yearly tournament and called it Pirate Chess, as he always reckoned the Mailers were a bunch of pirates. With, of course, himself as Captain Sparrow, I took to this variation and won most of the games and tournament after tournament. Everyone in the tournament was given names – boys will be boys and as we were living in little Wratting at the time, I was affectionately dubbed "The Ratting Rotter". When we moved back to Kedington, the lads decided to rename me "The Kedington Kraken"!

Epilogue

I decided to write my memoirs to enable our kids, grandkids and all that follow to understand our history. Something I deeply regret that both Eileen and I were deprived of. We were both born at the tail end of large families and as such never knew our grandparents. What grieves me most is that the opportunity was lost to glean information about the family heritage from our parents because we were too young to fully understand its importance. We were not only too young, but were struggling to build our own lives, earning a living, building a home and bringing up and providing for a family of our own.

By the time our lives had become more comfortable and we had time to reflect and wonder just what sort of lives they had it was too late and they were gone. I can only imagine that their lives were even harder than ours. Our parents were all born on or around 1900 – well over 100 years ago, at the time of writing this. They lived though two world wars, a Great Depression and Gawd only knows what other trials they suffered. Makes our upbringing seem like a real picnic.

Where am I now in the year 2010?? Living in Suffolk, Married to Eileen for 50 years, three Daughters and 10 Grandchildren, looking forward to more adventures to come and writing them down. Although I'm dyslexic and find reading difficult I have no such problems with writing and it has become a passion with me.

Life doesn't end when you clock off at the factory or office, It is an ongoing adventure, retirement! there's no such thing.

Bob Oliver

About the Author

Bob Oliver, born in 1938 in North London, eighth child in a family of ten, he learned to cope with the blitz, rationing, sadistic school teachers and picking up 'fag ends' from the streets for his 'roll-ups'

He survived this largely due to the warmth and love of the family he was lucky enough to be born into,

His mother dedicated to keeping her flock clean and fed and a hard working Father who made sure there was always food on the table and instilled in his children. a strong work ethic, which they carried all through all their lives.

Bob left school almost illiterate but took a basic literacy course in the Army where he found a deep love for writing and with his inborn sense of humour recorded his (not unfunny) life stories for his much loved children and grandchildren.

He decided to write his memoirs to enable his kids, grand-kids and all that follow to understand how lifestyles have changed and what it was like growing up through the Second World War as an ordinary working class person.

The Author now lives in Suffolk, is not famous he is not a celebrity just an ordinary working man.